June Ally

Also by Peter Shelley and from McFarland

Brittany Murphy: Her Life and Career (2022)

Ann Miller: Her Life and Career (2020)

Gene Hackman: The Life and Work (2019)

Joanne Woodward: Her Life and Career (2019)

Philip Seymour Hoffman: The Life and Work (2017)

Anne Bancroft: The Life and Work (2017)

Neil Simon on Screen: Adaptations and Original Scripts for Film and Television (2015)

Gwen Verdon: A Life on Stage and Screen (2015)

Sandy Dennis: The Life and Films (2014)

Australian Horror Films, 1973–2010 (2012)

Frances Farmer: The Life and Films of a Troubled Star (2011)

Jules Dassin: The Life and Films (2011)

Grande Dame Guignol Cinema: A History of Hag Horror from Baby Jane *to* Mother (2009)

June Allyson

Her Life and Career

PETER SHELLEY

McFarland & Company, Inc., Publishers
Jefferson, North Carolina

All photographs are from the author's collection.

ISBN (print) 978-1-4766-8768-1
ISBN (ebook) 978-1-4766-4864-4

LIBRARY OF CONGRESS AND BRITISH LIBRARY
CATALOGUING DATA ARE AVAILABLE

Library of Congress Control Number 2022057197

Front cover image: June Allyson, 1955 (Photofest)

Printed in the United States of America

McFarland & Company, Inc., Publishers
Box 611, Jefferson, North Carolina 28640
www.mcfarlandpub.com

Table of Contents

Introduction 1

1. Beginning 5
2. Hollywood 21
3. Marriage to Dick Powell 45
4. *Little Women* 65
5. *The Glenn Miller Story* 90
6. *You Can't Run Away from It* 114
7. Divorce 134
8. David Ashrow 150
9. *That's Entertainment! III* 175

Appendix 183
Bibliography 191
Index 201

Introduction

June Allyson looks like my mother, which probably explains why I find her so appealing. Film history has been unkind to Allyson, denigrating her as a twinkly-eyed smiling and tearful girl next door or perfect housewife wearing Peter Pan collars and starched skirts. Worse, as the old lady who shilled adult diapers. But she was big box office in the 1940s and 1950s. While not a great singer (her vocals often had to be sweetened), Allyson was a good dancer, a fine actress and a gifted comedienne. A star has a signature look and hers was the petite blonde who had more glamor thanks to MGM than the standard spunky, tomboyish gal. She also had a signature sound—that husky speaking voice that was the result of a chronic bronchial condition and enlarged vocal cords; it was dubbed her Million Dollar Laryngitis. The voice was so important to Allyson's persona that, when it was altered temporarily in 1961 after polyps were removed from her vocal cords, she didn't sound like herself and the performances lost their uniqueness.

The actress' rise in feature films is said to have come from the timing of her appearance during America's involvement in World War II, when the public supposedly admired the wholesome and virtuous, which matched MGM's goal of being the studio that made family films. The actress said she appealed to both sexes. Women were not threatened by her as the other woman and men wanted Allyson as a mate because she would always have dinner ready, never complain too much and be there for them. She was thought to be the embodiment of niceness—pretty, unassuming and uncomplicated—and the non-existent thing people called average. If the actress could be a success, anyone could.

But the truth is that she was more than average, apparent in the way Allyson was posed as a rival to Judy Garland in the 1940s. Garland was four years younger and had come to MGM seven years prior but Allyson's rise was in counterpoint to Garland's fall. The actress admitted that she did not have Garland's talent but Allyson had enough for the studio bosses to say this new girl could step right into Garland's shoes if

Garland didn't behave. Garland saw this as a silly threat, but her growing unreliability stemming from emotional problems made the star a risk to any production and therefore replaceable. Allyson was more reliable and only tried to refuse one role in her time at MGM—*The Three Musketeers* (1948)—though she eventually did play in the film. There were projects that Garland began and Allyson was considered to replace her, an example being *Annie Get Your Gun.* It was when there were projects where Garland replaced Allyson, like *In the Good Old Summertime* (1949) and *Royal Wedding* (1951) where the actress' power was now real.

She began her career in a series of film shorts alternating with chorus work in Broadway shows. It was one of those fateful theatrical opportunities that brought attention to Allyson: Betty Hutton contracted measles and Allyson was promoted from understudy to star in *Panama Hattie* in 1940. This led to a featured part in *Best Foot Forward,* and Hollywood when the cast was transported for the movie version made in 1943. Allyson had a rocky start in Tinsel Town and, after playing supporting roles, was nearly dropped by MGM. But wise counsel from Dick Powell led to her taking the "plain Jane" sister lead in *Two Girls and a Sailor* (1944), which was a hit. She alternated between featured, supporting and leading roles though the leads were surprisingly few: *Two Sisters from Boston* (1946), *Little Women* (1949), *Too Young to Kiss* (1951), *The Girl in White* (1952), *You Can't Run Away from It* (1956), *The Opposite Sex* (1956), *Interlude* (1957) and *A Stranger in My Arms* (1959). The actress also had her own television series from 1959 to 1961. After this, there were more TV guest spots, small roles in films and a return to the stage—and even Broadway in *Forty Carats*

Allyson's supporting role in the film *The Shrike* (1955) was seen as a shocking change of pace for her although a modern viewing makes the character seem not as radical as it was at the time. The lesbian murderer in *They Only Kill Their Masters* (1972) was another departure from her "perfect housewife" image. Other roles included college students, a Philharmonic string bass player, secretaries, nurses, a librarian, schoolteachers, illustrator, zookeeper, boxing promoter, pianist, doctors, party girl, actress, heiresses, singer, information assistant, nun, lawyer, fashion designer and head of a stuffed toy animal division. She even got to play blind, a ghost, a mental patient and a mad blackmailer in her television series, blind again on *The Love Boat,* and a con artist on *House Calls.* Allyson was always believable, except for one misstep in the comedy *My Man Godfrey* (1957) where the actress is charmless and unfunny. Allyson could do accents when required though this wasn't often and also appeared in period in *The Three Musketeers* (1948), *Little Women* (1949) and *The Girl in White* (1952). But despite her own misgivings as a musical performer, she is best represented by three musical numbers: "The Young Man with a Horn" from *Two Girls and a Sailor,* "Varsity Drag" from *Good News* (1947) and "Thou Swell" from *Words and Music* (1948). Honorable mention to "Now Baby Now" from *The Opposite Sex* (1956).

The actress' life had some scandal. She married, divorced and remarried her first husband Dick Powell and did the same with her second husband Glenn Maxwell. Allyson had an emotional but non-physical affair with Alan Ladd while they were both married to others, and in her later life she had a problem with alcohol. The actress' departure from a long-term contract with MGM did not end her career, like it did with others, and she was able to continue to star in films for other studios for the next decade. In addition, Allyson became a great spokesperson for MGM after she left, appearing in various documentaries about the studio, and also a spokesperson for Depend, bringing the problem of incontinence out of the shadows.

This is the first book to span the actress' career. Her 1982 memoir has been an invaluable source but it lacks comprehensive and consistent coverage of her work. This book cannot be considered the definitive study since some of the work is not available for viewing, with perhaps the biggest regrets being Allyson's episode of *This Is Your Life* and the *Biography* episode on Dick Powell. For the unavailable shows, as much information as possible has been provided. Accessing the aforementioned sources and any associated biographies and books on co-workers allowed me to consider differing views of some of the events in the life and career and to highlight any apparent inaccuracies. My research had me review the available interviews that she gave for DVD special features and newspapers and magazines, accessing the archives of *The New York Times,* and ebay.com collectibles and entertainment memorabilia and the Getty Images website for photographs of the actress at events. Interviews on YouTube.com and the Official June Allyson Web Site were helpful.

The book is written as a biography, with the actress' career presented in the context of her life. Each film, television, stage and radio show appearance is mixed into the biography. I have provided an analysis of the work when possible, positioning Allyson's place in the project, commenting on her look and performance, and quoting any comments I have found by the star as well as those about her by co-workers. I have also given the critical reaction that the work received. This book comes with an appendix of Allyson's work on stage, film and television and a bibliography of reference sources.

1

Beginning

According to studio biographies, she was born Jan Allyson to Arthur and Clare Allyson in Lucerne, Westchester County, New York. Actually, there's no such town. The truth is that Allyson was born Kathryn or Katrina Ann Eleanor Frances Van Geisman aka Eleanor "Ella" Geisman on October 7, 1917, in a three-room tenement on 143rd Street and Third Avenue, near St. Anne's Avenue in the Bronx. She was delivered by her aunt in the building where her father worked. Allyson said the name was of Dutch origin though it is believed that her paternal grandparents were immigrants from Germany. She was the daughter of Clara Provost, who was French, and Robert Geisman, who was Dutch, though later studio biographies listed her as being born to French-English parents. The girl had a brother, Henry, who was two years older. She was raised as a Catholic.

Her father worked as a janitor or building superintendent. An alcoholic, he left the family when the girl was young. Some sources describe Robert's departure as abandonment while another source claims there was an agreement to divide the children so that he took Henry and Clara had Ella. The children only saw each other once thereafter, on the Christmas their parents unsuccessfully attempted reconciliation. Allyson also said that after her father left, it was 12 years before she saw him again. But in her memoir, she wrote that when she was six or seven, he visited, waiting outside with a bicycle for her. Sometimes Robert would call and she would take the subway to meet him, and he would not be where he said he would be. Sometimes she would see him reel out of a cheap bar and go to her, and they would walk around, him treating her to an ice cream sundae. Sometimes she would have to wait outside the bar while he made a quick trip in and out.

Being poor, Clara and Ella were forced to live with her (Ella's) grandmother, in an apartment on Lucerne Street in the Throggs Neck section of the Bronx. Her mother took whatever job she could:

telephone switch operator, restaurant cashier, even a printer job making personalized checkbooks for $20 a week. The restaurant job was best because it allowed her to sometimes bring home food. The income was not enough for a babysitter so Clara left her daughter in the care of her grandmother, who became the center of her life. The old woman told Ella she would be something important in the world, and Ella believed it. Her grandmother took the girl to her first movie, to the zoo and on little trips as far north in the Bronx as Van Cortlandt Park. There Ella saw her first flowers, and the air didn't smell of gasoline.

After Clara obtained a divorce, she rented an $18-a-month railroad apartment of her own and brought her daughter to live with her there. They were still poor and, having no bath, heated water on a coal stove and bathed in a washtub. Ella collected boxes and crates from grocery stores and delicatessen, to be broken up and burned in the stove. The girl found herself alone in the apartment a good deal of the time while her mother worked to support them. This gave her a lifelong fear of being alone and of the dark.

Clara and Ella relocated often, which meant that Ella found it hard to make friends. Her greatest fear was that her mother would send her away for good. She had once sent her to a farm, supposedly for her health. There she learned how to milk a cow. She was also sent to stay with a stern aunt who showed her a photo album with a picture of her father that the girl took and put under her pillow. When she lied about taking it, her aunt wanted her gone. Ella was shuttled around to numerous aunts and cousins throughout New York City, and they were equally unkind. Later in life she refused to name them publicly, fearing they would try to capitalize on her name. They wanted no part of her as a child so she wanted no part of them as an adult.

The girl wore glasses from the age of five but never in public. She was a pretty tough little kid who knocked down a boy who wouldn't stop tormenting her. She was gymnastic, able to do a split while crossing her eyes. Her father enrolled her in a local tap-dance school but after three lessons, she was barred from attending for non-payment. Life again changed when her grandmother died suddenly in the night of a coronary occlusion. Ella locked herself in her room for three days and was inconsolable.

Allyson has given differing accounts of the freak accident that occurred where she was age eight, nine or 12. It was a blistering hot summer day and she had been taken to Coney Island. Blissfully happy, she had a new wire-haired terrier named Teddy, a bicycle and a new pink taffeta dress. Riding her bicycle home, she pedaled down the street with her cousin or a neighborhood boy. They dared each other to ride beneath a tree that had been struck by lightning and damaged in a storm. The children either rested beneath a loose tree limb, or just as they passed under it, it crashed down on them. Ella's bicycle was totaled and the dog killed or the boy killed. She was knocked unconscious, with half of the bones of her body broken, including a fractured skull and broken back, or her spine injured and pelvic region badly damaged.

Ella's mother heard the crash and rushed to help, then fainted. The girl awakened to find strangers around her. No one knew who she was; this was the source of a recurrent dream where she would reply that she was nobody. The girl was taken to Fordham Hospital, where her mother told her she probably wouldn't last until morning, and if she did she would never walk again. Clara sued to collect damages from the city. The tree disappeared in the night so that its existence could be denied. Clara was eventually awarded $100.

For five months, the girl stayed in the hospital in traction wearing a cast that extended from shoulder to hip. She was then confined to a wheelchair, having to wear a heavy steel brace to support her spine and a girdle with straps under her arms to hold the back straight. The one good thing about her hospital stay was that Ella had her first crush: a doctor who made her want to live and become a doctor herself. She learned to walk again with the aid of Marie Spinosa aka Spinoza, a swimming instructor. Later studio publicists claimed that Ella emerged as a star swimmer, though they also said the injury came from her running down a hillside and tripping over a log. Spinosa became her best friend; years later, Allyson was maid of honor at Spinosa's wedding. Dancing was also part of her corrective exercises to build her muscles, and she was eventually able to dance wearing the brace. The girl ended up with a limp, resulting in others calling her a freak and Gimpy. By the time the brace came off, she weighed only 42 pounds.

Therapy was expensive and things became desperate at home. Sometimes her mother didn't eat dinner because there was only enough food for one. One day the girl came home from school to find their furniture out on the street because they had to move again.

Her mother married Arthur Peters, manager of the transportation department for the Loft Candy Company. They now lived in a new apartment at 1965 or 1975 Bryant Avenue. Peters' salary was too low for the three of them to live on so Clara had to continue working. They were joined by Arthur's son Arthur Peters, Jr., whom Allyson always said she loved more than her own brother.

After finishing eighth grade at P.S. 14, Ella entered Theodore Roosevelt High in the Bronx. The other children made fun of her deep-throated, low-pitched voice, calling her Foghorn and similar unpleasant names. Its huskiness was due to recurrent bronchitis and enlarged vocal cords and she was told that any competent surgeon could have stripped them in 15 minutes and made her a soprano. But the cost was out of the question. She hated the sound, not knowing that the unusual timbre would lead her to fame.

Ella's dreams of being a famous doctor or a celebrated actress were replaced by wanting to be a professional dancer. She saved money from ghostwriting homework for her classmates (the left-handed girl had to learn to write with her right hand for the forgeries). She also got money from running errands and her weekly allowance. Ella paid in advance for a dance course, but when she arrived for her first lesson, a sign on the door read "Closed for Bankruptcy." She enrolled in the Ned Wayburn Dancing Academy and entered every amateur dance competition in the neighborhood with the stage name of Elaine Peters, but won none of them.

At the new Loew's Paradise on the Grand Concourse in the Bronx, Ella finally learned how to dance by watching the film *The Gay Divorcee* more than 15 times. She would play hooky and spend whole days in the movie house, taking along the lunch she had packed for school, and arriving home at the right time. She also managed the cost of tickets by inveigling the boys into taking her to dance movies. Her idols were Fred Astaire and Ginger Rogers, whose dances she copied. Ella boasted to her school friends that she could dance as well as Rogers, though the truth was that all she could really do was jump up and down a lot. (Plus she didn't have movie star looks, being skinny and rather plain, with a lisp and a stutter.) It was on screen that she first saw the famous juvenile singer Dick Powell.

Working on a career, she answered every newspaper ad wanting chorus girls and dancers for Broadway musicals though Ella was rejected again and again. But she did get into movie shorts in New York.

Swing for Sale was a ten-minute musical short shot in Brooklyn by director Joseph Henabery for the Warner Bros. Vitaphone Corporation. It was released on February 27, 1937.

Pixilated was an 18-minute comedy short with a screenplay by Arthur Jarrett and Marcy Klauber and directed by Al Christie. It was made for the Educational Films Corporation of America and distributed by 20th Century–Fox. This was shot at the Astoria Studios in Queens and released on March 19, 1937.

Ups and Downs was a 21-minute musical short based on a story by Jack Henley and Cyrus Wood and directed by Roy Mack for the Warner Bros. Vitaphone Corporation. She is billed as June Allyson (perhaps retroactively) and plays the supporting role of June Daily, daughter of a stockbroker. At the Hotel St. Plaza, tap-dancing elevator operator Hal Smith (Hal Le Roy) is friends with June. She has what appears to be peroxided blonde short hair which has a side part. June dances for Hal in the elevator, then they dance together on "Rhythm Personality" by Cliff Hess and with the ensemble on "The Dancing Financier" with music by Saul Chaplin and lyrics by Sammy Cahn. Her best number is perhaps "Rhythm Personality" where June wears a floor-length dress and cape. The number has them dance together in her apartment, in an elevator, and then in the Café Grill which has a bandstand orchestra. Le Roy is showcased as the better dancer but Allyson keeps up with him and her singing voice is pleasant. For "The Dancing Financier," June wears a white suit with white tie, black blouse and beret. The dances were arranged by Ned McGurn. The short was released on October 9, 1937.

Dime a Dance aka *Happyland* was an 18-minute musical comedy short for the Educational. The story was by Arthur Jarrett and Marcy Klauber and the director was Al Christie. Waitress Esmeralda (Imogene Coca) wants to get a job at the dance hall where Harriet (Allyson) is the cashier. Allyson receives third billing after Coca and Danny Kaye, who plays Eddie the sailor. The short was released on December 23, 1937, with the tagline "A Wallflower Turned Cavewoman." Again Allyson's hair looks peroxided. She is funny and her performance is more naturalistic compared to the mannered comic style of Coca.

Dates and Nuts was a 19-minute Educational musical comedy short. It had a screenplay by Parke Levy and was directed by Robert Hall. Herman Timberg, Jr. (Tim Herbert), and Pat (Pat Rooney, Jr.) attend a dance at a co-ed school. Allyson plays Wilma Brown, Herman's girlfriend. It was released on December 31.

In the summer of 1937, Allyson was hired by a theatrical producer (she said he was either wonderfully gallant or conveniently myopic) for a

$50-a-week job as a singer–tap dancer at the Lido Club in Montreal. She didn't know about stagecraft and the difference between American and Canadian money flustered her, but it was a professional engagement.

"Sing for Sweetie" was an 18-minute Educational musical comedy short, shot at General Service Studios in Hollywood. The screenplay was based on a story by Marcy Klauber and Arthur Jarrett and the director was Al Christie. Shot under the working title *Not Now,* the story centers on Edward Carroll (Lee Sullivan), a young tenor with Johnny Johnson's Orchestra who is in love with Sally Newton (fifth-billed Allyson). In one scene she wears the same costume as in *Ups and Downs.* She is funny in a scene in which she tears up a photograph of fiancé Snodgrass (actor unknown) in favor of one of Edward. The short also features what might be Allyson's first screen kiss. It was released on April 15, 1938.

The Prisoner of Swing was a 21-minute Vitaphone comedy adventure short written by Eddie Forman and Cyrus Wood, based on Anthony Hope's Ruritanian novel *The Prisoner of Zenda* in which a commoner takes the place of a lookalike king. United Artists had released a film version of the novel in 1937. Here Mr. Razzenstill (Hal Le Roy), a saxophonist and dancer specializing in swing music, comes to the kingdom of Sulvania and finds he looks exactly like King Rudolph. Allyson, third-billed, plays the part of the princess, who is first seen pushed by the king when she curtsies to him. She wears a blonde sculptured wig with braids that is presumably meant to recall Madeleine Carroll, who played Princess Flavia in the UA film. We see her and the king waltz to Johann Strauss' "G'schichten aus dem Wienerwald, Op. 325" ("Tales from the Vienna Woods") at the royal ball. When Razzenstill (part of the orchestra) breaks into swing, so does she. Allyson also dances as part of the number "Coronation of the King of Swing" with music by Saul Chaplin and lyrics by Sammy Cahn performed by the Lester Cole Singers and the Gae Foster Girls. Allyson sings "Pardon Me If I Say It with My Feet" (also by Chaplin and Cahn) with Le Roy, who dances for her. Directed by Roy Mack, the film was released on June 11, 1938.

Although the timeline seems doubtful, Allyson claimed to have still been a 15-year-old schoolgirl when auditioning for a Broadway musical comedy. She also offered two versions of the story. One had a girlfriend bringing the newspaper advertisement (for a job in the chorus) to her attention, with a quarter bet riding on June's chances. Another version has the ad given by two friends who escorted her to the audition to watch. At the tryout were a hundred girls who looked taller, considerably older, well-endowed and vastly more sophisticated. She did not know to bring sheet music to give to the piano player. When he asked her what she wanted to sing, Allyson answered, "What do you want to hear?" and the whole place erupted in laughter. She finally called out a popular song of the day and he played it down low enough for her to sing comfortably. In another rendition of the story, Allyson said that when the player asked what she wanted to sing, she said, "Play anything." She didn't know the song he played and just sang whatever came into her mind.

By a miracle, Allyson was asked to come back the next day and then for two more days. On the third day, the piano player groaned as she stepped up and played the same song until a voice said, "Hold it." The speaker said that this girl had to be hired because otherwise she would keep coming back and he couldn't stand it. Allyson claimed that she was called back six times which made her realize it was being done for laughs. She said that on the last day, she was among six contenders. The voice she said belonged to Richard Rodgers (who was apparently not involved in this particular Broadway show). Rodgers *was* involved in a later Broadway show, *Panama Hattie*, about which Allyson has repeated the same audition story. But then she also claimed that the voice was Cole Porter at that audition.

Whoever the voice was, Allyson said she won the quarter bet, helping to offset the cost of the subway trip to Times Square and back. The show was *Sing Out the News* and she was credited as June Allyson, though again perhaps retroactively. She reported the origin of the name in two versions. In one of them, one of the show's two choreographers said her name had to be changed. Asked what name she liked, the girl suggested Allison (her brother's second name). He thought Allyson would be a good first name but wanted a different surname as well. She couldn't think of one. The choreographer asked a chorus boy what month he liked. The boy said June and the choreographer announced that June Allyson was it! She liked it and was grateful the boy did not like August or October because she did not want to be named Auggie or Oggie.

Another source claims that the choreographer wanted her name changed because he could not be bothered to remember her real one.

Allyson's second version has the name come from George Abbott. Abbott told her she just didn't look like an Ella Van Geisman and he suggested June because she was kind of sunny, and Allyson as a variation on her brother's name. Allyson would also say that *she* chose the name June because that month was pleasant and pretty.

Allyson was in the chorus but did not sing. The show was a topical revue produced by Max Gordon and in association with George S. Kaufman and Moss Hart with songs by Harold J. Rome and sketches by Charles Friedman, (plus two sketched supplied by Kaufman and Hart). It was also staged by Friedman. The show had a tryout in Philadelphia at the Forrest Theatre for two weeks from August 29, 1938, and then opened on Broadway at the Music Box Theatre on September 24 and ran till January 7, 1939. It received critical praise for being a neatly written and attractively produced satire about the bourgeoisie and the New Deal.

Fellow chorine Miriam Franklin coached Allyson in professional dancing. Under the name Miriam Nelson, Franklin wrote in her book *My Life Dancing with the Stars* that her coaching helped Allyson get into *Sing Out the News*. Nelson claims that the producers told her they liked the girl but she needed a routine to use at an audition and the more experienced dancer taught her a jazz number which led to her casting.

Clara was less than thrilled, concerned because her daughter had not finished high school. One source claims that the girl left high school prematurely after completing two and a half years, when the death of her stepfather necessitated her going to work. In a 1957 *Saturday Evening Post* interview, Allyson reported that she quit school at the end of her sophomore year. However in a *New York Times* interview (February 10, 1952), Allyson said that she did finish high school.

The show required daily performances in addition to the auditions Allyson also attended to try for bigger roles. She now carried sheet music for a Judy Garland song to sing.

She made more Vitaphone shorts. The 18-minute *The Knight Is Young* had a screenplay by Cyrus D. Wood and Eddie Forman and was directed by Roy Mack. In it, sign painter Hal (Hal Le Roy) Hal meets June (Allyson) through her apartment window and they have a mutual love of dance. The film opens with a shot of June dancing in her apartment to "Just a Simple Melody" by Saul Chaplin, with Allyson's blond hair looking more natural than peroxided. The actress is sweet and vulnerable even if she over-gestures when explaining that she can't leave her apartment because of owed back rent. Allyson duets with Jimmy

(Norman MacKay) on "What Do You Hear from the Mob in Scotland?" with music by Chaplin and lyrics by Sammy Cahn (the window blind cord above her head is distracting). She also dances with Le Roy to "Bob White (Whatcha Gonna Swing Tonight?)" by Bernard Hanighen at the Sign Painter's Ball. As in *Ups and Downs,* the dance is designed to showcase Le Roy since at one point Allyson stops dancing altogether to watch him. The short ends with a shared closeup of the two, June talking to the camera to tell us that "everything turns out right at the end of the picture." It was released on October 29, 1938.

The 20-minute short *Rollin' in Rhythm* (working title: *Roller Skates*) was also directed by Roy Mack. Allyson is billed as Band Vocalist. It was released on April 15, 1939.

Allyson decided to try a modeling call, not that she thought she could be a model but because they might use her in a crowd scene where space needed to be filled. Allyson had no portfolio or even a photograph to show but she was one of the four girls picked out of a crowd of 30. Her measurements were taken for a bathing suit, but the suit was an unsexy tennis outfit for the "before" in a before-and-after advertisement. That was the end of her modeling.

Allyson appeared in the musical *Very Warm for May,* composed by Jerome Kern with a libretto by Oscar Hammerstein II. The Broadway show was also produced by Max Gordon and staged by Vincente Minnelli and centered on the antics of a summer theater troupe. After an out-of-town tryout, it opened at the Alvin Theatre on November 17, 1939, and ran until January 6, 1940. Allyson played the part of June. The show received mixed reviews.

An original cast recording was discovered, though it is said to be incomplete as it was taken from a promotional radio show and was not an attempt to faithfully record the full score. The album received a Grammy nomination for Best Cast Show Album when it was finally released in 1985. There was also a loosely adapted film version, the MGM musical *Broadway Rhythm* (1944), but neither Allyson nor the character of June appear in it.

Next was the musical comedy *Higher and Higher* with music by Richard Rodgers, lyrics by Lorenz Hart, and book by Gladys Hurlbut and Joshua Logan. It centered on Zachary Ash (Jack Haley), a butler in a ruined first family. The show was produced by Dwight Deere Wiman and staged by Logan. It opened at Broadway's Shubert Theatre on April 4, 1940, and closed on June 15. Allyson appeared as one of the Specialty Girls. The show's cast was praised and it was said it had some of the most joyous dancing in recent years. It had a return engagement at the Shubert from August 5 to 24. Allyson did not appear in this production, nor was she in RKO's 1943 film version.

Her last short was for Warner Bros.: the eight-minute *All Girl Revue,* written by Eddie Forman and Cyrus D. Wood and directed by Lloyd French. The story had women put in charge of the city government for a day; the temporary mayor (Allyson) must go to the train station to greet an opera singer. She is a brunette and top-billed below the title. With the Harrison Sisters, Allyson sings "We've Got to Make the City Pretty" with music by Saul Chaplin and lyrics by Sammy Cahn; it is reprised as they perform on City Hall steps behind the dancers the Gae Foster Girls. She remains on the steps as two other Chaplin and Cahn songs are reprised, "Information, Please," sung by Edith Brandell, and "I Love a Long Note," sung by Beverly Kirk. Allyson has a funny line when the opera singer Madame Beverly (Kirk) points out she is only a day mayor and Allyson replies, "Certainly not a nightmare." The Madame's insulted reaction provokes an added laugh. The film was released on June 22, 1940.

Allyson found show business to be a hard life. At one audition, she fainted after three days of not eating. If she was hired, Allyson was soon fired from many chorus lines for being too small, too young, too innocent-looking, and for her ridiculous self-taught dancing. Once she danced off the wrong side of the stage, wondering where everybody else was. Another time she had to be kicking right-left, right-left but she kicked left-right and was fired. Sometimes Allyson was put on probation and told to shape up by the next rehearsal. It seemed some directors would give her a bit part out of pity, just to keep her from disrupting the chorus line with her bungling. She said she was in more flops than one could imagine. Somehow, without being able to dance or sing, she got by. Richard Rodgers often kept her from being fired, even though every dance director wanted to do so.

Her next stage show was the musical *Panama Hattie.* This show had songs by Cole Porter and book by Herbert Fields and B.G. DeSylva, who also produced. The title character, Hattie Maloney (Ethel Merman) owns a night club in the Panama Canal Zone where she also performs. The show was directed by Edgar MacGregor and had pre–Broadway tryouts at New Haven's Shubert Theatre on October 3, 1940, and then at the Shubert Theatre, Boston, on October 8.

This time Allyson was saved from being fired by Merman, who even let Allyson do a little schtick with her. Allyson claims that Richard

Rodgers picked her to understudy for the show's second lead Florrie (Betty Hutton), although Rodgers is not credited on the show. He doubted that the girl would get the chance to go on but the experience would be good for her. Allyson studied every move Hutton made and memorized every line.

The musical premiered on Broadway at the 46th Street Theatre on October 30, 1940, and closed on January 3, 1942. It received critical praise. Allyson was billed as one of the Dancing Girls and reportedly had one line in the opening number: "Hello, sailor."

Being an understudy was not enough for Allyson, so after each show at 11 p.m. she dashed over to the Copacabana to dance in the chorus line at the shows performed between midnight to 3 a.m. In the middle of *Panama Hattie*'s run, Hutton came down with measles and Allyson had to go on. The dates are unknown but Allyson said she played the role five or ten times. Merman let her share the star dressing room since otherwise Allyson would have been running up and down three flights of spiral stairs to the chorus dressing rooms. Merman also had a bouquet of spring flowers delivered to the dressing room.

There were stories that before she went on, Allyson wired all the important producers, columnists and critics, urging them to come and see this great new talent. She was supposed to have signed telegrams with the names of the show's stars Merman and Arthur Treacher. George Abbott did come and she almost threw him out. The show had a practical-joking chorus boy, Freddie Ney, who often (falsely) whispered to cast members that producers were out front to scout them. One night after the show, there was a knock on Allyson's dressing room door, the voice saying it was Abbott. Allyson figured it was Ney and replied that she was Sarah Bernhardt and that the $75 a week he was offering her to be in his new show was not enough and he should go away. He kept raising the salary until it reached $150. Allyson opened the door out of sheer exasperation and discovered that it really was Abbott. She almost fainted and said she would work for him for nothing, purely for the chance. But he kept his word about the salary.

Hutton recovered from the measles and returned to the show, but then left for Hollywood. Allyson thought she would now get a chance to play her part but the producers decided they wanted a "name." MGM made a film version of *Panama Hattie* with Ann Sothern in the title role in 1942.

Betsy Blair, another Dancing Girl, described in her book *The Memory of All That* how she shared a room at Manhattan's Henry Hudson

Hotel (home of the American Women's Club) with Allyson and fellow chorus girl Jane Ball. They were making $45 a week and the room cost $27 a week for three. Allyson said she lived for the first six weeks on money pooled from her friends and the allowance from her mother and Arthur Peters. Allyson and Ball had asked Blair to room with them, but first Blair had to have them meet her parents. Blair found Allyson to be exuberant and adorable with her gravelly voice, and both girls used their charm to melt away any objections Blair's father had to her living in the city. They also reassured her mother that they would look after Blair, emphasizing how hard they would work and that they would go to dance class every day. When the girls were ready to move in, the hotel offered them a room that would house four, for the same price. Secretary Clare Moynihan joined them. She owned a winter coat which was shared when one of the other girls had a job interview or a date.

The hotel was an all-female residence which permitted gentlemen visitors between 6 p.m. and 8 p.m. but the door always had to be kept open. (Blair said that no men were allowed upstairs in the rooms and not even in the elevators.) There were no cooking facilities, according to the New York fire code, but Allyson had a hot plate. She hid it on the fire escape when the security officer came knocking. Allyson was finally caught dead to rights as she tried to wave away the odor of frying eggs through the open window. He didn't turn her in but warned her not to burn the place down when she used her hot plate.

Blair reported that Allyson had the ambition and drive to get ahead. Being the smallest one in the chorus, she was the last one onstage and at the end of the line when they danced offstage. George Abbot observed that when the chorus boys had to throw her high, Allyson was so light that she disappeared under the proscenium. Afterwards she went into the washroom and threw up. The cast always knew when there was a movie star in the audience, and Allyson would contrive to trip and fall to get noticed. When she got up again, her charming confusion got a hand.

By this time, Allyson had acquired a boyfriend, Tommy Mitchell, a tall, lean singer who resembled James Stewart and had appeared in *Sing Out the News*. His old conservative family in the South frowned on him dating a chorus girl but Tommy loved her too much to ask her to give up her ambitions. Allyson bought him an inexpensive camera—her first gift to a man—because he was also a photographer. She also gave Tommy her virginity. She told her roommates that it was like sitting on a telephone, which ended the conversation.

She also dated Van Johnson (they had the same agent, Martin Jurow). In his book *Van Johnson: MGM's Golden Boy,* Ronald L. Davis reported that they had met at the apartment of a mutual friend and quickly became soulmates. Johnson was a dancer in the chorus of *Pal Joey,* the musical which was playing at the same time on Broadway. Allyson wrote that their dates were not romantic (without mentioning that he was gay) but fun. The couple got together after shows and went to the Rikers Automat; each paid for their own meal. Davis wrote that on matinee days, they would often meet for a hamburger between shows. Allyson said that when Johnson bought her a box of chocolates they shared them, she eating the dark ones and he the light. They were avid movie fans, the girl believing that Margaret Sullavan was the screen's greatest actress and trying to emulate her. The couple would sit through three or four screenings, watching them more to learn than to be entertained. Together they dreamed of someday becoming actors and acted out scenes they had seen, critiqued each other's performances, and did the scenes again. The two talked about being film celebrities and wanting to play in a film together.

Because audiences liked Allyson in the role of Florrie, Richard Rodgers offered her the role in the national road company and she accepted. But she would not do the tour. Casting the new musical *Best Foot Forward,* George Abbott needed a funny little girl to ham up some scenes with the budding comedy star Nancy Walker and offered it to Allyson. The show centered on a self-centered actress (Rosemary Lane) who peps up her career by attending a college prom. Allyson declined the offer because of her commitment to *Panama Hattie,* though she had yet to sign a contract. Abbott went to Richard Rodgers and he fired her, considering the Abbott offer to be the superior opportunity. It appears that Ann Barrett played Florrie on tour.

Best Foot Forward had songs by Hugh Martin and Ralph Blane and a book by John Cecil Holm. Abbott was the producer-director. Allyson played Minerva. She had a duet with Kenneth Bowers, "What Do You Think I Am?"; sang the show-stopping "The Three B's" with Walker and Victoria Schools, and sang the opening song "Don't Sell the Night Short" with Walker, Students and Girls. There was an out-of-town tryout in mid–September 1941 at the Forrest Theatre in Philadelphia. The production opened on Broadway on October 1 at the Ethel Barrymore Theatre and ran till July 4, 1942. The show was praised as highly enjoyable, staged with professional skill, with Allyson described as a sunny blonde with considerable charm. It appears that no original cast recording was made of the whole show but there are recordings of some of the songs.

One night the cast heard that in the audience was Dick Powell, who had come to see Rosemary Lane. Allyson saw him when she peeped through the curtain. When he appeared backstage after the show, Allyson was too shy to join the crowd around him and watched from the spiral staircase above. She noticed that Lane and Powell were both looking up at her with Lane later reporting that he had noticed the little midget, the cutest thing anybody ever saw, with veins that stuck out like a garden hose and who boomed with a big, husky, funny voice. He had guffawed through her whole routine though he doubted the show's producers meant it to be as funny in that way. Lane called to her to come down and she did; Lane said Powell had asked to meet her. Allyson put out her hand and he held it as he grinned. Her mouth was open but nothing would come out. So she broke into a smile before the moment passed and someone else grabbed Powell to talk to him. Allyson wrote that his wife Joan Blondell was with him but the women were not introduced. Blondell wrote about the meeting in her book *Center Door Fancy,* claiming Allyson simpered and cooed that she slept with a fan letter from Powell under her pillow every night. But Allyson had no letter from him and had never written to him or any other star. Blondell also wrote that Allyson was a tramp dressed as a little kid, and a call girl in New York with exhibitions being her specialty.

At a formal luncheon that afternoon, Powell was struggling with a stubborn hunk of chicken and felt someone's eyes on him. When he looked, he saw Allyson convulsing with laughter at him.

Powell's backstage visit raised Allyson's status in the show's company. Rosemary Lane had previously been kind but now drew closer, fascinated at how he had singled Allyson out and insisted on meeting her. She shared many confidences about the actor, who was her dear friend and a nice man, unlike the usual arrogant movie stars.

An MGM scout saw *Best Foot Forward* and recommended the studio buy the whole cast as a package, minus Rosemary Lane and Victoria Schools. Allyson felt she was not good enough for Hollywood with her barrel-house voice, slightly bowed legs and skinniness. But she was wrong. Even the very wise and experienced experts in Hollywood would not be able to explain just what she had.

20th Century–Fox had her make a screen test, which Allyson thought was terrible and which made her weep in despair when she saw it. Fox sent it to other studios. MGM producer Arthur Freed saw it and he ordered her to be signed immediately.

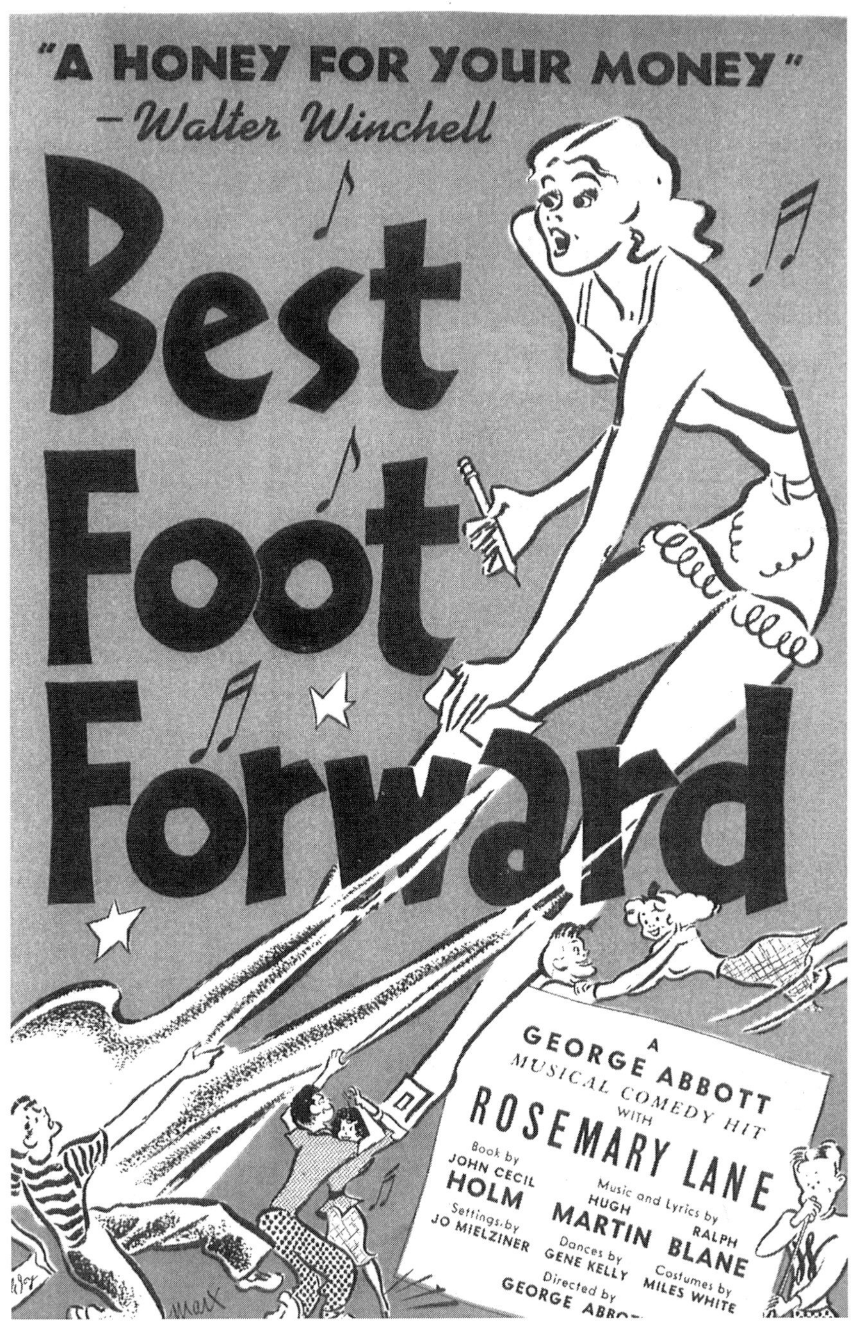

Flyer for *Best Foot Forward* at Broadway's Ethel Barrymore Theatre from October 1, 1941, to July 4, 1942.

Allyson made her last visit to her mother, promising to make it up for their long years of desperation and to help to take care of her half-brother Arthur. She borrowed a scruffy little suitcase and stuffed into it everything she owned, including some costume jewelry and photographs of those dear to her. Tommy went with her to the Pennsylvania Station train. Allyson noticed that people were staring, then realized she was still wearing bedroom slippers, having left her only good shoes sitting beside her bed. The girl only had $21 in her purse and now had to spend $10 on new shoes even before she even received her first Hollywood paycheck.

2

Hollywood

When Allyson arrived in Hollywood, there was a studio representative to meet her. Luckily he recognized the girl because otherwise she would have to use her remaining money to get to the hotel that was booked for her. Allyson learned that the film's start date had been postponed, which meant a six-week layoff.

The film cast gathered to meet Arthur Freed and then he asked her to stay behind. Freed had concerns, primarily about her voice. He wanted her to go straight home and wait for a doctor he would send, but Allyson said she was not sick; this was how she always sounded. He said that on the lot, they had Lillian Burns, who could teach her how to speak like a girl and how to smile with her eyes open, since the girl's eyes was his second concern. The third were her teeth, but on the lot was a wonderful dentist.

The dentist thought her teeth were healthy and wouldn't touch them. Lillian Burns, after trying for days to get Allyson to smile with her eyes open, decided she couldn't do anything about the eyes or the speaking voice. Allyson believed that Van Johnson was the one who convinced MGM that Allyson's million dollar laryngitis would make her a star.

Since she was on the payroll, they decided to put her in something: *Girl Crazy* (1943). It was said that she was signed for the part *because* of the unusual sound of her voice. This was the second movie adaptation of director Alexander Leftwich's Broadway show with music by George Gershwin, lyrics by Ira Gershwin and book by Guy Bolton and John McGowan. It opened at the Alvin Theatre on October 14, 1930, and closed on June 6, 1931. The first film version was made by RKO and released in 1932.

Scripted by Fred F. Finklehoffe, MGM's *Girl Crazy* centered on Danny Churchill, Jr. (Mickey Rooney), a young philanderer who is sent to a college somewhere in the West. Danny organizes a show to save the school from closure due to falling enrollments. Busby Berkeley was the director when it began shooting on January 4, 1943, but was replaced by Norman Taurog in early February. After filming ended in early April, additional scenes were shot in May. Location footage was shot in Palm Springs but otherwise it was shot at MGM in Hollywood. Allyson appears in one scene as part of the number "Treat Me Rough" with Rooney, the Music Maids, the Stafford Sisters and Tommy Dorsey and His Orchestra. Berkeley's firing meant that Allyson's schedule was changed, so that she had to shuttle back and forward between this film and *Best Foot Forward* which was now being shot. Charles Walters was the film's credited dance director but choreography for the number was by an uncredited Jack Donohue. Allyson sings and moves but does not dance in her part. The number is part of Dorsey's opening night performance at Teddy Mitchell's 100 Beautiful Girls 100 nightclub.

Allyson's singing here is broader and flatter and it appears that the style and her physicality was influenced by Betty Hutton. She is presented as a homely girl in contrast to the more elegant way that the Music Maids and the Stafford Sisters are dressed by costumer Irene.

Allyson with Mickey Rooney in the "Treat Me Rough" number from *Girl Crazy* (1943).

Allyson's knee-length dress with its ribboned straps and skirt hem pinned up to one side looks homemade and the ribbons in her brunette shoulder-length hair add to the image. Allyson sings that she wants to be treated rough but she is shown to be the one treating *men* rough. She musses the hair of a male patron sitting at a table below the stage and then goes to Danny, pinches his cheek, grabs him at his table and pushes him away. Allyson reappears for the end of the song, advancing on Danny when he is on the stage floor after being treated rough by the other girls.

The director was satisfied with the first take of "Treat Me Rough," which was a lucky thing as Allyson didn't know if she could have lasted a second round. After the take, she went to the rest room and threw up. She had always found singing a song hard, being unable to read music, but now Allyson also had to contend with the complexity of movie acting and try to remember all the things she had to do. She learned not to eat much until the end of the day, starving herself to soothe her nerves, and ending up with low blood sugar. On the film, she befriended Rooney and Judy Garland, who both made her feel she belonged in Hollywood.

Rooney was surprisingly sensitive to her needs in her first movie scene and, like a big brother, helped her through a nerve-wracking day. A master craftsman, Rooney could have upstaged her but he was a generous human being. Rooney wrote in his book *Life Is Too Short* that Allyson had unusual blond good looks and a sexy, almost croaky voice, but she was never anything more to him than a little sister.

Allyson caught three buses every morning to get to MGM, which took about two and a half hours. One day it was pouring rain and a chauffeur-driven limousine stopped on Wilshire Boulevard where she was waiting for the third bus. The limousine would pass her every day but this time the back door swung open and Allyson heard Judy Garland's unmistakable voice say, "Will you just get in the car!" Acknowledging Allyson's reticence to get in the car, Garland laughed, saying, "What did you think I was going to do, kidnap you?!" Garland told her she would see Allyson every morning at the bus stop and Allyson explained how she had no car. So every morning after that for six months, Garland's car would come and pick her up. If Garland finished early, she would send the car back for Allyson; even on the days when Garland was not working, she would still send her limousine to take Allyson to the studio and back.

Garland had been Allyson's idol and here she was, plain as an old shoe dressed in slacks and with little makeup, talking to her as if they were old friends. She was fun (and no star attitude), which put Allyson totally at ease. Garland became the girl's mentor and showed her the ropes. The pair got together between scenes in Garland's dressing room and talked for hours, discovering how much they had in common, such as having fathers with drinking problems. Through the years, they would cry on each other's shoulders and laugh together as their fortunes zoomed up and down. Their friendship lasted a lifetime.

Girl Crazy was released on November 26, 1943, with the taglines "LOVE OR LUNACY? It's the wild cry of a 'girl-crazy' cowboy ... but one clear-eyed daughter of the west ropes and ties him!" and "The Big Musical with Broadway Flair and a Western Air!" It was praised by *Variety,* T.S. in *The New York Times,* and John Douglas Eames in *The MGM Story.* The film was a box office success.

Allyson moved into her first apartment, a $40-a-month place on Wilshire. It was basic but had a kitchen so she could cook eggs and now pancakes, her new culinary triumph. When she got the check for her first week, she danced around the room with it. It was for $125 with $12.50 (ten percent) going to her agent. She could now send money to Clara in New York. Allyson made very few friends, though when being alone at night became too frightening, Allyson rapped on the neighbor's door to ask to sleep on their day bed.

She had to report to the studio every day. If Allyson wasn't working, she would watch other people work as a form of training: stars like Spencer Tracy, Katharine Hepburn and Ingrid Bergman. It was also fun to walk around the lot. Allyson learned to view the studio personnel as her new family. The stars were not competitive; there was no one she didn't get along with. Her contract meant Allyson had to take whatever script was given to her. If she turned it down, she would be put on suspension without pay so Allyson rarely turned anything down.

The Technicolor musical comedy *Best Foot Forward* had a screenplay by Irving Brecher and Fred Finklehoffe (with uncredited work by Dorothy Kingsley) and was directed by Edward Buzzell. After dance director Charles Walters held rehearsals in November and December 1942, the movie was shot between January 18 and March 24 at MGM and on location at St. John's Military Academy in Wisconsin. Allyson plays Ethel but is incorrectly credited as Minerva, one of the girls bused in for the Winsocki Military Institute senior prom. She sings and dances as part of three numbers: a new Hugh Martin–Ralph Blaine song, "Wish I May Wish I Might"; "The Three B's," which she had done in the stage show, and the reprise of "Buckle Down, Winsocki." Her best number is "The Three B's," performed at the prom by Allyson, Gloria DeHaven, Nancy Walker, the MGM studio chorus and Harry James and His Orchestra. She is costumed in the same white floor-length puff-sleeved Irene dress that all the girls wear, though she has a purple ribbon pinned to her waist. She and Walker and DeHaven are juxtaposed by their hair color as much as by the three B's of the song. Allyson has dark blonde, shoulder-length hair. Walker, black-haired, likes the boogie-woogie and DeHaven, a reddish-brunette, likes the blues. Allyson's solo has her first seen at an angle (she has been dipped by one of the dancing cadets) and her part continues with her thrown about in a comic way, with one boy flipping her completely over him. Her singing is more broad and flat. Allyson also has a few lines of dialogue and one scene with Lucille Ball, who replaced Rosemary Lane. She is funny in the way she pronounces the name Schlesinger and gets the two lines, "As Shakespeare once said, 'Who steals a name steals very little. But who steals this steals trash.'" The stage show songs "What Do You Think I Am?" and "Don't Sell the Night Short" were not heard in the film.

Best Foot Forward premiered in New York on June 29 with the tagline "Metro-Goldwyn-Mayer's Honey of a Musical." It was praised by

From left, Allyson, Nancy Walker and Gloria DeHaven in front of cadets, doing the number "The Three B's" in the 1943 film version of *Best Foot Forward*.

Bosley Crowther in *The New York Times* and Pauline Kael in *5001 Nights at the Movies*. The *Variety* reviewer described Allyson as a "looker and good vocalist." It was a box office success. When it was remade as an episode of NBC-TV's musical television series *Max Liebman Spectaculars* on November 20, 1954, "The Three B's" was performed by Pat Carroll, Hope Holiday and Candi Parsons.

Allyson would remain friends with Gloria DeHaven but the person who was the most important on the film was Lucille Ball, whom she found to be wonderful—tall, slightly tough-talking but glamorous. In his book *Ball of Fire: The Tumultuous Life and Comic Art of Lucille Ball*, Stefan Kanfer reported that Allyson paid Ball a visit and expressed envy at her house and garden.

Allyson believed that, after Fred Astaire, Charles Walters was the best dancer in the world. He knew exactly what to do with people, how to put them together and work with them. Walters reported that rehearsals revealed a healthy ongoing rivalry between Allyson and DeHaven, with the two vying for attention. He said Allyson, as a kid from the theater, was unusual in that the camera did not bother her. He counselled her that she had a good chance in the business. The girl had everything the camera liked—looks, height, and style—but she had to do something about that husky voice. Walters felt that if Allyson had two sentences in a row to speak she would put everyone to sleep. He later laughed at how wrong he could be.

Allyson's next film was the Technicolor musical comedy *Thousands Cheer* (1943), produced by Joe Pasternak and directed by George Sidney. This was shot with the working titles *Private Miss Jones* and *As Thousands Cheer* from November 9, 1942, to February 1943 with additional shooting in May 1943 at MGM. The screenplay was by Paul Jarrico and Richard Collins, based on their story "Private Miss Jones." The story centered on Kathryn "Kitty" Jones (Kathryn Grayson), a soprano with Jose Iturbi's New York orchestra. The daughter of a colonel, she goes to an army camp for recreational duty and falls in love with private Eddie Marsh (Gene Kelly). As part of the MGM Parade, Allyson appears as herself in the camp show that features Hollywood stars. Allyson sings part of "In a Little Spanish Town" (music by Mabel Wayne, lyrics by Sam Lewis and Joe Young), played by the Bob Crosby Orchestra. Her hair is again worn shoulder-length with a ribbon and she is dressed in an Irene powder-blue knee-length long-sleeved dress with a white collar. The first part of the song has her singing softly with Gloria DeHaven, and then they support Virginia O'Brien after she gets a solo.

The film was released on September 13 with the taglines "30 Stars * 3 Bands," "Love Story of an Army Camp," "The STARiffic Musical Hit!" "It's STARiffic in Technicolor" and "MGM's Greatest Musical Show." It was praised by *Variety* and by Thomas M. Pryor in *The New York Times*. A box office hit, it was Oscar-nominated for Best Cinematography, Color, Best Art Direction–Interior Decoration, Color and Best Music, Scoring of a Musical Picture.

Allyson said that her part in the film was nothing to cheer about. In his book *Gene Kelly: A Life of Dance and Dreams*, Alvin Yudkoff wrote that Kelly and Allyson chatted and laughed during production, reminiscing about the Henry Hudson hotel where she had lived with Betsy Blair (now Kelly's wife). They compared the fortress mentality of the all-girls' residence to the free-flowing sex of the movie colony.

Pasternak wrote in his autobiography *Easy the Hard Way* that he first met Allyson one day walking into the MGM commissary. He pushed the door open and found her sprawled on the floor. He helped her up and apologized; Allyson dusted herself off and smiled, saying she was not hurt. Pasternak noticed her intriguing throaty voice, brightness and sparkle as the girl said how she recognized him and had been meaning to call on him. Pasternak invited Allyson to lunch and soon he decided he was going to put her in a film. He told the *Thousands Cheer* writers to work her into the story because she just breathed talent and would help the film. The next day the writers went to Pasternak's office to meet the girl and they were equally impressed. Later she admitted to the producer that their meeting was no accident as Allyson rushed to the door when she saw him coming. Her fall was deliberate, done to get noticed because no one was going to notice her for her singing or dancing or beauty. The girl didn't necessarily want to be a star—she just wanted to be an actress. In response to her confession, Pasternak said he admired people who know what they want and how to get it. He called Allyson the most conscientious young actress he had ever met. She never "faked" and was always prepared. She was destined to rise to the top as God had given her an acting talent and she had helped Him considerably with hard work and firm purpose.

Allyson claimed to have been with Van Johnson on March 31, 1943, the night he had a car accident that resulted in facial scarring and the implantation of a metal plate in his head. She said they had attended an acting seminar at the studio and left in separate cars. According to another source, Johnson had his accident after attending a screening of MGM's *Keeper of the Flame* (1942).

The black-and-white musical comedy *Meet the People* (1944) was produced by E.Y. Harburg, who wrote the lyrics to some of the songs. The material had been produced as a play by Sol and Ben Barzman and Louis Lantz in Los Angeles and as a musical with music by Jay Gorney and lyrics by Henry Myers and Edward Eliscu which ran on Broadway at the Mansfield Theatre from December 25, 1940, to May 10, 1941. The film was shot from June to September at MGM. The screenwriters were S.M. Herzig and Fred Saidy and the director was Charles Riesner. It centered on Broadway star Julie Hampton (Lucille Ball) who is interested in a musical tribute to the war industry written by William "Swanee" Swanson (Dick Powell), an idealistic worker at Morgan Shipyards as well as a playwright. Allyson is billed sixth as Annie. She has shorter hair with a side part; sometimes Annie has bangs. Allyson appears in six scenes: She is among the crowd at the Morganville train station bidding farewell to Swanee, at the shipyard launching party where she pours drinks and takes plates from Swanee and listens to the Commander (Bert Lahr) and ensemble sing "Heave Ho" (music by Harold Arlen, lyrics by Harburg), dancing at the Liberty Ship Deck Dance where Vaughn Monroe and His Orchestra perform "In Times Like This" (music by Sammy Fain, lyrics by Harburg), backstage at the shipyard launching show where she has one line to Powell, and as part of the finale which features "It's Smart to Be People" (music by Burton Lane, lyrics by Harburg) and the title song (music by Gorney, lyrics by Myers).

Allyson has a dialogue with Lahr and Ball at the Ritz roadhouse, where she tells Julie. "For the past hour, he has been dining with you by remote control." Her best showcase is part of the number "I Like to Recognize the Tune" which is also in the Deck Dance. Allyson performs the song (music by Richard Rodgers, lyrics by Lorenz Hart) with Virginia O'Brien, Ziggie Talent, Monroe and His Orchestra, the King Sisters and others. Here Allyson wears a floor-length long-sleeved white Irene dress and sings and dances; she is also used as a comic foil to the others. Annie is called a "musical termite" who doesn't like the scat and swing variations that are used by the orchestra and other singers, although at one point she does her own scat riffing. She is handled by Monroe and Talent and ends up falling back on the floor. Allyson's voice is presented as melodious and her performance is funny.

The film was released on June 1, 1944, with the tagline "Metro-Goldwyn-Mayer presents the gayest musical!" It was not a box office success.

The dance direction is credited to Sammy Lee, Charles Walters and Jack Donohue. Brent Phillips in *Charles Walters: The Director Who Made Hollywood Dance* wrote that "I Like to Recognize the Tune" was directed by Walters.

Kay Thompson was the film's vocal arranger and Allyson reported that she helped her overcome the terror of recording songs. Allyson couldn't stand the sound of her own voice and Thompson came up with two cardboard coverings that Allyson could put over her ears when they were recording. Then later Allyson could mouth to the track for the camera as if she liked her voice. In his book *Kay Thompson: From Funny Face to Eloise,* Sam Irvin wrote that Thompson did not warm up to Allyson, and vice versa. Thompson's curt indictment was "Never trust a woman who wears a Peter Pan collar." Irvin reported that later in life, the arranger mocked Allyson by imitating her "high, whiny voice."

Allyson writes that she wasn't given a script or told who else was going to be in it. She was just handed a song for another cameo appearance and told to learn it. She commented on the song "I Like to Recognize the Tune" by telling Lucille Ball, "I'd like to recognise where I am going. I think it is nowhere. That's where." When Allyson again saw Dick Powell in person, she fell in love with him immediately. She would always call him Richard, not Dick, because Allyson hated the diminutives of proper names. One day on the set, she saw Powell standing talking on a box portable telephone and smiling at her. Wanting a closer look, Allyson walked over to him, to look at his blue eyes. He put his hand over the receiver and asked her if something was wrong. Allyson said she was waiting to use the phone, but felt crushed, believing he did not remember meeting her before (on the stage version of *Best Foot Forward*). Powell said he would be off the phone in a minute and after he hung up, Allyson still stood looking at him in a daze. The man looked back as if to ask "What is wrong with you?" and then walked away. She dialed numbers and hoped no one would answered. When Powell walked back, Allyson hoped it was to tell her that he did remember her. But he wanted to use the phone again and stood absently waiting for the girl to finish. She hung up the receiver, telling him that nobody was home.

Allyson got palpitations every time Powell looked at her but she felt she was getting nowhere with him. And besides, he was a married man. She was thrilled when Powell invited the cast to his home for a barbecue. Curious to see how a real movie star lived, Allyson met Joan Blondell and her mother. Mrs. Blondell could never remember Allyson's name and referred to her throughout the evening as "that cute one." She sat and monopolized Allyson for what seemed like hours, telling her endless stories about her daughter. It wasn't exactly what Allyson had come for, but she was all ears to learn anything and everything about Powell's wife.

Powell had a reputation for helping beginners after having done so for Jane Powell—no relation. He held sessions with a little band of ambitious youths and discussed how to get ahead in Hollywood. He also told them to feel free to call him if they needed counsel on a specific problem. Allyson told him how hurt she felt when he didn't recognize her at the phone and he just laughed. There was still no romance.

Allyson was also concerned about her film career. She feared she might never be anything more than a bit player, singing songs in cameos. She wanted to give up but Lucille Ball wouldn't let her. Ball felt the girl had worked too hard to get where she was and was sure that Allyson was going to progress. Ball gave herself as an example but Allyson felt they were in two different situations. Ball had a full life, with husband and friends, and was a star. Allyson was lonely and frustrated. She decided that after the next commitment, she would go back to New York. She was starting to get somewhere on Broadway; Hollywood was not for her. She also wanted to study to be a doctor before it was too late.

As part of the war effort, Louis B. Mayer decided to send Allyson, Nancy Walker and Gloria DeHaven to entertain and cheer up the troops in wartime hospitals. This idea terrified Allyson. The three were required to each take a different ward. Usually there was great applause but one day after she had sung and done a dance routine, there was complete silence. Confused and frightened, Allyson wondered if they hated her and whether she should continue. Finally one man yelled out "Sing it, June," so the girl sang another song and danced some more—but again there was silence. Suddenly Allyson realized what the problem was: It was an amputation ward with boys that had lost arms. She pulled herself together and called for requests, staying on to sing whatever song they wanted. But after Allyson left the ward, she fell to pieces.

MGM assessed her and decided they could do without her. She had made it through six months of probation but was not considered worthy of the next step, which was a seven-year contract. With Dick Powell as a mentor, her plan to leave Hollywood had changed; she was now ready to stay and fight for a movie career. But the MGM front office saw her as a failure: She wasn't pretty or sexy. She sang fairly well but they already had Judy Garland, Jane Powell and Kathryn Grayson. She didn't dance that well. But Joe Pasternak felt that Allyson had something and stepped in to save her. He went to Mayer and said to take a look at a test they had done talking to her. He said to ignore how she was dressed and walked but to see how the girl spoke and listened and to watch her eyes. Mayer watched the test and agreed she had something. He didn't know what it was but he let Pasternak use her in a new film, *Two Girls and a Sailor.*

With her head momentarily out of the noose, Allyson called Powell at home. Joan Blondell answered and didn't seem interested in her situation. Worse was that Blondell said that if Allyson wanted Powell, she could have him. Allyson was embarrassed that Powell's wife was aware of her feelings, but did not tell Powell what his wife had said when he got on the phone. She asked him if he would read the script for the new film and help her with it.

They discussed the script over lunch at the Brown Derby. Powell felt that Allyson shouldn't play the part she had been cast in: the beautiful younger sister to plain sister Gloria DeHaven. Powell felt the plain sister was the better part and suggested she go to Mayer and say that she wanted to test for the role of the plain sister—and, to help convince him, to wear no makeup in the test. According to Allyson, she cut her hair (already short from *Meet the People*) for the test. Although fearful of contradicting Mayer, Allyson trusted Powell's judgment and went to see the studio head. Mayer agreed to let her test. When he saw the result, he agreed that she should play the plain sister. Allyson was happy that at last she had a real screen role. When the girl bumped into Lucille Ball in the commissary, she thanked Ball for convincing her to stay in Hollywood.

The black-and-white musical comedy *Two Girls and a Sailor* (1944) was produced by Joe Pasternak and shot from mid–September to December 24, 1943; additional scenes were shot in late February 1944. It had the working titles of *The Tale of Two Sisters* and *Two Sisters and a Sailor.* In the screenplay by Richard Connell and Gladys Lehman, Patsy Deyo (top-billed Allyson) and her younger sister Jean (DeHaven) set up a private canteen to entertain servicemen. Allyson again appears with her hair short with a side part. Patsy is juxtaposed against her sister who is man-crazy and whom men find more attractive. They are rivals for the "Sailor" of the title, John "Johnny" Dyckman Brown III (Van Johnson); Patsy likes him but he likes Jean better. The romantic rivalry is demonstrated in a seven-minute dream sequence with outlandish sets and costumes, Jimmy Durante wearing a moustache, a Navy band playing "Anchors Aweigh" and a fashion parade and a performance of "You,

Dear" (music by Sammy Fain, lyrics by Ralph Freed, performed by Buddy Moreno with Harry James and His Orchestra). The dream turns into Patsy's nightmare: Johnny proposes marriage but then leaves her for Jean. The two girls have a catfight, with face-slapping, until Patsy awakens. The narrative has Patsy state that Jean is the prettier of the two, which no doubt explains Johnny's preference for Jean, though it is Patsy who is shown in her slip in one scene as she changes clothes. Patsy gets the funny line to Jean, "I've had to pinch you in Paducah, Peoria, Tacoma, Topeka, Johnstown, Jamestown, Augusta, Maine and Georgia!" She is sincere in dramatic moments and insincere when she encourages Frank Miller (Tom Drake) to pursue Jean so that Patsy can have a better shot at Johnny. Allyson also has a scene where she cries because the sister act is ending. She gets her first feature film kiss with Johnson, and director Richard Thorpe gives her some closeups.

Allyson sings and dances with DeHaven in three numbers: "Sweet and Lovely" by Gus Arnheim, Harry Tobias and Neil Moret at a vaudeville theater (the song is heard again in the finale), "A Tisket, a Tasket" by Ella Fitzgerald and Van Alexander at the Humpty Dumpty Inn, and "A Love Like Ours" with music by Alberta Nichols and lyrics by Mann Holiner at the Club Floriano with Harry James and His Orchestra. The first number is notable for Allyson dressed in male drag of top hat and tails. She gets a solo number "The Young Man with a Horn" (music by George Stoll, lyrics by Ralph Freed), performed with Harry James and His Orchestra at the revamped Wigson's Warehouse. Here Allyson dances with a soldier (actor unknown); her dancing is perhaps more impressive than her singing, where she uses a broad style. Allyson is funny when she is made dizzy by the soldier's jitterbugging. The number has her in a white floor-length Irene dress with gray-colored lace sleeves. "The Young Man with a Horn" is also reprised in the finale. Pat Hyatt was reported to have voice-doubled for Allyson in the finale. The film's dance director was Sammy Lee.

Two Girls and a Sailor was released on April 27, 1944, with the taglines "M-G-M's Ship-Shapely Musical" and "Star-Spangled BANTER... with JOY AHOY!" It was praised by Bosley Crowther in *The New York Times* and by John Douglas Eames in *The MGM Story*. A box office success, it received an Academy Award nomination for Best Writing, Original Screenplay.

Allyson reported that on the set, she received a package that contained a hand-sewn felt jacket from a sailor in the Pacific. This came in handy as she found the temperature so cold that she feared she would

Van Johnson and Allyson in *Two Girls and a Sailor* (1944).

come down with pneumonia or the flu. Allyson could now huddle in the warm jacket and, thanks to the unknown fan, she did not get sick. For years Allyson used the jacket and kept it in her dressing room for luck.

There was an incident with flying teeth in one scene. In the empty warehouse, Jimmy Durante was hiding and supposed to frighten the two girls. He let out such a bloodcurdling sound that DeHaven screamed for real and the caps she wore over her teeth went sailing by Allyson before landing on the floor. The horrified look on Allyson's face was seen in the film.

Allyson had a fan who collected everything about her life, and through the years became one of her best friends: Ronnie Dayton. She met him when her brother graduated from Culver Military Academy. He knew she would attend and went to get her autograph. He later became a stand-in, which made it easier for him to spend time with Allyson. He sent her cards on every occasion and she would invite him to dinner occasionally. Dayton commented on her cooking by answering invitations with "Only if you promise to burn it."

Allyson said that Van Johnson was the funniest man in the world, though very serious when he was working. In his book on Johnson, Ronald L. Davis wrote that the actor and Allyson renewed their friendship during production and occasionally ate dinner together in fancy restaurants, sharing the expense as they had done at the Automat in their Broadway days. Sam Irvin wrote in his book on vocal arranger Kay Thompson that when they were shooting "Young Man with a Horn," Allyson didn't want to put on earphones to hear the music as her hair had just been done. Thompson lost patience, saying to forget about her hair as they had work to do.

Allyson appeared in the group portrait celebrating MGM's 20th birthday, which appeared in *Life* magazine on September 27, 1943. Perhaps to indicate her low status among the stars, Allyson was seated in the fifth of six rows, between Frances Gifford and Richard Whorf.

David Rose was married to but separated from Judy Garland and he and Allyson began dating, often double-dating with Betsy Blair and Gene Kelly or picnicking on the studio grounds. Garland did not mind but Louis B. Mayer did. He was a very moral man who didn't like it when his stars dated married men. When Allyson told him Rose was a lovely, gentle person and a gifted composer from whom she was learning a lot about music, he told her to buy a book instead. She liked Mayer because he was the strong father figure she'd never had, and he treated his stars like his children. Mayer was concerned that Allyson was becoming the subject of gossip, just when she was hitting it big. There was a rumor of nymphomania—she wasn't Goody Two Shoes but Goody Round Heels—and that Allyson was actually a 43-year-old midget.

Mayer suggested that a more appropriate person to date was Van Johnson, whom every bobbysoxer in the country was swooning over. She agreed to go on a series of official dates to premieres and industry functions with the studio's publicity department manufacturing a big romance and even panting for them to be married. Allyson got a taste of how popular Johnson was when she saw crazed fans waiting in the hundreds for him, outside the studio gates or wherever the couple went, ready to tear off his clothes and yank his hair. She and Johnson tried to spend Christmas and birthdays together and she felt he was the kind of friend who loved you whether you were up or down. One birthday present she received from him: a miniature painting of a clown with a birdcage on his hat and an umbrella over the bird.

Mayer also approved of Allyson dating Peter Lawford. Though she was never as close to him as she was with Van Johnson, Allyson grew very fond of Lawford in a mild romantic way. They had a lot of fun together. She loved his devil-may-care attitude and was fascinated by his British accent and his terribly British titled parents. Another man that Allyson said she dated at ths time was John F. Kennedy, whom she also met at the studio.

MGM was confident that *Two Girls and a Sailor* would be a hit and sent Allyson and Nancy Walker to New York on a personal appearance tour. Dick Powell said he had seen the film and that she was going to be a star. Allyson gave two versions of the tale. One had him calling her hotel room at midnight asking to meet him in the lobby. The other had him coming to her room and suggesting they go out to dinner. They ended up having a cup of coffee. When Powell asked her on a date, she refused because he was married. He fetched a newspaper from the hotel's newsstand and showed her the headline "Joan Blondell and Dick Powell Separate." Powell took her to Sardi's or 21.

In Los Angeles, they began going to parties together. Mayer called her in to tell her that, since Powell was a married man, dating him was another bad idea. It didn't matter that he was getting a divorce. It still didn't look good. But Allyson was in love. They were careful when they went out in public, with a private refuge being the home of Lucille Ball. Allyson met Powell's acquaintances, whose talent and success made her insecure. He helped by coaching her how to behave, and on his birthday on November 11, she gave him two pearl-handled antique guns. Powell gave her the nicknames Flattop, Pumpkin Head, Idiot Child, Idiot Head and Junie Face, and the book *Messer Marco Polo* by Donn Byrne for inspiration. On page 44, Powell wrote her name in the margin next to the sentence "She is as warm in the sun in early June ... but we all think of her as Golden Bells, the little girl in the Chinese garden."

Powell moved in with his father at Toluca Lake and took Allyson to meet him, telling his father this was the girl he loved. She discovered that Powell was a take-charge kind of man and as a result her whole lifestyle changed. She moved to a larger apartment, with a bedroom. He hired a live-in housekeeper, Bess Van Dyke, so that the couple could have dinner together at her place. Bess was a great companion. Allyson continued her education by getting armloads of library books on etiquette and she cut out pictures from magazines that showed tables set with lovely silverware and linens. Powell also taught her what he thought was good taste and what was not so that soon Allyson was ready to sit at elegant formal dinners.

They also had *fun*. When he asked what her philosophy on life was, she said it was if you see someone without a smile, give them yours.

Powell almost fell off his chair laughing at that and told her to never change.

She had promised to go to a party at Ronald Colman's and asked Powell to take her but he said that if he gave her a sign, that meant they had to leave immediately. At the party, Powell was the most social creature there and she just walked around clinging to him, afraid to say a word. They stayed the whole evening. Powell urged her to drift around and talk to people on her own. She didn't know what to talk to them about and felt she was an introvert in training to be an extrovert. Sometimes she would clown around and act as if she were having a great time and other times she just sat in a corner. But she learned to hold her own socially, though ironically once she did, Allyson found the thrill was gone and she preferred to stay at home to just enjoy Powell and a few friends.

Allyson was determined never to be on the studio's drop list again. She had been in a hit movie and now people were starting to imitate her croaky voice and lisp. No one knew that Allyson would spend hours checking through a script and changing words with the dreaded "s" sounds to something easier for her to say. She felt she was a star and finally belonged at MGM, loving the premieres and the parties. She acceded to the publicity demands made on her, which she saw as part of her job. Fifty percent of the success of any star came from publicity. Louis B. Mayer always made sure that you never faded away unless or until he was ready for you to fade away. Allyson was told what to say on every interview and wasn't allowed to get mad despite admitting to having a temper. When the actress saw a camera, she automatically smiled. She was never photographed with a cigarette, a drink, a cup of coffee, or even a glass of water because someone might think it was liquor. And if she were, these photos were never published. The studio had complete control of her image. Portraits were taken at the studio for magazine covers though the press had access when home layouts were done. The stars were sheltered and not compensated for any merchandising like paper dolls or publicity cards.

On July 30, 1944, Allyson appeared on the radio show *Command Performance* before an audience of 400 WAVES and sang "A Love Like Ours." On September 13, she was back on the show, with Gloria DeHaven promoting *Two Girls and a Sailor.* They read mail from men in the armed forces and duetted on "A Love Like Ours." On January 31, 1945, Allyson was the mistress of ceremonies on the radio show *Mail Call.* She also sang "Don't Fence Me In" (music by Cole Porter, lyrics by Porter and Robert Fletcher) and "A Love Like Ours."

On April 17, it was announced that Allyson would re-team with Gloria DeHaven and Jimmy Durante in an MGM musical to be produced by Joe Pasternak, *You Are Beautiful* (previously known as *The Joy of Living*). It appears this film was never made.

The black-and-white musical comedy *Music for Millions* (1944) was produced by Joe Pasternak and shot from May 22 to September 5, 1944. The working titles were *Dear Barbara* and *100 Girls and a Man*. The screenplay by Myles Connolly has six-year-old "Mike" aka Monkey (Margaret O'Brien) join her sister Babs (Allyson), who plays string bass in Jose Iturbi's Manhattan Philharmonic orchestra. Allyson is billed third after O'Brien and Iturbi. The role of Babs was first planned for Lana Turner, then Susan Peters and Donna Reed, before Allyson was cast. She wears her hair in a longer shoulder-length style. Since Babs is pregnant in the narrative, costume designer Irene dresses her in bulky jackets and coats, though she is seen in her slip in one scene. The film sees Allyson play a straight dramatic role, though she sings with the crowd as Andrew (Jimmy Durante) performs "Umbriago." In her best scene, she tells Iturbi that she wants to have her baby for her soldier husband, who is fighting in the Pacific war theater; she fears he is dead. She makes Babs' distress moving. Director Henry Koster gives her several closeups in the film.

The film was released on December 18 with the taglines "Warm, Tender Romance! Deep, Lasting Faith!," "A MUST on Every Moviegoer's List!," "The Picture That Has Everything!" and "M-G-M's picture of warmth and charm ... a love story that smiles through tears, about people you'll love!" *The New York Times*' Bosley Crowther wrote that Allyson played most sweetly. The film was a box office success and received an Academy Award nomination for Best Writing, Original Screenplay.

Allyson commented wryly on her ability to cry on camera, saying that once she had to cry in a film, she was never asked to sing again. This was not true but Allyson believed that she was a better crier than singer. To cry, Allyson would simply tell herself that she was not going to cry and the tears always started flowing.

Margaret O'Brien and Allyson were known around MGM as The Town Criers with any role that called for a lot of tears automatically earmarked for one of them. This put them in a class by themselves and they formed their own mutual admiration society. In one scene, O'Brien pronounced sword as saw-ward and Allyson imitated her on camera. The crew thought that was funny but the director did not. She also found herself talking like O'Brien on dates. O'Brien reported that Allyson was very nice to her, always very sisterly, and they remained friends afterwards.

Koster said Allyson was good to work with, a great talent, and he mentioned her marvelous gravel voice. Koster made three films with her so they were very close for a while. For years, she and Dick Powell would go to Koster's house.

On June 10, Allyson appeared on the *Old Gold Comedy Theater* radio show in the episode "Tom, Dick and Harry." This was a 22-minute version of the 87-minute 1941 RKO comedy. Telephone operator Janie (Allyson) receives marriage proposals from conservative car salesman Tom (Don DeFore), millionaire playboy Dick (Reginald Gardiner) and bohemian auto mechanic Harry (Bill Williams), and must make a choice. Janie was played by Ginger Rogers in the film. The radio episode was directed by Harold Lloyd. Allyson's performance includes a funny drunk scene.

Her next film was the black-and-white romantic comedy *Her Highness and the Bellboy* (1945), produced by Joe Pasternak and shot from December 11, 1944, to late January 1945, with reshoots from February 7 to mid–February. It had the same screenwriters (Richard Connell and Gladys Lehman) and director (Richard Thorpe) as *Two Girls and a Sailor*. Jimmy Dobson (Robert Walker), a bellboy at the grand Hotel Eden in New York, gets a second job as personal attendant to Princess Veronica (Hedy Lamarr), a visiting European beauty. Third-billed Allyson plays the supporting role of Leslie Odell, Jimmy's neighbor and friend. In her one scene with Lamarr, Lamarr winks at her and Allyson smiles back. Leslie is bedridden and crippled, said to be a former dancer who is now depressed and paints Santa Claus dolls. Allyson sings three times and dances five times (the dance direction was Charles Walters). She sings one line of "The Fountain in the Park (While Strolling Through the Park One Day)" (by Ed Haley), part of "Honey" (by Richard A. Whiting, Seymour Simons and Haven Gillespie) and "Dream" (by George Stoll and Calvin Jackson). The film gives the actress an extended (seven-minute) dream sequence, perhaps her best scene. It begins with Leslie getting out of bed, walking to a floor-length mirror and talking to her reflection. She dances and does a cartwheel, then proceeds to walk up a large staircase to the court of a king ("Rags" Ragland, who plays Albert Weever in the rest of the film). Leslie does some comic dancing, imitating the royal ballet dancers, and then a giant frog appears and her pajamas are transformed into a low-cut feathered floor-length Irene ball gown with straps worn with a tiara. The frog is transformed into Jimmy and the couple sings "Honey" and waltz before he kisses her. Allyson makes Leslie vulnerable, and her laugh is infectious. Director Thorpe gives her multiple closeups.

The film was released on September 11, 1945, with the tagline "A Royal Command to Love!" It was praised by *Variety* but lambasted by *The New York Times'* Thomas M. Pryor, who wrote that she looked beautiful and pathetic. The film was a box office success.

Allyson found working with Robert Walker a strange and exhilarating experience. He was a very sad man, intense and moody, difficult but only for himself and self-destructive. He would disappear from the set, not to be found for hours. Often he went to a bar just around the corner at lunchtime to drink and sometimes did not come back. Once he was found sitting on the roof. Another time he somehow smashed his hand through a mirror and took himself to a doctor. A lot of stitches were required and the actor didn't come back to work for several days. Walker was involved in a love triangle and felt his personal life had been wrecked by David O. Selznick's obsession with his (Walker's) wife Jennifer Jones. Although Walker always seemed to be hiding some hurt, shooting a scene with him was a once-in-a-lifetime experience. No other actor Allyson ever worked with could make a scene so true.

Allyson wished she could have helped Walker but she was preoccupied with her own problem: She was pitted against her greatest competition of that era, Hedy Lamarr, who was said to be the most beautiful woman in the world. Allyson admitted that she was not a big star like Lamarr, who had this aura and untouchable quality that one didn't infringe upon. You did not talk to Miss Lamarr until she talked to you. It was nothing that Lamarr did, it was just something you felt. Allyson would just stare, entranced, and was impressed by how Lamarr used an intimate little smile to turn a man on. When Allyson tried it, people laughed at Junie the clown and Junie trying to look cute. She would never be Junie the sexpot and it was a joke among MGM officials that she was the only one on the lot whose cleavage the Hays Office never had to come down to check. Lamarr commented that though she had star billing, the June Allyson part was really better.

The black and white comedy *The Sailor Takes a Wife* (1945) was produced by Edwin H. Knopf and shot from mid–March to late May 1945. It had the working titles *John and Mary* and *For Better, For Worse.* The screenplay was by Chester Erskine, Anne Morrison Chapin and Whitfield Cook, based on the unproduced Erskine play *Happily Ever After.* The director was Richard Whorf. In New York City, John (Walker), a sailor waiting to ship out to Europe meets 18-year-old secretary Mary (Allyson) at a servicemen's canteen and they impulsively marry. Costumed by Irene, Allyson wears pigtails and ribbons in her hair for sleeping. She dances with servicemen at the canteen, with another sailor (Johnny Lane) in particular. The role allows the actress to perform slapstick including trying to open a stuck window, being repeatedly hit in the back by an opening door, struggling to put a pillow in a pillowcase, accidentally hitting Freddie (Hume Cronyn) in the face with his hat, and later draping the mink coat he has given her over him. She also imitates Mr. Ambor (Reginald Owen) and Lisa (Audrey Totter) with a Romanian accent. Mary gets two funny lines. When she first shows John their apartment, she comments, "Isn't it wonderful? We've already got ice cubes." And when Mary packs her bag to leave him, she says, "You don't think that I'm going to live with a husband who brings his lady friends home and commits orgies?" Allyson makes Mary sincere and funny.

The film was released on December 28, 1945, with the tagline "FOR BETTER...OR WORSE...IT'S THE HILARIOUS SIDE OF MARRIAGE!" It was praised by *Variety* and by John Douglas Eames in *The MGM Story*. Bosley Crowther of *The New York Times* wrote of Allyson' attractive personality. The film was a box office success.

In Beverly Linet's book *Star-Crossed: The Story of Robert Walker and Jennifer Jones*, she quotes Allyson on Walker. Allyson made it her personal mission to keep Walker from retreating into his shell during the long waits between setups.

Her next film was the black-and-white musical comedy *Two Sisters from Boston* (1946), produced by Joe Pasternak (under the working title *Brighton Beach*) from June to October 1945. The Myles Connolly screenplay, set at the turn of the century, focuses on a Bostonian, Martha Canford Chandler (Allyson), who visits her sister Abigail (Kathryn Grayson) in New York. Abigail works at the Golden Rooster, a burlesque house in the Bowery where she is known as High "C" Susie. Allyson is billed second after Grayson though Allyson plays the leading role. She wears what is presumably a wig of long hair in the period style that includes a sculptured updo. The role has the actress playing the piano and doing slapstick, including being pulled around, carried when unconscious, repeated fainting, and hiccupping. Allyson screams and cries, gives Martha moments of sincerity, and is funny. Her best scene is perhaps when Martha sings and dances to "After the Show" (music by Sammy Fain, lyrics by Ralph Freed) alongside chorus girls and Jimmy Durante. The number is designed to convince Lawrence Tyburt Patterson, Jr.

Allyson and Robert Walker in *The Sailor Takes a Wife* (1945).

(Peter Lawford), that Martha is High "C" Susie to protect Abigail's reputation. It begins with Martha in a Helen Rose dark-colored knee-length sparkly dress with a shoulder ribbon that is stripped off her by the chorus girls so that she has to perform in a frilly leotard. Then the girls dress her in a light-colored, floor-length, long-sleeved low-cut sparkly dress with feather boa and dark-colored feathered hat. Martha transitions from being humiliated to enjoying performing. The dance director was Jack Donohue. Henry Koster commented that he loved both girls and felt Allyson the better actress and Grayson the better singer.

The film was released in April 1946 with the tagline "SHOO AWAY THOSE BLUES!" It was praised by *Variety.* Bosley Crowther in *The New York Times* wrote that Allyson charmingly demonstrated that her talent in the comedy department was extensive and captivating. The film was a box office success.

Allyson writes that Grayson had the patience of Job, remaining unruffled no matter what was happening on the set. If the director blew up or she had to repeat a difficult song because her acting partner fumbled, Grayson smiled her sympathetic smile and carried on. Allyson saw herself made of weaker stuff, unable to stand temperament around her. She admired Grayson as a woman and her singing talent.

Working with Peter Lawford was like going to a party since he made a game of whatever he did. Lawford was funny and witty and he used many strange Briticisms for things he knew would crack the Americans up. In his book, James Spada wrote that during filming, the actor now found himself quite taken with Allyson and she responded to his advances despite her marriage to Dick Powell. Lawford was said to have been crazy about Allyson, describing her as a little China doll, sweet, nice and intelligent. She was completely helpless and this acted as a spur to the protective and resourceful male in him. The couple occasionally stole chances to be together at the house of Jackie Cooper, where Cooper said Allyson had Powell pick her up so it looked like she was just visiting Cooper and his wife. Whenever the Powells had a party, Lawford would be invited with Allyson insisting he bring a girl with him as a decoy. Lawford said it was hard for him to go to these parties since he was unable to touch her or talk to her the way he wanted to. She and Lawford were discreet but rumors about their romance cropped up and soon blind items appeared in gossip columns. Then the MGM bosses forbade him to make a trip to New York because Allyson was going to be there at the same time. According to Spada, the romance was over before it had a chance to explode into the public eye, ending with ill feelings on bad sides. Lawford's later manager reported that the actor then hated Allyson and used to say the most uncomplimentary things about her.

Powell had helped her career and now she wanted to return the favor but after reading a script he liked, Allyson said he was wrong for the part. Powell disagreed and made the crime drama *Murder, My Sweet* (1944) which was a hit and transformed his persona from musical comedy crooners to hard-boiled characters.

She had trouble leading Powell to the altar. Allyson wasn't interested in dating other men but he didn't seem to appreciate the fact that she turned down their offers. Allyson tried goading him by accepting the offers and Powell played along. He would go to the same restaurant she would be at on the date and sit at another table. Powell would look the man over and then give the thumbs down, knowing they were not for her. Still he did not propose. Allyson wondered if the problem was that he was used to more sophisticated ladies so she went to Bullock's and bought a slinky black gown, long false eyelashes and put her hair up. Powell was taking her to Ciro's but, when he saw this brand of sophistication, Powell said she looked like everything he was trying to get away from. Allyson returned all scrubbed, with just a touch of lipstick and her usual Peter Pan collar, and Powell said the real her was like being in a fresh breeze.

Allyson's biggest competition for Powell's attention was not another woman but his boat the *Santana*, a 64-foot yawl. They spent weeks on its maintenance with Powell's friend James Cagney until he finally invited her out to Catalina. Everything was fine in the quiet bay and a little less fine in the open ocean but things got really rough on the way back when she got seasick. Allyson and Powell also went out on the boat with Humphrey Bogart and Lauren Bacall. One day Bogart looked over at the women sitting on the deck and said to Powell that they had picked the two babes with the croakiest voices in Hollywood. Powell confided that Allyson got mistaken for a boy on the telephone all the time.

Allyson believed her frustration with Powell led her to get a bad case of shingles, though she was also working too hard. When she almost fainted on the set, the studio doctor discovered Allyson had low blood sugar. He prescribed rest and to start eating right. Louis B. Mayer supervised the girl's diet and made her eat in the executive dining room. Predictably, a rumor started that she was having an affair with Mayer who, it was said, enjoyed dating starlets. She spent more time on the boat and at Lucille Ball's house. Allyson saw how Ball's marriage to orchestra leader Desi Arnaz was like cars that passed in the morning: When she was leaving for the studio in the early morning hours, he would be coming home.

Allyson and Powell tried to stay out of public sight and, one night, went for dinner and dancing to an out-of-the-way nightclub where Mayer's spies were not apt to find them. Powell was divorced but not talking about marrying Allyson after they had been seeing each other for a year. He drove her home and they sat in the car a while and kissed. Powell got out but before he could come around to help her out, she stopped him and wanted to know his intentions. At first he laughed and said, "I never discuss trends without talking to my business manager." Then Powell told her he loved her very much but he had no intention of ever getting married again. Her heart was broken and Allyson burst into tears and said she didn't think they should see each other again. Allyson wouldn't even let him walk her to her door. Do you have any better offers?, he called out. Two she said defiantly, though there was really only one: Tommy Mitchell, who had returned to New York from military service. It always took Powell an hour to drive back to Toluca Lake and he always called to say he was home safely. The phone rang at the usual time and she answered sobbing, which made Powell hang up. Later there was a pounding on her door and he said that if she wanted to get married, they would get married. Allyson felt it was the most unromantic proposal ever uttered until he added, "You know I love you." She threw her arms around him, saying, "I love you, Tommy," not realizing her gaffe. Powell asked who the hell Tommy was and when Allyson explained, he roared with laughter and so did she.

3

Marriage to Dick Powell

Powell obtained his final divorce decree from Blondell on July 27 and it was announced on August 12 that he and Allyson had filed notice of their intention to wed. Following Hollywood protocol, Powell leaked the news to Louella Parsons. Louis B. Mayer sent for Allyson. In no uncertain terms, he said she could not marry Powell because it would ruin her career, but Allyson didn't care. Mayer predicted she would end up having to take care of him because of Powell's advanced age. Mayer threatened to put her on suspension but she still didn't care, and stalked out. Allyson suddenly realized there was another problem and went back to Mayer. He beamed, sure that she would now agree not to marry Powell. Instead she asked Mayer to give her away because she didn't know where her real father was. Mayer was dumbstruck and then said he would be happy to give her away.

Allyson called Tommy in New York and told him the news, though he had read about in the newspaper. He had the same objections as Mayer about Powell's age and said to call him once she had gotten him out of her system. These negative reactions gave Allyson second thoughts, especially how people were saying she was a homewrecker as Powell had left Joan Blondell for her. But Powell reminded his fiancée that Blondell had first left *him* and the marriage was not a happy one anyway.

The wedding was planned for August 19 at the Holmby Hills house of Bonnie and Johnny Green. Bonnie had been a member of the Copacabana chorus line with Allyson, and Johnny was MGM's musical director. Johnny would stand in for Powell's father, who was now in a nursing home, and Bonnie for Allyson's mother, who had remarried and couldn't make the trip.

The night before, Allyson was in a state of nerves. She feared that Powell would not turn up because of the cold he had caught doing stunt work in icy waters. She dropped a platter and cut a gash in her finger when picking up the pieces. Her maid of honor Jane Wilkie took her to a drug store where Allyson was administered first aid and a hospital emergency room where it took seven stitches to close her up.

Powell was late for the wedding. The judge performed the ceremony in the house's living room. His best man was A. Morgan Maree, who handled Powell's money (and Allyson's). Allyson's housekeeper Bess was there, as was her agent Johnny Hyde, who made Allyson feel tall because he was so tiny. There was one momentary hiccup: When the judge asked her if she took this man, Allyson got confused and asked, "Who?" There were chuckles all around her.

The reception was held at the LaRue restaurant. The couple then went to the apartment that would be their home for the time being. Allyson had bought a knockout nightgown made of white satin with a filmy white robe and satin slippers and delayed the inevitable by feeding her husband three glasses of milk and soda crackers. The next day they went to the *Santana* where they made love and she accidently set fire to the galley. But a call from the nursing home got them to return, and they learned that Powell's father had died. After her marriage, Allyson received hate mail from people feeling she should have wed Van Johnson.

On October 1, she was on the cover of *Life* magazine as part of the promotion for *Her Highness and the Bellboy.* Allyson was posed in a rural setting, wearing a sweater and with her hair windswept.

The Technicolor musical biography *Till the Clouds Roll By* (1946) was produced by Arthur Freed and shot off and on between October 8, 1945, and May 23, 1946, at MGM and on location at the Los Angeles County Arboretum & Botanic Garden. The working title was *As the Clouds Roll By.* The screenplay was by Myles Connolly and Jean Holloway, based on George Wells' adaptation of a Guy Bolton story. The director was Richard Whorf though the uncredited Vincente Minnelli did the Judy Garland numbers and George Sidney did the Hollywood finale sequence. It was based on the life and music of Jerome Kern (Robert Walker). Since the actors are billed alphabetically, Allyson is top-billed. She appears in two musical numbers with Ray McDonald and the chorus, staged and directed by Robert Alton. Allyson dances as Mary in the title song sung by McDonald in the Broadway show *Oh, Boy!* (lyrics by Guy Bolton and P.G. Wodehouse) and sings and dances as Jane in the show *Leave It to Jane*; in the latter, she, McDonald and the chorus do a medley of the title song and "Cleopatterer," both with Wodehouse lyrics. The second number is the better showcase with its red, white and blue candy color costume design by Helen Rose. Jane wears a white long-sleeved blouse with blue knee-length skirt with red and white underskirt, red bow tie, red belt, red hair ribbon, white socks and black shoes. "Cleopatterer" has that broad flat singing style favored by vocal arranger Kay Thompson. At one point it features the undulating hands of the chorus in the foreground as Jane sings. Allyson's hair length changes in some shots so it is apparent that the medley features footage from retakes shot at a later date. According to the Hugh Fordin book *The Movies' Greatest Musicals: Produced in Hollywood USA by the Freed Unit*, her numbers were shot in November–December 1945.

The film was released on December 5, 1946, with the tagline "The mammoth musical of Jerome Kern's dramatic life story!" It was praised by *Variety* but lambasted by Pauline Kael in *5001 Nights at the Movies.* The film was a box office success.

By now Allyson could be shooting scenes for three films all in the same day and, to help her, the studio supplied a bicycle so she could travel from one set to another. If there was a crying scene, it was shot last.

She and Powell lived in a big house in Bel Air but Allyson wasn't a good housekeeper. She didn't know how to order food or plan meals or how to handle personnel. Allyson was intense about becoming a successful wife. Once, instead of one cord of fireplace wood, she ordered seven; they sat around looking like a beached whale until Powell sent back six. When he had to go to New York to make a speech, Allyson packed for him but forgot the pants. Another time she forgot to get a pair of pants to the cleaners that he needed for the next day. Allyson found Powell a joy to live with, always either whistling or

Allyson doing the title song number in *Till the Clouds Roll By* (1946).

singing. He talked a lot and cried with happiness, and also cried over the deaths of people he did not know that were struck down in their prime. If Powell felt anger coming on, he would say "God is love" and just slow down, or work on his boat.

Powell was determined to make a good sailor out of his wife so they were out on the water quite a lot. Allyson learned to operate the boat and one day she had a wonderful time as the captain with the breeze in her face and a glorious view. As Allyson steered, a tiny blue sailboat appeared to their right and Powell told her to hit it. The kids in the boat jumped overboard and Powell fished them out of the water, later paying them for the damage done in the collision. The kids were thrilled to meet the two stars but Allyson was mortified about what she had done and apologized. Powell seemed more bothered by how the boat now needed a patch job. Humphrey Bogart was determined to own the boat and his persistence paid off when one day he caught Powell in the right mood. Powell said his friend had worn him down and the Bogarts invited the Powells on the new maiden voyage. Bogart was all smiles but Lauren Bacall told Allyson in a low sour voice, "Thanks a lot," because she hated the boat.

Powell's love of his boat was replaced with a love of planes but Allyson was a very uneasy rider. He prevailed on to her to climb into a cockpit with him and fly, but she noted that the fuel gauge said they were out of gas. They were over the Muroc Field Air Force base where private planes were forbidden to land and, when he radioed in, they were directed to a small base nearby. Allyson begged him to call the Air Force back. He feared losing his license but called in a mayday as they were out of fuel. Powell landed the plane and angry officers marched toward them. He told his wife it was her show because he understood the army didn't shoot women. She climbed out and the men recognized her and invited her to lunch. She left with the men and Powell trailed behind until Allyson stopped and told the men that she wanted them to meet him. After they refueled, Allyson did an imitation of being the pilot with Powell as her co-pilot. But a high wind meant that they had to take off crossfield instead of downfield, so Powell assumed piloting duties, pulling back on the controls and she disappeared under the panel. Powell thought the officers knew who was really flying the plane.

Allyson learned how her husband did everything better than she—swimming, playing tennis, golf and skiing—though when they went to Sun Valley ski lodge, he couldn't wait to get to the ski slopes and broke a shoulder while Allyson was still unpacking in their suite. They had agreed to meet for lunch at the Round House but she got a phone call from Powell, who was in the hospital.

Now that Allyson was married, there were no more money worries. Powell would say to have any store send their bill to the house and he would pay for it. Allyson had dreamed of having an Adrian suit but was afraid the elegant salon might ask her to leave, as Tiffany had the time when the girl first came to Hollywood and went there wearing pigtails and flat shoes. But now the salespeople made her feel at home, congratulating Allyson on the success of *Two Girls and a Sailor.* She ordered a suit made of white cashmere, never inquiring about the price. At home she modeled the suit for Powell. When Allyson told him she did not know how much it cost, he told her to take go back and find out. If it was more than $250, Allyson would have to leave it there. The cost was $1500 and she told them her husband didn't like the suit and it was given back. When they offered to show some others, Allyson said she would bring Powell in, but never went back.

To make up for the Adrian humiliation, Powell bought his wife a fur coat that had been made for someone else, who was dissatisfied. The coat fitted like a tent and Allyson had to roll up the sleeves to make cuffs, but was afraid that if she complained, it would be taken away from her. Powell controlled her spending so that if she wanted to buy something, he would ask if Allyson really needed it, which made her not want it any more.

Powell thought he knew the woman he had married but now learned of her desperate feeling of inadequacy. It wasn't just the difference in their ages (he was nearly twice as old as she) but that he was a responsible mature man and Allyson was still a child. She was afraid of everything—cats, people who didn't like her, being alone, the dark, illness. She was always going to him to dispel some specter that had been raised. Allyson confessed she was afraid of Hedda Hopper because she had said mean things about her, as when Hopper blamed the actress for Powell giving the news of the marriage to Louella Parsons and not her. He advised her to just smile and be sweet in return and let the people who were mean shame themselves. Allyson needed constant reassurance of Powell's love, wanting to be with him every moment. He wanted to be with her too, but he was aiming to get to be so successful that he could finally relax, saying it was as much for her as it was for him. She heard him tell friends that he had to get up at 5 a.m. and sneak into his bedroom-study to get any paperwork done, but Allyson believed it was also that her husband was used to a lot of space around him.

When the couple had dinner with Richard Rodgers, she continued the myth of coming from Westchester in order to give herself the social background that she never had. When Powell reminded her that she came from the Bronx, he got a kick under the table. Her husband said Allyson had to grow up, and assured her that people loved her and didn't care what her beginnings were. But she was still afraid and deeply ashamed and this led the woman to see a psychiatrist. In less than a year, she would be discharged with the assurance that the man had done what he could. And that, with Powell's tireless comfort, was a very great deal.

One of the biggest adjustments was having Powell's children from the marriage to Joan Blondell with them. One day he asked Allyson to pick up his daughter Ellen. Blondell wanted her to live with them, and so did the girl. He predicted Ellen would love her because they were about the same size and she would be like a little sister. Ellen lived with the couple for a while and then stayed periodically from then on, but the two women were never the sister team Powell had hoped for. His son Norman also stayed occasionally.

On January 7, 1946, it was announced MGM planned a screen musical remake of their 1935 comedy, *Ah Wilderness!* It was to be produced by Arthur Freed and directed by Rouben Mamoulian, with Allyson and Ray McDonald in the juvenile leads. Songs would be by Harry Warren and Ralph Blaine. The musical was eventually made as *Summer Holiday* (1948) with Gloria DeHaven and Mickey Rooney.

The rumor factory and gossip columnists gave the Powell marriage six months and on their six-month anniversary they had a party with a huge cake with the lettering **Who Said It Wouldn't Last.**

On March 11, 1946, Alllyson appeared on *Lux Radio Theater*'s version of the 1943 MGM musical comedy *Presenting Lily Mars*. Allyson played the title character, a small-town Indiana girl who dreams of being a stage actress, the role played by Judy Garland in the film. Allyson does not sing any of the songs Garland sang in the film. She was interviewed by producer William Keeley after the show and said that singing and dancing had given her her start in the theater, but that dramatic roles were what she liked best.

Next was the black-and-white romance *The Secret Heart* (1946), produced by Edwin H. Knopf and shot from May 27 to August 1, 1946, with retakes in late September. The screenplay by Whitfield Cook and Anne Morrison Chapin (adapted by Rose Franken and William Brown Meloney from their original story) centered on real estate operator Lee

Adams (Claudette Colbert), the widow of banker and brilliant pianist Larry and stepmother to his children. Allyson, playing the role of Larry's 17-year-old daughter Penny, is billed third after Colbert and Walter Pidgeon. Penny is a straight dramatic role for her though she dances in one scene. At 28, Allyson is perhaps too old to play a teenager. Penny wears her hair in pigtails and with ribbons from costume designer Irene to suggest youth. She is said to have psychosomatic heart trouble and to be in love with the memory of her father; her arrested development allows Penny to transfer her father fixation onto Chris (Pidgeon). This naturally makes her jealous and pouty when he is more interested in Lee. Allyson is funny when indignant over her hair being mussed when her dancing partner "Brandy" Reynolds (Marshall Thompson) twirls her. Penny gets a funny line to Lee, who she sees dancing with Chris after turning off the music: "I never saw anything so silly. Oh, Lee, you're just making yourself ridiculous ... and cheap." The screenplay also gives her self-awareness as Penny admits to Chris that she can make people unhappy and is unhappy too, and she apologizes to Lee for her behavior. With her darting eyes, the actress is sometimes funny when showing Penny's neurosis. She is touching when she recalls how much she loved her father. The role has her playing the piano, holding and playing with a dog, an attempted suicide scene on a clifftop, and fainting. Allyson uses stillness for shock and her best scene is perhaps when Penny transitions from telling Lee how she is in love, to anger and hurt when Lee thinks it is Brandy and not Chris that Penny loves.

The film was released on December 25, 1946, with the taglines "You'll share the intimate secrets of an amazing love affair!," "SHE had no right to love him ... but she did!" and "SHE had the right to love him ... but hesitated!" *Variety*'s reviewer wrote that Allyson gave out with what was undoubtedly the best emoting of her career. The film was lambasted by John Douglas Eames in *The MGM Story*. It was a box office success.

Allyson reported that she was so enamored of Walter Pidgeon that she could barely talk to him. He lived next door to the Powells but the actress had never spoken to him because, being such a big star, he intimidated her. She would call him Mr. Walter Pidgeon and he finally told her to call him Uncle Walter.

Allyson had been nervous about the part and about acting opposite Claudette Colbert, whom she idolized. The actress said Colbert's authority and polish intimidated her, and that she was the most professional person Allyson had ever worked with. She felt Colbert sensed her

Allyson and director Robert Z. Leonard on the set of *The Secret Heart* (1946).

insecurities and was compassionate and helpful, giving her moral support and acting tips. Allyson found herself copying many of Colbert's ways, like the habit of appealing to the Almighty in French and going around saying "Mon Dieu!" Colbert knew exactly what she was doing, exactly where the camera and the lights were, and how her face should be photographed and how and where to look. Allyson didn't know these things so they were wonderful to learn. She also felt Colbert's obsession about being photographed with her best side was unwarranted as she was gorgeous on any side. The older, elegantly dressed actress gave her fashion advice. To a party at Colbert's, Allyson had worn a three-quarter length brown woolen skirt and white blouse while all the other women wore floor-length gowns, many shimmering with sequins. Colbert suggested she should dress up more. Allyson explained that Powell hated her wearing fancy clothes, which is why she dressed plainly in Peter Pan collars and casual girly skirts. Colbert said you didn't have to wear fancy clothes to be dressed up. The two women became great friends.

Shot around the same time (from May to August 1946) was the black-and-white *High Barbaree* (1947) aka *Enchanted Island,* produced by Everett Riskin. The screenplay was by Anne Morrison Chapin, Whitfield Cook and Cyril Hume, based on the Charles Nordhoff–James Norman Hall novel. The director was Jack Conway. Alec Brooke (Van Johnson), a World War II Navy pilot on a bombing mission, has been shot down in the Pacific and is lost at sea. Allyson plays Nancy Frazer, a Navy nurse and Alec's Iowan childhood friend. She is presented in contrast to the tall, slinky blonde Diana Case (Marilyn Maxwell), Alec's pre-war fiancée who also happens to be the daughter of his boss at an aviation company. Diana may be wealthier than Nancy, but her taste in Irene-designed clothes are flashier and a little tacky compared to the white dresses Nancy wears. Nancy has one low-cut short-sleeved sparkly dress for a dance but even the sparkles are understated. The role has Allyson dance with Johnson, though clumsily, and ride in a rotating plane with him. She makes Nancy funny; for example, her reaction to a toy plane that is a cigarette lighter. The actress has her best scene when Nancy talks obliquely about being in love with Alec while they dance. Director Jack Conway gives Allyson several closeups.

The film was released on May 1, 1947, with the tagline "Six Great Stars! A Thousand Unforgettable Moments!" and "M-G-M Presents a NEW Dramatic Role for VAN!" It was lambasted by Bosley Crowther in *The New York Times,* who wrote that Allyson goes completely soggy, and John Douglas Eames in *The MGM Story.* The film was a box office success.

The original ending for the film had Johnson hearing over his radio that the ship on which Allyson was serving had been sunk. Johnson then died and the picture ended. Preview cards demanded that Johnson live so a new ending was shot; it had Allyson surviving as well.

On November 20, it was announced that MGM intended to remake their 1930 musical comedy *Good News* as a vehicle for Allyson and Johnson. There had been talk of the film being made with Judy Garland and Mickey Rooney in October 1939 and in December 1946 but that had not happened. Arthur Freed was to produce the new film with the original songs of Ray Henderson. The Broadway show had run at Chanin's 46th Street Theatre from September 6, 1927, to January 5, 1929.

In December, Powell found a house on Cliffwood Drive in Brentwood Park. He wanted to knock out walls and extend the front 100 feet. He and Allyson had to sleep on the floor with only a tarpaper wall against the elements. Powell had a decorator fill the house with antiques, lovely furniture and braided rugs; she was happy with whatever her husband chose. But when it was finished, Allyson thought Powell would let her add a few touches of her own, like expensive antique chairs and tables, and a painting, but he sent them back. The only thing he liked were the lamps, like a solid brass antique scale of justice she had converted into a four-foot-tall lamp as a wedding present. Now Allyson made everything she found into a lamp: an early movie projector, old telephones, churns and some of Powell's old hunting rifles. But buying him clothes was different. At first he beamed at what she bought him but Allyson never saw him wear any of the fanciful ties or unusual shirts. One day she discovered that he gave them away as gifts and rewards to prop men and butchers and bakers and even the lawn man.

Powell and Allyson were gracious when their exes came to dinner—Tommy with his new model bride, and Joan Blondell. For Blondell, they had steaks grilled outside and Allyson left Powell inside to chat with his former wife. It began to rain and, once the time the steaks were ready, Allyson entered like a maid with wet hair to find Powell and Blondell sitting at either end of the table. Allyson bit her lip to stop from bawling and found a place to sit. But the next time Blondell came to dinner, Allyson was sure to have a butler. In an evening gown, she stood at the head of the table to indicate where their guest was to sit.

Joan Crawford, who lived in the house around the corner, sent the couple roses when they moved in. She kept sending notes inviting Allyson to lunch, which Allyson turned down, intimidated by the great star. But Powell said to go because she could learn from Crawford. Allyson didn't have to say anything, she could just listen. On the day Allyson went, she was the only guest and didn't have to worry about what to say as Crawford talked, leading her into a sitting room. Crawford ordered a servant to get her daughter Christina, who curtsied formally, saying, "How do you do?" Lunch was announced and they went into the dining room but Allyson felt uneasy with the child sitting there saying nothing and her mother treating her as if she didn't exist. Allyson also felt that Crawford had no interest in *her*, since she only talked about herself, so the feeling of being afraid to talk was replaced by the feeling of not being permitted to. Allyson's face froze into a permanent smile as she tried to follow Crawford's patter. They walked out into the large foyer and Crawford paused and asked if she had noticed how quiet Christina was. Crawford explained that the girl was getting the silent treatment, then told Christina to go upstairs and bring down a wrapped box. When the girl returned, she was told to sit on a bench and hold the box until the party she had been invited to was over, as punishment for talking back. Allyson found this humiliation nauseating and hurriedly left the Crawford house, almost stumbling as tears blurred her vision.

She never returned the luncheon invitation to Crawford and was never her friend, though Allyson and Powell would see her many times at parties like those thrown by Hedda Hopper. These were a must for Hollywood stars to please the queen of the press; *not* attending might cause some nasty rumor to be launched. But although Allyson dutifully attended these parties, prodded by her husband, Hopper still knocked her in her column. Hopper wondered if the Peter Pan collars were favored because there was something wrong with her neck. Allyson showed up at the next party in a very sophisticated black satin low-cut sheath dress to prove her wrong. This resulted in Hopper writing that she didn't know whether Allyson was coming or going, referring to her lack of bosom, and asking what Allyson was trying to prove.

The Powells loved being at home. They would curl up in front of the fireplace, even if it had no fire. He would sip a martini, spinning dreams of producing and directing great movies and she would nibble on goodies, telling him about her day at the studio. So it was a shock when one day Powell introduced her to the house's new owners: He was selling because he wanted to double his investment. Powell drove Allyson to their new home in Copa de Oro. It was an estate done in English Tudor with a two-acre yard behind a big iron gate. Powell rebuilt the house and had the walls covered in silks and tapestries. This time Allyson was determined to have a hand in the decoration and ordered furniture which he sent back because it was Early American. Allyson also erred when she planted sweet peas on the front lawn.

The one thing missing from Allyson's life was having her own child. It seemed all her friends had one—Judy Garland, Dinah Shore, Frances Bergen. As their babies arrived, no one made a bigger fuss than Allyson. She haunted their nurseries and Garland would yell, "Hide the baby. Here comes Junie." She became a godmother but that wasn't the same as being a mother.

She tried to concentrate on her blossoming social life and the joy of being a hostess with the aid of her majordomo butler Frank. After getting the okay from Powell, Allyson invited everyone she could think of and sometimes the guest number was 75. He manned the phone to pull the evening together (including a small band for dancing) and she would get all the credit. Half of the Hollywood colony was entertained at the Powells: the Bogarts, Louis B. Mayer and his daughters Edie Goetz and Irene Mayer Selznick, Merle Oberon, Lana Turner, Louella Parsons. Judy Garland was always the center of attention and, when she sang, Allyson sat on the floor worshipping her. One evening Judy wanted to play Guess Who? Allyson went first and leant her head to one side and pounded her ear but nobody could guess that she was doing Esther Williams. When Allyson stood wringing her hands and looking to Heaven, they all guessed it was Margaret O'Brien. Judy wiped tears from her eyes and waved goodbye to do June, and Allyson fixed her by dancing down the Yellow Brick Road clumsily while singing "Off to See the Wizard" off key. Garland sang at everyone's parties except for the Powells because they had no grand piano to accompany her.

Frances and Edgar Bergen were right at the center of their group of friends and Jack Benny, Joan Fontaine and George and Gracie Burns were also guests. Ronald Reagan and wife Jane Wyman were two of the most interesting new friends she acquired through marriage to Powell. The Reagans and George Murphy and his wife Julie were among their first dinner guests, and the Reagans and the Powells made several trips together. Jane asked to be shown around the house so they could get away from the men talking politics. Allyson took her upstairs to see the separate bedroom suites. Powell's was also used as a sick bay where either of them could recover from colds. Allyson's bedroom suite was in misty rose as opposed to Powell's masculine browns and beiges. June had a niche for her collection of stuffed animals, witches and Raggedy Ann dolls.

Allyson met Polly and Leonard Firestone. Polly took the time to teach her the finer points of distinguishing between good taste and mediocre and just plain bad taste. Another couple, Jane and Justin Darts of Dart Industries, took a trip to Honolulu with the Powells. The joke among the husbands was that they didn't need a detective to find their wives because their matching cars were a dead giveaway. They both had wild-looking Thunderbirds; Jane's was bright yellow and Allyson's hot pink.

The Powells were charter members of a square dance club with George and Julie Murphy, the Firestones, the Bergens and the Darts. They wore square dance costumes and met at each other's houses, serving country-style food on checkered tablecloths. There were hoe-downs with an authentic square dance band. Julie Murphy was Allyson's square dance teacher. When it came to bridge, that was another matter. When Allyson was finally ready to play, she trumped Julie and then never played again.

For Allyson, it was fun to venture out into Hollywood society as Mrs. Dick Powell. One evening they attended a party at Mary Pickford's house Pickfair. When they arrived, they saw that everyone was dressed to the hilt while Allyson had just thrown on a Peter Pan dress and wore no makeup. She felt like the ugly duckling in a room full of swans. But it didn't bother Pickford, who made a big fuss because she had heard so much about the little girl who had been compared to her. At a party at Frances Bergen's, Allyson stood at the buffet table and cleaned up the whole platter of imported and expensive *pate de foit gras*. Others placed a bit of it on a cracker but she piled each cracker higher and higher until there were only bits left on the serving platter. Bergen materialized by her side and asked to see her in the other room. She was exasperated because Allyson had left none for anybody else. Allyson offered to have her butler Frank bring some over but Bergen thought that would be too late because by then the guests would have gone. Allyson followed her friend around apologizing and their friendship survived but Bergen never served the pate again when Allyson was around.

Powell took his wife to visit Marion Davies, who was an old flame. When they arrived at Marion's mansion, it almost broke Allyson's heart to see that Marion had been drinking. Allyson could still see the beauty in her face with enormous, very sad eyes. The Marion in the photos with Powell that he had shown her no longer existed. From then on, they kept in touch with her by letter.

Allyson was back on the radio show *Mail Call* on January 22, 1947. She sings "A Love Like Ours" but it appears to be a repeat of the recorded performance of the January 31, 1945, *Mail Call* broadcast.

Her next film was the Technicolor *Good News* (1947), shot at MGM and on location in Burbank from March 10 to May 23 with reshoots on May 27. Betty Comden and Adolph Green based their screenplay on the play by Lew Brown, Lawrence Schwab, Frank Mandel, B.G. DeSylva and Ray Henderson. As well as using the play's songs (music by Henderson, lyrics by Lew Brown and DeSylva), there were new songs by Hugh Martin, Ralph Blane, Roger Edens, Betty Comden and Adolph Green. At the co-ed Tait University in 1927, Tommy Marlowe (Peter Lawford), captain of the football team, falls for fellow student and assistant librarian Connie Laine (Allyson). Allyson is top-billed though her part is supporting to Lawford's. The role sees her perform in five musical numbers. She sings part of "Lucky in Love" by Henderson, Brown and DeSylva; recites "The French Lesson" by Edens, Comden and Green; sings "The Best Things in Life Are Free" by Henderson, Brown and DeSylva; sings "Just Imagine" by the same; and she, Lawford and the chorus sing "Varsity Drag" aka "The Varsity Drag" by same.

Allyson's best showcase is "Just Imagine." Director Charles Walters starts with a closeup of her sitting on a bed, then has her lie down in a medium shot. She does not have the voice of Judy Garland for a ballad and it was reported by one source that Allyson was dubbed for this number (and for "The Best Things in Life are Free") by Patt Hyatt. However the performance is still touching. Her hair is shorter though purists will note that Sydney Guilaroff's hair styling is not period. Costume designer Helen Rose dresses Connie in pastels in opposition to the primary colors worn by Pat McClelland (Patricia Marshall), Connie's rival for Tommy. Pat is presented as the vampy brunette bad girl to Connie's virginal blonde good girl, with Pat manipulating men for her own benefit. Connie does her own manipulation to get Pat away from Tommy and interested in Beef (Loren Tindall). Allyson's age of 29 playing a college student is less an issue than when she had recently played a teenager. Connie is funny when she stages a fake conversation with Cora the cook (Connie Gilchrist) for Pat to overhear. She gets a funny line after Tommy decides not to take her to the prom: She says she will read her favorite book, *Les Miserable.* The role also sees the actress speak French, cry, and whistle. It was reported that Robert Alton staged the film's two big production numbers, "Pass That Peace Pipe" by Martin, Blane and Edens and "Varsity Rag" while Walters did all the others. Kay Thompson again did the vocal arrangements.

The film was released on December 4, 1947. It was praised by *Variety,* which reported that Allyson was most appealing and lent considerable charm to her role. Pauline Kael in *5001 Nights at the Movies* describes her as goofy and blithe. Bosley Crowther in *The New York Times* wrote that Allyson, while soft and beguiling as a sweetheart, can't sing worth a fig. A box office success, the film received an Academy Award nomination for Best Music, Original Song for "Pass That Peace Pipe."

A song with music by Edens and lyrics by Comden and Green, "An Easier Way," was cut prior to release but it can be seen on the DVD of the film. The number is mostly sung and danced by Allyson, with parts also sung by Marshall and chorus girls. Allyson is funny in it, particularly when the song references Cleopatterer, Pollyanna and the modern flapper.

Since Peter Lawford spoke French fluently and Allyson did not, he had to teach *her how to teach him* to speak French in the French lesson scene. She felt this did not come off as her French accent was atrocious.

Allyson hated the slow ballads that were not for a no-voice like her, but loved working with Charles Walters, loved the music and the dancing, and said it was a happy film. She also called it one of her three favorites.

Allyson and Peter Lawford in front of the chorus in the "Varsity Drag" number in *Good News* (1947).

In the 2004 video documentary *That's Entertainment!: The Masters Behind the Musicals,* Allyson said she was thrilled when she heard that Walters was going to do the film. He knew exactly what he wanted and how to get you to do it. He was so talented because he could dance better than anybody and could teach you better than anybody. And the man loved what he was doing, which she thought always made a big difference.

Brent Phillips writes in *Charles Walters: The Director Who Made Hollywood Dance* that rehearsals began on February 12 and Allyson was determined to establish herself in an Arthur Freed musical. She told Freed that she loved Walters but wasn't sure he was ready to direct a whole film. Freed reminded her that someone gave Allyson *her* start so she soon adjusted her attitude and later acknowledged that Walters was good. His way of directing was to play the characters the way he believed they should be played as the stars observed. In his book *The Movies' Greatest Musicals: Produced in Hollywood USA by the Freed Unit,* Hugh Fordin wrote that Allyson shared her misgivings about Walters with MGM vice-president Benny Thau. This matter was important to her because she considered the film to be her first big movie musical. Thau reportedly called Freed, and Freed called Allyson into his office. Freed wouldn't replace Walters except if he was unhappy with the rushes.

James Spada writes in his book on Lawford that the actor found it a strain to work with Allyson after the breakup of their romance. His stand-in Ken DuMain recalled that Lawford took some petty snipes at her, saying that she was considerably older than the age she professed to be.

Next was the black-and-white romantic comedy *The Bride Goes Wild* (1948) produced by William H. Wright and shot from June 17 to August 1947. The screenplay by Albert Beich centered on Greg Rawlings (Van Johnson), a best-selling children's book author who clashes with Martha "Marty" Terryton (Allyson), a Vermont schoolteacher who has won a contest to illustrate his next book. Allyson is funny as the prudish teetotaling character who wears her long hair in a bun. She gets drunk, thanks to Greg's attempted seduction of her at Joe's, a sea-themed bar. Martha gets a haircut in reaction to Greg's brunette former girlfriend Tilly Smith (Arlene Dahl). Martha also expresses her jealousy by wearing a duplicate of Tilly's outfit—a Helen Rose floor-length low-cut sleeveless dress with a striped head shawl. Martha's fiancé (Richard Derr) is a manual training teacher and a good-looking and physical man, and this works against the stereotype that Martha is a virgin. Greg's immediate attraction to Martha helps to dilute the comparison between Martha and Tilly as a bad girl vamp. We may question why Martha repeatedly forgives Greg for his deceits though that has more to do with the conventions of the romantic comedy genre where the battling couple will inevitably come together.

The role sees Allyson also wear a wedding gown, use a swing and takes part in some slapstick: pushing over a table, inadvertently closing a door in Greg's face and falling into a hole in the ground (the use of a stunt double is apparent). In one scene, her extended crying is funny when she tells Greg's publisher John McGrath (Hume Cronyn) that Greg got her drunk, with the funny lines "He got me pie-eyed!" and "He took me to a grotto and he blew in my ear." This scene is perhaps her best.

The film was released on March 3, 1948, with the tagline "M-G-M's Picture of Happy-go-lucky Love!" It was praised by Bosley Crowther in *The New York Times,* who wrote that Allyson was remarkably appealing. The film was a box office success.

Allyson wrote that the actors couldn't stop laughing in the scene when they were supposed to be falling in love, amused by the word "clavicle," particularly as Allyson had an aunt who once fell off a roof and broke her clavicle. Director Norman Taurog's anger made them laugh more but then he started to laugh too, threw up his hands and told everyone to go home knowing they would never get anything done that day. The next morning, he wouldn't let the two actors speak off-camera and refused to give them a run-through before shooting. Taurog shot them separately, with the actors speaking of the dialogue director's cues, and the scene got done. But, forever after, Allyson couldn't hear the word *clavicle* without grinning.

On November 4, 1947, it was announced that MGM had purchased an option on screen rights to *Alexandra,* a novel by Gladys Schmitt, and they assigned George Haight to prepare a screen adaptation, probably a vehicle for Allyson. The story dealt with a young woman, unappreciated as a child, who falls in love with a reprehensible actor but recovers from the affair. The film was never made.

Next was the Technicolor action-adventure *The Three Musketeers* (1948), produced by Pandro S. Berman and shot from January 25 to May 5, 1948. The screenplay by Robert Ardrey was based on the Alexandre Dumas novel which had already been adapted for film multiples times. The new version showed the hectic adventures of D'Artagnan (Gene Kelly), a young man who comes to Paris to become a Musketeer in 1625 and his indestructible friendship with Musketeers Athos (Van Heflin), Porthos (Gig Young) and Aramis (Robert Coote). Allyson, billed third, plays the supporting part of Constance, a maid of Queen Anne (Angela Lansbury); she has more scenes than the top-billed Lana Turner, who plays Lady de Winter. Allyson wears her hair shoulder-length in style with a braided headband, which is perhaps a wig by Sydney Guilaroff and Larry Germain. Constance's pastel-colored costumes by Walter Plunkett contrast her as the light brunette good girl with the primary clothes used for the blonde bad girl Lady de Winter. The actress' face is obscured in a cloak the first time we see her and composer Herbert Stothart uses themes from Tchaikovsky to underscore her scenes. She doesn't employ a French accent but that's acceptable given that none of the other actors playing French people use one either. Her best scene is perhaps Constance's death, where director George Sidney has her face sweaty, supplemented by the tears of D'Artagnan. Death is signaled by a fallen hand.

The film was released on October 19, 1948, with the taglines "Mightiest of All Romantic Adventures! ... Storming its way to the screen with unbelievable excitement!" and "THE COMPLETE ROMANCE...THE FULL NOVEL!" It was praised by *Variety,* who wrote that Allyson had sweet charm. Pauline Kael in *5001 Nights at the Movies* said that Allyson looks like a little girl done up in Mama's clothes. The film was a box office success and nominated for the Best Cinematography, Color Academy Award. There were many more versions of the Dumas story made for film and television after this one.

Deborah Kerr was offered the role of Constance but Allyson was cast after production had begun. She did not want to do the film, not feeling comfortable in a period piece. She feared she would look silly in the sweeping robes. But Mayer told her she would do the film, and its success made her think she knew nothing about casting. The film was a reunion with Gene Kelly, who had choreographed *Best Foot Forward* on Broadway. The relationship between Allyson and Kelly now changed because the actress felt she had to be as good as he was and never could be.

Allyson reported that Lana Turner was super to work with, although late a lot. In the prison scene where Lady de Winter begs Constance for a knife so she can kill herself, Allyson was mesmerized by Turner's tears. In her book *Lana: The Lady, the Legend, the Truth,* Turner wrote that Allyson was terrified by her in the scene.

Next was the Technicolor biographical musical comedy *Words and Music* (1948) produced by Arthur Freed and shot from April 4 or

Allyson checks her costume behind the scenes on *The Three Musketeers* (1948).

13 to July 14, 1948, with reshoots on August 7. Allyson's casting was announced on April 9. The working title was *The Lives of Rodgers and Hart.* The screenplay was by Fred F. Finklehoffe, based on Ben Feiner's adaptation of a story by Guy Bolton and Jean Holloway. It was based on the lives and music of songwriting partners Richard Rodgers (Tom Drake) and Lorenz Hart (Mickey Rooney). The actors are billed alphabetically so that Allyson is top-billed. Her unnamed character only appears in one scene, singing and dancing with Ramon and Royce Blackburn (dubbed by Pete Roberts and Eugene Cox) "Thou Swell" a song from the Rodgers and Hart musical, *A Connecticut Yankee.* Allyson is dressed in a Helen Rose white long-sleeved ankle-length bejeweled dress with a sheer top over a white leotard and layered skirt, with white ballet slippers and a white tiara. She wears her hair in a short style. She sings well though it is her dancing that is more impressive here. The film was directed by Norman Taurog but the musical numbers were staged and directed by Robert Alton. At point he has Allyson walk over the shoulders of medieval knights arranged like a staircase.

The film was released on December 9, 1948, with the taglines "14 Stars! 22 Songs! 2 Love Stories! 14 Spectacular Scenes!," "22 Terrific Rodgers and Hart Tunes! 2 Exciting Love Stories! 5 Great Broadway Musicals Rolled Into One! 14 Spectacular Girl-Filled Production Scenes! 14 Sensational Singing and Dancing Stars! and Color by Technicolor," "The BIGGEST musical!" and "M*G*M presents a spectacular musical, packed with the beloved hits of the famed song-writing team of Rodgers and Hart; their own story, with all the adventure, romance, high life of the Great White Way." Pauline Kael in *5001 Nights at the Movies* wrote that Allyson's number was a bright spot in her career. The film was a box office success.

It was announced on June 13 that the movie rights to "Celebration," a forthcoming magazine story by Richard Mealand, had been purchased by MGM as a possible farce-comedy vehicle for Allyson and Van Johnson. The story dealt with an artist, his ex-wife, his fiancée and his 80-year-old aunt, and it was expected that William H. Wright would produce the film. This film was never made.

4

Little Women

The Technicolor *Little Women* (1949) was produced and directed by Mervyn LeRoy and shot from June 29 to September 1948. The screenplay was by Andrew Solt, Sarah Y. Mason and Victor Heerman, based on the Louisa May Alcott novel. The novel had been made as a British silent film in 1917, an American silent in 1918, and an American made-for-TV in 1946, but most notably as a feature by RKO in 1933. The story centered on the four daughters of a New England family who fight for happiness during and after the Civil War. Allyson is top-billed playing the leading role of Jo, the second oldest of the March sisters. Her age is not given so the fact of the actress being 31 and playing someone who is presumably a teenager is less of an issue. Jo is a tomboy and has a more adult attitude about life as opposed to her sisters, who are more traditionally girlish. Allyson's hair is dark brunette here and worn long down to her waist with bangs, though Jo has her hair cut short in a plot point. The passage of time is represented by the growth of her hair. Allyson said this was her own hair dyed but the longer style is presumably a wig by Sydney Guilaroff. Costumes are by Walter Plunkett. Jo's pantaloons being exposed is an example of some of the slapstick the actress does to express Jo's boyishness, like jumping over a fence and having the back of her dress scorched by fire. She uses masculine physicality and a loud voice. The role sees her shovel snow, play croquet and push Laurie (Peter Lawford) when he makes a romantic advance. Allyson sings "Merry Christmastime Is Here" (composer unknown) and "It Came Upon a Midnight Clear" (music by Richard Storrs Willis, lyrics by Edmund Hamilton Sears) *a cappella* with Margaret O'Brien (who plays sister Beth), Elizabeth Taylor (who plays sister Amy) and Janet Leigh (who plays sister Meg). She also sings one line of the song "M'appari" from the opera "Martha" (music by Friedrich von Flotow) and dances the polka to Johanna Strauss' "Brautschau." The actress gets a funny line to Laurie: "Meg is too young and far too clever to wonder about who wonders about her." Allyson expresses the pain of Jo's disappointment over Aunt March (Lucille Watson) choosing to take Amy to Europe instead of her but her best scene is perhaps when she shows her disapproval of Meg dating john Brooke (Richard Stapley). The actress transitions from laughing after being chased by Laurie to angry stillness when seeing John. Director LeRoy only gives Allyson two closeups.

The film was released on March 10, 1949, presented as the Easter attraction at New York City's Radio City Music Hall as part of MGM's Silver Anniversary Celebration. The taglines were "THRILLS OF YOUNG LOVE!" and "M-G-M's New Color by Technicolor Romance!" According to *Variety,* Allyson's irrepressible cavorting and thesping dominated the film. Bosley Crowther in *The New York Times* compared her unfavorably to Katharine Hepburn in the 1933 film. The film was a box office success. It was Oscar-nominated for Best Color Cinematography, and won for Best Art Direction–Set Decoration, Color.

Allyson could understand why MGM would want to make *Little Women* because it was known as the studio that made the family pictures. She felt every child should see it and it was one of her three favorite movies. She loved making it because she saw herself as Jo (who wanted to be the world's greatest writer) because the actress once wanted to be the world's greatest poet. She hated wearing the long, clumsy period dresses which matched the character's hatred of them. Jo having to run in the snow, jump over a fence and fall down was her favorite scene. The blades of the ice skates she had around her neck hit Allyson in the face but she continued. The second time the actress jumped was an improvised moment as she thought the director was going to say *cut.*

Mervyn LeRoy wanted her to test for the part and the actress refused because, every time she tested, Allyson never got the part. LeRoy went to Louis B. Mayer demanding she test but the actress out-sat him and got the part.

The four stars acted like real-life sisters, only wanting the best for each other and not trying to be better. At lunch they all talked about Mayer and laughed at Elizabeth Taylor's defiance of him, thinking it was a miracle she was still employed. Allyson loved eating with her co-stars in the studio commissary but said she also had lunch with Mary Astor (who played Marmee), with food prepared by Allyson's home cook. The actress was embarrassed for Astor, whom she considered a bigger star than herself, since Allyson had the star dressing room. Mayer decided that Allyson was getting too thin and thereafter made her lunch at the MGM executive suite where she ate matzo ball soup, steak, mashed

Allyson (left) and her stand-in Elaine Russell on the set of *Little Women* (1949).

potatoes and ice cream. One day when all four stars were sitting around talking in Allyson's dressing room, Taylor glanced at her and said she would give anything to look like Allyson. Allyson couldn't imagine that the most beautiful woman in the world said that but it kept her going for years.

The hardest she ever cried was in the scene when Jo realized Beth was doomed to die. Allyson cried so hard she had to be sent home. She got into her car still blubbering and continued to cry for hours. In his book on Margaret O'Brien, Allan R. Ellenberger reports that the take of the scene where Jo reveals her long hair has been sheared was repeatedly spoiled by laughter from Allyson and Peter Lawford every time she took off her hat and he saw her hair.

Janet Leigh wrote in her memoir *There Really Was a Hollywood* that she had first seen Allyson in June 1946 in the MGM makeup room when Leigh was waiting to be made-up for her first screen test. She described Allyson as sweet and adorable and one of her favorites. Leigh had seen every movie Allyson had ever made and she was now so close to her that she could have reached out and touched her but records that there was no conversation between them. Leigh said that when making the film, Allyson was the ringleader of the four actresses, who misbehaved and fought and giggled, though they blended beautifully to weave the web of sisterhood. Leigh turned 21 during filming and a surprise birthday party was thrown on the set with Jerry Lewis, Dean Martin and Gloria DeHaven as Allyson's guests.

Mary Astor reported that Allyson giggled a lot, which distracted the older actress and did not amuse her. She also said that Allyson chewed gum constantly and irritatingly and the young actress' silliness wore her down. Kitty Kelley wrote in her book *Elizabeth Taylor: The Last Star* that Peggy Lynch was an MGM player and the girl-next-door type, her potential to become "the next June Allyson" a reminder to Allyson not to get out of line.

MGM's publicity department now promoted Allyson as a star, describing her as the sort of girl who, if the occasion arose, could milk a cow or fly a plane. She was meticulously neat and liked roses, sliced peaches, Chinese food and classical music. Allyson never went to the hairdresser and set her own hair her own way and washed it every morning in the shower. She found that as hard as singing and dancing were, movie acting came easy. There was no trouble memorizing lines. Allyson was able to look at a script for 20 minutes and have everything set in her mind, thanks to a photographic memory. She saw herself walking through it and saying the lines and becoming the character so it was very easy for her. Usually one take was all Allyson needed to get everything right. She could not audition, because she had so little faith in herself. She never watched film rushes, feeling it would affect her performance the next day if there was something she didn't like.

Directors learned not to challenge her. They had to approach the actress gently and if they patted her on the head she would do anything they requested. But if they screamed, Allyson would flee to her dressing room. She was not a Method actor and did not improve with a lot of rehearsals. If any kind of emotional scene requiring anger or crying was rehearsed, the actress would only walk through it, though this was sometimes unfair to the other actor in the scene who wanted to know what she was going to do. To do her best acting, Allyson had to know the time was now, in order to give a natural reaction. If she had an emotional scene to play, the actress might still be sniffling and feeling sad when she got home, but mostly she could leave it at the studio.

She had a career and parties and friends but what the actress now wanted most was a baby. It had been reported that she was pregnant when was making *Little Women* and that pregnancy had forced her to drop out of the musical comedy *In the Good Old Summertime* (1949) which went into production in November 1948 with Judy Garland replacing her in the role of Veronica Fisher. This pregnancy also reportedly saw her drop out the musical comedy *Take Me Out to the Ball Game* (1949), with the part then re-cast with Esther Williams. But these reports were either false or Allyson miscarried, something she doesn't mention in her memoir. The actress wrote that her doctor had said that because of her childhood injury, she might never conceive due to the broken pelvis, but Allyson was still very young by nature's clock and miracles happen. Powell suggested adoption and she agreed to this as an alternative. He had commented that he didn't think Allyson was cut out for motherhood but since she wanted it so badly, he groaned in mock horror at the prospect of having another child to raise. Many of her friends had adopted: Ronald Reagan and Jane Wyman, George and Gracie Burns. The Tennessee adoption agency the Powells used was reportedly recommended to them by Joan Crawford.

On August 10, while *Little Women* was still in production, the agency delivered a two-month-old girl to the Powell home. Powell was home to greet her, thinking if the nurse arrived to find only the butler home, she would not hand over the child. Powell called her on the set all day every hour to report that the nurse had yet to arrive. Then the call came that the baby was there and Allyson said she was on her way home. The actress ran out of the sound stage in costume and didn't tell anyone she was going, knowing they would try to stop her from disrupting the shooting schedule. Allyson drove home as fast as she could and ran into the house and up the stairs to find the nurse holding the baby. The nurse allowed her to hold the girl and Allyson could hardly breathe. She was beautiful. The actress had to return to work later in the day and told the cast and crew the joyous news. That night Allyson didn't sleep and sat looking at the baby sleeping in her crib. The girl would be named Pammy. Powell quipped that now he had three daughters: Ellen, Pammy and June.

The Powells hired a nurse who assured Allyson that Pammy behaved just like any other baby, crying no more and no less, gasping no more and no less. At night the new mother watched the child and listen to her breathing. When Allyson couldn't hear the baby, she pinched her, ashamed at her action but relieved to hear Pammy respond with annoyance or a cry of pain.

Regis Toomey was godfather and Claudette Colbert godmother. Colbert bought a lace christening gown from Paris but Pammy vomited all over it on the way to the christening. Allyson wanted to go home so the gown could be washed. Powell said that Colbert would understand, but the actress insisted that Colbert never know so they went home. The gown was washed and they hurried to the church, where Pammy pulled Colbert's string of pearls, which broke all over the place.

MGM announced that Allyson would star in *Forever* based on the novel by Michael Crann but the film was never made. Her next film was the black-and-white biographical romance *The Stratton Story* (working title: *The Life of Monte Stratton*), produced by Jack Cummings and shot from late October to December 28, 1948. The screenplay was by Douglas Morrow and Guy Trosper, based on a story by Morrow. centered on Monty "Country" Stratton (James Stewart), a star major league baseball pitcher who loses a leg in a hunting accident but becomes determined to leave the game on his own terms. Allyson, second-billed, plays Ethel, who becomes Monty's wife. She is back to wearing her hair in a short style with a side part, one time worn in pigtails. Costumes by Helen Rose include an odd dark-colored high-necked long-sleeved sweater with matching dark-colored pants worn when Ethel plays catch with Monty. The role sees the actress interact with a baby for the first time on screen, and she also dances with Stewart, Bill Williams (who plays Eddie Dibson) and Bruce Cowling (who plays Ted Lyons). Director Sam

Wood gives her some slapstick as when Ethel gets hit in the head with socks by Monty and when she falls on the ground in the playing-catch scene. Allyson doesn't have anything that challenging to do, since Ethel is devoted to Monty but essentially a passive character. Her best scene is perhaps her silent reaction to seeing Monty when he first stands after his accident: Wood has her in closeup and then uses a camera tilt-up to show Monty's full body. Wood provides other closeups of the actress, including a bizarre one as Ethel laughs as Monty hugs her.

The film premiered in Cleveland, Ohio, on April 21, 1949, opened in New York on May 12 and received a wide release in June with the tagline "James Stewart–June Allyson, In the True Romance of the Year." It was praised by Herm in *Variety* and Thomas M. Pryor in *The New York Times,* who wrote of Allyson's affecting contribution to the film. The film was a box office success and won the Academy Award for Best Writing, Motion Picture Story. In the trailer, Allyson (in her MGM dressing room) tells the theater audience that doing the film was especially interesting because the story was true.

For the role of Ethel, Janet Leigh was first announced, then Donna Reed; Reed and Stewart had co-starred in 1946's *It's a Wonderful Life.* This idea was dropped because of the box office failure of that film. According to Marc Eliot's Stewart biography, Stewart vetoed Reed's casting as he had not enjoyed working with her. In Michael Munn's book *Jimmy Stewart: The Truth Behind the Legend,* the actor claims that he liked Reed personally and thought she was a good actress but he felt they had no chemistry in the former film and it suffered because of this. Stewart needed a hit film and he wanted the actress to play Ethel as someone who was 110 percent supportive of her husband and he wasn't convinced that Reed could pull that off. The actor asked for Allyson because he knew she had made a success at playing the girl-next-door in a succession of films. Her reputation was also one of an easy-to-work-with, sweet-natured girl. What you saw on the screen was what you got off the screen. He felt they made a good screen team.

Allyson turned down the part three times but Powell made her do it. She loved doing it and said that it was her best film. They had the real Monty Stratton and his wife as consultants; they were marvelous people, and the way they accepted their tragedy made things very easy for the actors. Stewart was different from any other actor Allyson knew. He was embarrassed to see himself on film and wouldn't look at rushes or go to premieres. He also had a great sense of humor. In the baseball backyard practice scene, she had to fall on the ground and they did 15

James Stewart holds up Allyson in a publicity shot from *The Stratton Story* (1949).

takes. Allyson asked why, which made the crew laugh. When she would be talking to the director before each take, Stewart was putting tiny, pointed pebbles on the ground where she had to fall. After so many takes, the actress had a sore bottom for weeks. On one occasion, Stewart wiggled his fingers and said that that was all the exercising he did, fearing he would lose weight. Stewart said Allyson was the most gullible person in the world and he was always finding a new way to put her on.

The chemistry they had was based on how the pair liked each other, though it was not romantic. Even in public, when they would see each other he would come pick her up and kiss Allyson in front of everyone. In their dialogue scenes they would unintentionally forget the script and just talk, eventually come around to making sense, and that was usually the take that was used. Allyson felt what worked was when he looked at her as if wondering "Is she for real?" Eliot wrote that they had known each other before either of them were married and at one point they even considered marriage. The actress reported that in the minds of audiences, she and Stewart became inextricably linked as screen partners and many times fans approached her in public and asked where her husband Stewart was. Not wishing to disappoint them, she generally told them that he was busy elsewhere that day.

On set they were always laughing at the antics of Frank Morgan, who always called her a brat. One day he arrived slightly tipsy and the director had to tell him to hush as she was in the middle of a scene. In response, Morgan boomed "What for? She can't act anyway."

Stewart's wife Gloria said that Allyson was Jimmy's perfect wife in movies and she was his imperfect wife in life. Powell referred to the celluloid Stewart-Allyson relationship at a banquet introducing Stewart as his wife's husband. Stewart and Powell chuckled as they compared notes on their helpless wives and how they had to fix everything around the house or it would stay broken forever.

When Allyson had an appointment with Helen Rose for a costume fitting, she found her friend Esther Williams being fitted with a gold-sequined glamor suit. Allyson asked if she could ever wear a suit like that in a film and Williams replied that they didn't make them with Peter Pan collars. But, Williams added, be glad they didn't because Allyson didn't have to get wet.

In February 1949, Louis B Mayer gathered all of his 58 stars under contract together on the studio's biggest soundstage with executives and exhibitors at a gigantic luncheon for MGM's 25th anniversary jubilee. Film was taken of the contractees, plus a group photograph. The black and white surviving footage is incomplete. The stars are shown entering the soundstage individually and in alphabetical order introduced by George Murphy but with Wallace Beery first seen so that Allyson is skipped over. She is also absent from the footage of the stars seated for the lunch; the actress does appear in the group photograph, seated in the front row in between Lionel Barrymore and Leon Ames.

The same month, Allyson was announced for the role of small-town farmer Jane Falbury in the musical romance *Summer Stock* (1950). Judy Garland had been announced for the part in December 1948 and then later reinstated to replace Allyson when the film finally went into production in November 1949. In February, it was announced that Allyson would star in *All Too Young*, which would be later made as *Too Young to Kiss*.

She was in contention for the role of Annie Oakley in the MGM biographical musical comedy *Annie Get Your Gun* (1950), produced by Arthur Freed. The film was based on the Ethel Merman–starring Broadway show with songs by Irving Berlin, which had run at the Imperial Theatre from May 16, 1946, to February 12, 1949. Production began on the film on March 7, 1949, with Judy Garland as Annie and the director Busby Berkeley. Berkeley was replaced by Charles Walters on May 3 or 5 (sources differ), and then on May 10 Garland was fired for repeated failures to report to the set and being responsible for substantial delays. MGM shut down production and searched for a replacement. Walters reported that Allyson was a popular choice but he preferred Betty Grable. Freed preferred Betty Hutton, and MGM's vice-president in charge of production Dore Schary preferred Betty Garrett. Freed won out and on June 21 Hutton was signed on a loan-out from Paramount.

Powell wanted Allyson to co-star with him in the United Artists drama *Mrs. Mike* (1949) but MGM refused to loan her out and Evelyn Keyes was cast instead. On April 10, Allyson appeared in the *Screen Director's Playhouse* radio version of the film *Music for Millions*. She repeated the role of Barbara "Babs" Ainsworth, who plays string bass in a symphony orchestra. This version was also directed by Henry Koster. He confessed to being an Allyson fan; he saw her as a new force in films—fresh, vital, spontaneous, and a highly talented actress. He and she chatted after the show. Allyson described Koster as a motion picture man of the world and one of the greatest directors in Hollywood and very sweet.

On April 21, she appeared in the *Hallmark Playhouse* radio version of the RKO romance *Kitty Foyle* (1940). Kitty is a hard-working white-collar girl from a middle-class family who meets and falls in love with a young socialite, but clashes with his family. In the show's intermission and after the show, Allyson promoted *Little Women*, which had been released on March 10. Hallmark celebrated the occasion with dolls of the *Little Women* characters. Allyson supplied some to her young friends, with each actress having autographed the doll which part they played. On May 19, she appeared in the *Screen Guild Theater*'s radio version of the film *The Bride Goes Wild*.

On July 5, it was announced that Allyson would play psychoanalyst Mary Belney in MGM's *The Big Hangover* (1950), a comedy with social significance, to be produced, written and directed by Norman Krasna. Allyson was replaced by Elizabeth Taylor. Her next film was the black-and-white comedy *The Reformer and the Redhead* (1950), written, produced and directed by Norman Panama and Melvin Frank. It was shot between September 21 and November 1, 1949. Based on a story by Robert Carson, it was set in Oakport, where hot-tempered Kathy "Red" Maguire (Allyson) enlists the services of attorney Andrew Rockton Hale (Dick Powell) to help her zookeeper father get his job back after he is fired for political reasons. She is top-billed but has less scenes than Powell. The actress has a wardrobe by Helen Rose and her hair is worn with a right side part instead of Allyson's signature left part. The

Dick Powell, a lion and Allyson in *The Reformer and the Redhead* (1950).

directors score an unintentional laugh when Andrew is shown to have a framed, uncharacteristically glamourous photograph of Kathy (her hair longer than in the film). In one scene, Kathy has a catfight with Lily Rayton Parker (Kathleen Freeman) which leaves Kathy with facial scratches, bruises and torn clothes. Stunt doubles and trick photography were used in the scene where Kathy and Andrew interact with lions. She demonstrates convincing anger for the part. Kathy's easy rapport with Andrew is presumably thanks to the couple being married in real-life. Allyson's best scene is perhaps when she delivers a funny monologue describing an average date between men and women. The film was released on May 5, 1950. It was praised by John Douglas Eames in *The MGM Story*. It was a box office success.

In early 1949, Lana Turner and Robert Taylor were set to star in the film, according to *The Hollywood Reporter*. Allyson worked harder with Powell than with any other co-star but was afraid the public would refuse to believe that she was anyone but what she was in real life—his wife. If Powell had not been in the film, the actress doubted she would have accepted the role because working with live lions terrified her, coming after a childhood phobia about cats. One day a lion got loose on the set and headed straight for Allyson. The trainer spoke quietly, telling her not to move, as if she could.

Allyson said the film only partially came off. Working with Powell was no different than living with him. He was the boss at home and the boss at work. On set, the man was very professional and insisted that she drive home rather than take a limousine. When the couple toured together to promote the film, there was violent reactions from fans, with one ripping off the sleeve of her beloved mink coat. But the worst was that one cut a big swatch of Allyson's hair.

On December 18, she appeared on *The Edgar Bergen with Charlie McCarthy* radio show. She said she would have adored living in King Arthur's time with their knights and shining armor. It would have been so much fun shopping for canned goods because in those days even the men were put up in tins. Allyson sings "Thou Swell" with a male chorus. She comments on her voice, having been told it has the range of Lily Pons and the vivacity of Mary Martin, though Allyson disagrees. She and Edger and Charlie go to the museum to see the King Arthur display in their armor room. Allyson gets a funny line to the museum guide about a 15-foot long prehistoric bone: "Think of the size of the prehistoric dog that buried it." In a King Arthur and his Knights fantasy scene, she plays a strolling player, Princess June and a child, with various

English accents. She also sings "I've Got a Lovely Bunch of Coconuts" by Fred Heatherton with a male chorus. Four days later, on December 22, she appeared in the *Screen Guild Theater* radio version of the film of *Little Women.*

Pammy's adoption came under question when the Tennessee agency was part of a Congressional investigation of the baby adoption racket. It was charged that some agencies were running a black market in babies, and Tennessee made angry noises about coming to take Pammy. Powell was accused in some newspaper accounts of having paid $1 million for her but he said the girl had been legally adopted in court and, if anyone came to get her, they should bring a very large cannon. But no one came. The Powells never hid from Pammy the fact that she was adopted; Pammy loved to hear the bedtime story of how Mommy had "adopinated" her.

They decided it was time for Pammy to have a little brother. Despite the Congressional investigation, the Powells went to the same Tennessee agency and found a boy. They were assured that after the usual lapse of time for paperwork and investigation, he would be theirs.

Allyson's next film was the black-and-white sports drama *Right Cross* (1950), produced by Armand Deutsch and shot from January 25 to early March 1950. The Charles Schnee–scripted story is set in New York, where boxing promoters Pat "Kitten" O'Malley (Allyson) and Rick Garvey (Powell) compete to sign up Mexican prizefighter Johnny Monterez (Ricardo Montalban), with whom Pat is romantically involved. (Gloria DeHaven was first slated for the role of Pat, then Ava Gardner.) The actress, top-billed, wears her short hair with bangs and her wardrobe by Helen Rose includes one notable dark, low-cut, short-sleeved belted pattern dress. The role sees Allyson dance with Johnny, whistle and have champagne splashed on her face by a waiter. She gets a funny line when Johnny asks how her father (Lionel Barrymore) is: "Very dead, thank you." Allyson transitions from Pat expecting Johnny to propose to her to disappointment that he won't marry her, and she makes the mistake of mixing business and romance and her jealousy of his love of boxing over her. Director John Sturges features the same glamor photograph of the actress that was used in *The Reformer and the Redhead* and it is just as uncharacteristic of the character she plays.

The film was released on October 6, 1950, with the tagline "The Star of *The Stratton Story* in a New, Powerful Romance!" It was praised by *Variety* and John Douglas Eames in *The MGM Story.* Thomas M. Pryor in *The New York Times* wrote that Allyson did nicely in the somewhat

(From left) Dick Powell, Allyson and Ricardo Montalban in *Right Cross* (1950).

trying role of the girl who was humiliated and exasperated by the muscled knucklehead. The film was not a box office success.

Allyson said that the film just did not come off. She was not jealous of Marilyn Monroe in an uncredited role as Dusky Ledoux; rather, she found the young actress to be the sweetest and most delightful person she had ever met. If you told Monroe you loved the blouse she was wearing, she would give it to you.

On February 13, Allyson reprised her *Stratton Story* role in a *Lux Radio Theatre* version of the film. On March 13, she reprised her *Little Women* role in a *Lux Radio Theater* version; at the end, she promoted the forthcoming *The Reformer and the Redhead.* She and Dick Powell presented the Best Cinematography award at the 22nd Academy Awards held at the RKO Pantages Theatre on March 23.

On April 6, it was announced that Allyson had been cast in a major part (originally intended for Lana Turner) in *Three Guys Named Mike.* But she was unavailable when the MGM romantic comedy started filming in July, and was replaced by Jane Wyman. It was reported that she underwent minor surgery on April 28 in St. John's Hospital. Her physician said the illness was not serious. Allyson was allowed to return home after a few days.

The Powells attended the May 6 marriage of Elizabeth Taylor and Conrad Hilton at the Church of the Good Shepherd in Los Angeles, followed by a lavish reception at the Bel-Air Country Club.

Allyson was cast in the musical comedy *Royal Wedding* (1951), produced by Arthur Freed and directed by Charles Walters. She was to play Ellen Bowen, the sister of Tom (Fred Astaire), whose dance act was booked in London during the Royal Wedding. The actress was delighted to be able to dance with Astaire and told him about seeing *The Gay Divorcee* many times; smiling wryly, Astaire wasn't sure he believed her. When Allyson added that she had crashed Broadway and even gotten to Hollywood on his training, he threw back his head and laughed. Rehearsals began in May. Though it felt good being twirled around the room and gliding over the floor with his masterful touch guiding her, she felt weak and nauseated. Allyson was losing weight and after eight days Powell finally told her to see a doctor. She feared that the operation she had had in April had ended with the surgeon leaving an instrument inside her, that they now needed to retrieve—but the news was that Allyson was pregnant. Not wanting to risk losing the child, Allyson knew she had to withdraw from the film. She regretted losing the chance to dance more with Astaire, but she wanted the baby more. She wanted to be polite and tell Astaire rather than let the studio do so. When Allyson called him excitedly with the news, there was a stunned silence and then a horrified voice asked, "Who is this?!"

She was replaced by Judy Garland in late May. Garland had been promised an eight-month vacation but was called back to the studio after three weeks. She told Allyson, "How dare you do this to me?! My first vacation in my entire life and you have to go and get...." Allyson couldn't use the word Garland used—pregnant. Allyson was almost sorry she was for a few minutes. After Garland was fired on June 17 for not reporting for rehearsals, Jane Powell stepped in. Allyson theorized that Garland was late or absent out of self-doubt, a perfectionist fearful that she wouldn't be able to deliver.

Garland would call Allyson in the middle of the night needing someone to talk to so Allyson would go to her place and listen. She felt responsible for her friend's predicament, which would lead Garland to what was reportedly a suicide attempt in June. Garland, broke, had gone to Louis B. Mayer after he had put her on suspension without salary and asked for a loan. She didn't have someone like Dick Powell to manage her finances and, like Allyson, was clueless about money. The MGM New York office refused to loan her money but Mayer himself lent her a few thousand dollars. Garland had never liked Mayer, and perhaps feeling bitter and in a drunken state, she stumbled into the bathroom and cut her neck with a piece of broken glass. When Allyson heard about it, she rushed to Garland's house. Garland said she didn't want to die. Garland was just exhausted and depressed and had given up feeling she could be Judy Garland any more.

The pregnant Allyson had her own problem: the boy they had arranged to adopt. Powell discussed the dilemma with a producer friend who offered to take him. It still hurt her to lose the boy and Allyson wondered, as they watched him grow up, if he ever knew they were almost his parents. Gloria Stewart was pregnant at the same time and one day the Powells were driving in the shopping area of Beverly Hills when they saw her tripping across the street recklessly. Allyson yelled at her to get out of the traffic and Gloria leaned into their car with a dazed and euphoric expression and said she was going to have twins, then floated off again.

Allyson announced her pregnancy in August and Louella Parson wrote that both the actress and Powell just walking on clouds, believing a miracle had happened.

On June 21 she appeared on the *Richard Diamond Private Detective* radio show episode "Mrs. X Can't Find Mr. X. aka Mrs. X Can't Find Her Husband." It was written by Blake Edwards and directed by Jaime del Valle. Allyson plays a woman from out of town who asks Diamond's help to find her husband in New York while refusing to reveal either of their names. The show's conceit is that Richard and others say the woman looks familiar but when she is revealed to be the real-life Allyson looking for the real-life Powell, it doesn't make any narrative sense. The treatment also overdoes the actress' crying so that what is initially funny becomes annoying.

Judy Garland was released from her MGM contract on September 29. Allyson commented that Garland just got lost somewhere and that there were too many demands on her. Allyson would get mad when people said unkind things about Garland or when they only seemed to remember all the unfortunate things that happened to her. Garland was one of the warmest, most loyal and funniest ladies Allyson had ever known. She had a magic all of her own and talking about Garland made Allyson cry.

Powell was preparing to star in the MGM crime drama *The Tall Target* (1951) with Adolphe Menjou. Menjou was especially interested in the time of June's baby's birth because astrology was his big passion. She was carrying all in front and every old wives' tale said this was a sign that the child would be a girl. The acid test was when some girlfriends hung Allyson's wedding ring from a string and held it over her stomach as she reclined on the couch. The way it swung made them agree it was definitely a girl although Allyson thought they were all wrong and she would name him Herman.

The doctor said the baby was due in mid–January but in late December Allyson was taken to St. John's Hospital. She was so nervous that the actress forgot her name when signing in. Powell whispered it to her and she wrote *June Dick Powell* on the hospital records. Then followed 18 hours of labor, and an emergency caesarean was required. The baby boy, born on December 24, looked just like his father. Powell and their friends had been going through agony in the waiting room after hearing Allyson was having difficulty so they were surprised to see her sitting up and yelling, "Merry Christmas everyone! I've got a boy!" When they got the new mother back to her room, she ordered two big club sandwiches and ate them. Powell gave her a new wedding ring, similar to the old plain one but gem-encrusted, and Allyson wore both of them. Powell was so happy being a new father while in his 40s. He left the hospital to go to the George Murphys to spend Christmas Eve.

Although Allyson was ready to go home, the baby had to stay in the hospital in an incubator for a time. Calling him Herman was really a joke since that was the name of one of the *Reformer and The Redhead* lions and that of an acting seal she once met. Allyson always planned on naming the boy Richard aka Ricky, after his father.

Allyson made her television debut on DuMont's family music show *The Arthur Murray Party* in the episode broadcast on February 4, 1951. Her next film was the black-and-white romantic comedy *Too Young to Kiss* (1951), produced by Sam Zimbalist and shot from April 15 or 16 to late May 1951. The screenplay was by Frances Goodrich and Albert Hackett, based on an Everett Freeman story. Allyson starred as Cynthia Potter, a talented pianist who passes herself off as a child prodigy to impresario Eric Wainwright (Van Johnson) in an audition for young musicians for a children's concert tour. The actress doubles as the 22-year-old Cynthia and her 12-year-old sister Molly. At the age of 34, Allyson can't really pass for either age, but her lack of height in contrast to Johnson, body language, the use of a child's dental plate and the wardrobe by Helen Rose all help for her play Molly. Rose's wardrobe for Cynthia gives the actress a more sophisticated look. Cynthia's shoulder-length hair—presumably a wig—is let down and worn in pigtails with bangs and hair ribbons. Cynthia being a smoker (the first time we see Allyson smoke on screen) is a plot point, as is her relationship with John Tirsen (Gig Young), particularly when he is seen kissing Molly. The role also sees the actress play the piano, hiccup, chew gum and ride a bike and a rollercoaster. Allyson is funny, especially when tantrum-crying as Molly, and she gets a lot of physical comedy. This includes being pushed by a boy with a violin case; being manhandled by Eric, Miss Benson (Kathryn Givney) and Danny Cutler (Larry Keating); bumping noses with Eric; and falling off a piano bench. The spanking that Molly inevitably receives is not funny. Director Robert Z. Leonard gives the actress four closeups. Allyson underplays her best scene, in which Cynthia agrees to give up her career, not implicate Eric in the hoax, and marry John.

The film was released on November 22, 1951, with the taglines "Too Funny to miss!," "M-G-M's hilarious answer to the question: WHEN IS A MISS TOO YOUNG TO KISS?," "When a glamour girl goes in for pigtails, there's trouble ahead for wolves" and "Is she a kid, or is she kidding?" It was praised by John Douglas Eames in *The MGM Story* but lambasted by *The New York Times'* Bosley Crowther, who wrote that Allyson's performance suggested that she was bucking to take over the role of Baby Snooks. A box office success, the film was nominated for the Best Art Direction–Set Decoration, Black-and-White Academy Award. Allyson won the Best Actress—Comedy or Musical Golden Globe Award for her performance. She felt that the film was awful.

Louis B. Mayer was either fired or he resigned from MGM (sources differ) and left on June 23 after 23 years at the studio. Allyson was sad to see him go and said that when Mayer left, he took the studio with him in spirit so the man really didn't lose.

On June 25, she appeared in the *Lux Radio Theater* version of film *The Reformer and the Redhead.* At the end, Allyson did an advertisement for Lux, the sponsor. She also reported how she and Powell had recently gone to New York, their first time east together in five years, to see the new Broadway plays. They also saw the MGM musical biography *The Great Caruso* (1951) and she said she wanted to get Mario Lanza's records of the arias.

Her next film was the black-and-white biography *The Girl in White* aka *So Bright the Flame* (1952), produced by Armand Deutsch and shot from October to November 1951. Director John Sturges' film had the working title *The Hobson Girl.* The screenplay was by Irmagard von Cube and Allen Vincent, adapted by von Cube and Philip Stevenson

Van Johnson and Allyson in *Too Young To Kiss* (1951).

from the book *Bowery to Bellevue* by Emily Dunning Barringer. Allyson's Dr. Emily Dunning decides to become a doctor at the turn of the century when women are not being made welcome in the field of medicine. The actress, top-billed, wears her hair in its natural short state as the young Emily. She also has a shoulder-length wig worn with bangs as the older doctor. Emily is slapped by Marie Yeomens (Mildred Dunnock) and slaps Dr. Ben Barringer (Arthur Kennedy), touches a skeleton and handles instruments in a surgical operation, relocates a dislocated shoulder, is on a sleigh ride and rides in a horse-drawn ambulance wagon. We also see her dance with Ben and Dr. Seth Pawling (Gary Merrill). She sings part of the Cornell Alma Mater song. In one scene, Allyson wears only a period slip and in another a period bathing costume. Her most notable outfit is the dark-colored suit she wears for ambulance duty—a jacket and ankle-length skirt with white blouse, dark-colored tie, cap and cape. The actress makes Emily funny and dignified. Allyson has an impressive silent reaction to the news of Ben leaving for Paris and his indirect proposal but her best scene is perhaps the rooftop dance sequence. Here the actress transitions from Emily dancing with Ben, distracted after having danced with Seth, and then flirting with Seth with the realization that the director of New York's Gouverneur Hospital where she interns still cannot accept her as a female doctor. In his book *Escape Artist: The Life and Films of John Sturges,* Glenn Lovell wrote that on *The Girl in White,* time was lost in production partly due to the actress' pregnancy.

It was released on May 23, 1952, with the tagline "If men can do it, women can do it better!" A.H. Weiler in *The New York Times* wrote that although the script did not give her many opportunities for incisive acting, Allyson did on occasion give Dr. Dunning the stature of a crusader. It was lambasted by John Douglas Eames in *The MGM Story.* It was not a box office success.

On November 9, it was announced that Allyson was to next star in MGM's musical comedy *One for the Road,* in which she would play a traveling saleswoman promoting safety razors in 1906, an era when women still were mostly homebound. Sydney R. Zelinka and Howard Harris sold the story and had been engaged by the studio to develop it into a screenplay under the supervision of producer Joe Pasternak. The film was not made. On February 10, it was reported that she had been recently named by the nation's motion picture exhibitors as their most important feminine commodity of the past year. Allyson said MGM had taken her out of musicals and were giving her dramatic roles, where she specialized in projecting rather spinach-flavored girlishness. Allyson had yet to play a bad girl but reported that 20th Century–Fox's Joseph L. Mankiewicz had wanted her to play Eve Harrington in the drama *All About Eve* (1950) but MGM refused to lend her out. Allyson being considered for the part is confirmed by Sam Staggs in his book *All About*

All About Eve: *The Complete Behind-the-Scenes Story of the Bitchiest Film Ever Made.*

Despite losing out on the part, she said MGM was wonderful at taking care of its own, always having a car waiting for her when Allyson needed it. Her dressing room was bigger than any apartment she had ever lived in.

It appears that Allyson attended the *9th Golden Globes,* held on February 21, 1952, at Ciro's, where Allyson was awarded Best Performance by an Actress in a Motion Picture—Comedy or Musical for *Too Young to Kiss.* She appeared on the *Olympic Fund Telethon* TV special, shot at Hollywood's El Capitan Theatre and broadcast on NBC and CBS on June 21 and 22, 1952.

On July 11, it was announced that Allyson would star in MGM's *Remains to Be Seen* for MGM. The Howard Lindsay-Russel Crouse comedy opened on Broadway on October 3, 1951, and ran at the Morosco Theatre until March 22, 1952. She would play the role Janis Paige played on stage—a singer with a cheap band who becomes involved in a murder case. (Debbie Reynolds was also considered for the part.) The film was to go into production after Allyson completed *Battle Circus.*

Battle Circus (1953), a black-and-white war romance, was produced by Pandro S. Berman and shot from July 21 to September 9, 1952, on locations in Virginia and California. The working title was *MASH 66.* The screenplay was by Richard Brooks based on a story by Allen Rivkin and Laura Kerr; Brooks also directed. At the Mobile Army Surgical Hospital 8666 in Korea during the war, Major Jed Webbe (Humphrey Bogart), a hard-bitten Army surgeon, and Lt. Ruth McGara (Allyson), a new nurse ready to save the world, become romantically involved. Allyson, second-billed, wears her hair in her natural short style with a side part. A shower scene has implied nudity. Ruth gets to drive a Jeep and perform nursing duties, and the role incorporates some slapstick, such as being repeatedly tossed around by Jed when the unit is bombed and falling in the mud. Allyson also gets to dance with Bogart; their chemistry is no doubt due to the actors being off-screen friends. Though she has a good scene talking a Korean solider (Philip Ahn) into giving up a hand grenade, her best is perhaps the comic one when she listens to advice from a lieutenant colonel (Robert Keith) about how to romance Jed.

The film was released on March 6, 1953, with the tagline "M-G-M's great drama of desire under fire!" In Alan G. Barbour's *Humphrey Bogart,* he described Allyson as an actress of extremely limited range. The film was a box office success.

In one scene, Bogart wipes something off of Allyson's nose while she is talking to him. She has a surprised reaction but continues with the scene. Bogart had the habit of greeting her every morning with "Here comes little Junie. Cuter than a bug's ear." It annoyed her and she begged him to stop saying it. Allyson had no problem with director Richard Brooks. Despite his reputation for being pushy and intimidating, he did not act this way with her, having found out early that he could get more out of the actress if he was gentler. Brooks reportedly said that there was no on-screen chemistry between the lead actors, and when Bogart had to kiss Allyson it was like he was kissing his maiden aunt.

Allyson wanted to continue playing serious roles and not be typecast in light romantic comedies or as the plain girl next door, the one men took home to meet their mother and always got her man. The actress complained that MGM fell back on typecasting and was not choosing her vehicles as well as she would have liked. To them, her name was enough to sell anything.

Remains to Be Seen (1953), produced by Arthur Hornblow, Jr., began shooting in October 1952 with a Sidney Sheldon screenplay based on the Lindsay-Crouse play. The director was Don Weis. A millionaire (Stuart Holmes) is murdered in the Park Avenue apartment house managed by Waldo Williams (Van Johnson). In the role of Jody Revere, Allyson's hair is shorter and given a more sculptured style. Helen Rose's costumes provide a more glamorous though tacky look for her. There is a notable evening dress that is sparkly and beaded, low-cut, sleeveless, and has a matching jacket. Allyson sings and dances with Johnson to "Toot, Toot, Tootsie (Goo' Bye!)" by Gus Kahn, Ernie Erdman and Dan Russo and sings "Too Marvelous for Words" with music by Richard A. Whiting and lyrics by Johnny Mercer as she dances again with Johnson. The actress' reported vocal deterioration is evident in the singing of the second song. The role sees her smoke, faint and do some slapstick as when Jody touches Waldo's ears and musses his hair as he plays the drums. Her best scene is perhaps when she is hypnotized and sleepwalks and moves between Valeska Chauvel (Angela Lansbury) and Waldo.

The film was released on May 15, 1953, with the taglines "M-G-M's Fright-FULLY FUNNY MIRTHQUAKE," "Broadway Stage Hit on the Screen!" and "It's FRIGHTfully funny!" It was lambasted by John Douglas Eames in *The MGM Story*. The film was not a box office success. It had been said that the problem was casting although Jody is a character that is similar to the spunky ones Allyson had played in the past.

Quoted in the film's pressbook, Allyson stated that she was glad to

Print ad for *Remains to Be Seen* (1953).

play a different kind of part. Supporting player Louis Calhern said the film was a milestone in her career since any young woman who wore strapless gowns and high-heeled shoes and sings a disturbing torchy song could no longer be considered the girl next door. Unless of course Calhern was living in the wrong neighborhood.

Van Johnson reported that she did not like the part of Jody and was going to ask for a release from her contract. Johnson told Allyson not to do that because the studio already had her release papers ready and waiting but she thought Louis B. Mayer would look after her. But when Allyson went to Mayer and asked for her release, he produced the papers ready for her signature. However, this encounter was more likely to have been with the new head of MGM, Dore Schary, as Mayer left MGM in August 1951.

Allyson was a guest on the March 1, 1953, episode of CBS-TV's New York–based variety series *Talk of the Town* aka *The Ed Sullivan Show*. As Humphrey Bogart was also a guest, the appearance was presumably done to promote *Battle Circus*. The director was John Moffitt.

When Powell woke up in the middle of the night with stomach pain, Allyson called his doctor who ordered an ambulance. Powell's appendix had burst. He was admitted to St. John's Hospital on February 20 with his wife reported to be in almost constant attendance by his bedside. Powell was operated on immediately but they weren't sure he could be saved. Howard Hughes sent his personal doctor to help and Powell went back for corrective surgery. The happiest sound Allyson ever heard was when she put her head down on his belly and there was a faint gurgling. The actress was photographed on March 4 with Powell's hospital nurse, Clarice MacKay.

Allyson attended the *25th Academy Awards* ceremony on March 19 at the RKO Pantages Theatre and broadcast on NBC-TV. On May 1, she reported she had ended her contract with MGM so she could accept other offers. MGM had wanted her to re-sign but the actress was not happy working under Dore Schary. Unlike Louis B. Mayer, he did not guard his stars and no one on the lot was happy about his taking over. The studio announced that its contract with her had been dissolved through mutual agreement with the break ending a ten-year association. She owed them one more film and they announced on May 18 that she would be teamed with Fernando Lamas in the romantic comedy *Honeymoon*, to be written and produced by Anatole de Grunwald. The film was to be made in London in the fall and the story would see its principals on a tour of the capitals of Europe. It appears this film was never made.

The day she left MGM, the front office sent a man to make sure she didn't take anything that didn't belong to her. He had a long inventory sheet of things in the dressing room that were studio property. Not wanting to feel humiliated, she took the sheet herself and went around checking things off to show that nothing was being stolen. The actress felt leaving MGM was like a child leaving home for the first time, suddenly stepping on emptiness after being on solid ground for so long.

It was reported that Allyson would play the female lead in the MGM romantic comedy *The Long, Long Trailer* (1953) but Lucille Ball was cast instead. One source claims that Ball was cast because she was also the film's producer with her husband Desi Arnaz but the film credits Pandro S. Berman as producer. Allyson had also been sought for the musical biography *I'll Cry Tomorrow* (1955), based on the book by Lillian Roth which told of her life as an alcoholic. Susan Hayward had brought the script to MGM and wanted Charles Walters to direct her, but he wanted Allyson. Walters' idea was to start with this innocent façade and have the fears gradually eat at the woman. Walters personally knew how tough Allyson could be and he felt she could have scored with the part, even getting an Academy Award. But the studio insisted on Hayward and Walters walked off the film. It went into production after Allyson left MGM; Hayward's performance earned her an Academy Award nomination.

5

The Glenn Miller Story

Her next film was the Universal's Technicolor musical biography *The Glenn Miller Story* (1954) produced by Aaron Rosenberg and shot from June 5 to late July 1953 on locations in Colorado and at Universal. The working title was *Moonlight Serenade.* The Valentine Davies–Oscar Brodney screenplay followed the trombone player and bandleader (James Stewart) from his beginnings to his death over the English Channel in December 1944. Allyson plays Helen Burger, Glenn's college sweetheart who becomes his wife. Hair stylist Joan St. Oegger duplicates the signature MGM Allyson short dark blonde style though it is not period when the narrative is set in the 1930s. Costumer Jay Morley, Jr., outfits are also mostly non-period and feature a particularly ugly white short-sleeved knee-length petticoated dress with a black belt and black-and-white diagonal-patterned skirt. The role sees the actress dance with Stewart. The credited dance director Kenny Williams was no doubt more responsible for the dance in the number "Tuxedo Junction" (music by Erskine Hawkins, William Johnson and Julian Dash, lyrics by Buddy Feyne). She sings lines from "Basin Street Blues" by Spencer Williams and recites "Pennsylvania 6-5000" with music by Jerry Gray and lyrics by Carl Sigman. Helen is another devoted wife like Allyson had played to Stewart in *The Stratton Story,* here encouraging her husband to find his unique musical sound. Her habit of stealing money from his pockets allows him to eventually afford to pay his own band. Allyson gets a drunk scene and is accidentally hit in the head by one of Glenn's autograph seekers." Director Anthony Mann gives her many closeups. Allyson's best scene is perhaps her last when Helen learns of Glenn's disappearance. Mann uses another extended closeup as she listens to "Little Brown Jug" by Joseph Winner on the radio.

The film premiered in Japan on January 4, 1954, and opened in the U.S. on February 10 with the taglines "It was a time that changed the world. And one man put it to music" and "Their love made such wonderful music!" It was praised by *Variety*, Bosley Crowther in *The New York Times* and Gordon Gow in *Hollywood in the Fifties*. Clive Hirschhorn in *The Universal Story* wrote that Allyson was winningly sympathetic. A box office success, the film was Oscar-nominated for Best Writing, Story and Screenplay and Best Music, Scoring of a Musical Picture. Nominated for Best Actress by the New York Film Critics Circle, Allyson tied with Judy Garland for *A Star Is Born*, Audrey Hepburn for *Sabrina* and Eva Marie Saint for *On the Waterfront*.

20th Century–Fox had been rumored to be planning a film on the life of Glenn Miller in early 1942 with Betty Grable as the femme lead, but the project went nowhere. In July 1953, *The Hollywood Reporter* wrote that Dinah Shore refused the role of Helen Burger.

This is one of the three films Allyson considered her personal favorites. She said James Stewart had told her there were two films he wanted to do and wouldn't do them without her, the second being *Strategic Air Command*. Stewart offered to send her the scripts but she said not to bother. The actress agreed to do the films because Stewart was pretty sharp, and in retrospect this was the best thing she could have done.

She described Universal as her good luck studio, since it was there she made her very first freelance film after exclusively working at MGM. When Allyson ended her MGM contract, the actress thought she would take it easy. Then suddenly she found herself being offered the best stories she had ever had, and couldn't turn them down. She also started earning bigger money, around $100,000 a film, though this had little meaning to her as Powell took complete charge of her business affairs. The money went into a common pot with her husband's.

On May 18, Allyson made the *Lux Radio Theater* version of *The Girl in White*. At the end, she promoted her newest film *Remains to Be Seen* and reported that her family had new additions: puppies. Dick Powell wanted her for *The Gibson Girl* but the film was never made. On July 30, it was reported that she would return to Universal to make in the romantic actioner *Foxfire*, to be produced by Aaron Rosenberg. Jeff Chandler was to co-star in the Technicolor story, to be adapted from Anya Seton's novel. Allyson first had to make her last film for MGM to wind up her contract: *Executive Suite*. Jane Russell ended up with the *Foxfire* role.

The black and white drama *Executive Suite* (1954) was produced by John Houseman and shot from August 24 to September 25, 1953, on locations in New York, Pennsylvania, and California and at MGM. The

William Holden and Allyson examine test strips in a still for *Executive Suite* (1954).

Ernest Lehman screenplay was based on the novel by Cameron Hawley. The story centered on the furniture-manufacturing Tredway Corporation, whose 56-year-old head dies suddenly from a stroke. The vice-presidents vie to see who will replace him. Allyson plays Mary Blemond Walling, the seemingly devoted wife of veepee Don Walling (star William Holden). Vice-president and treasurer Frederick Y. Alderson (Walter Pidgeon) asks her to tell Don to have the board meeting delayed so that he can secure the vote for Don, but Mary doesn't pass along the message. She does not want him to be the new president, knowing it will keep him away from her. Mary is seen eavesdropping on the meeting. The actress wears her standard MGM short hairstyle. Director Robert Wise goofs with continuity in a scene in a taxi where Allyson's changes slightly from shot to shot. Costumes by Helen Rose include a slinky nightgown. The role also sees her playing practice baseball with son Mike (Tim Considine). The actress doesn't get the emotional moments given to Barbara Stanwyck as Julia O. Treadway, Shelley Winters as Eva Bardeman and Nina Foch as Erica Martin. Most of Allyson's scenes are with Holden.

The film premiered at the MGM World Film Festival in South Africa on February 17, 1954. It was released in the U.S. on April 15 with the taglines "Behind the lighted tower windows the conflict of love and power is reckless and daring!," "The TRUTH about 'office wives'!," "M-G-M presents the cast of the year in the picture of the year!" and "GREAT NOVEL BECOMES SENSATIONAL SCREEN DRAMA!" It was praised by *Variety*, Jerry Vermilye in *Barbara Stanwyck* and John Douglas Eames in *The MGM Story* but lambasted by Bosley Crowther in *The New York Times*. A box office success, it received Oscar nominations for Best Actress in a Supporting Role (Nina Foch), Best Cinematography, Best Costume Design, Black-and-White, and more. Allyson was among those in the cast who won the Special Jury Prize at the Venice Film Festival for Ensemble Acting. It was remade as a 1976 television series, though without the character of Mary.

Allyson was thrilled to work with Stanwyck and admired how she faked smashing a wine glass on a bar. Stanwyck was so professional that she almost scared the other actors, especially Allyson. When Stanwyck had lived across the street from the Powells, Allyson never socialized with her. Allyson said she could never sit and talk to her because she was too big a star—Stanwyck overwhelmed her.

In his book, *Golden Boy: The Untold Story of William Holden*, Bob Thomas wrote that Allyson, unlike Holden, did not learn her lines before the first rehearsal (to which she was late). During an embrace, Holden glanced over his shoulder at Wise, with an expression of "What the hell is this?" since the actress was still holding her script. Her agent telephoned producer John Houseman that night to report that she was in hysterics, claiming that other members of the cast were persecuting her. The matter was smoothed over and Allyson was neither late nor unprepared thereafter. In his book on Barbara Stanwyck, Alex Madsen repeated the story of the call made to Houseman, but says it occurred after the actress' scene with Stanwyck: The older actress reportedly jeered at Allyson for being late and not knowing her lines.

On November 2, she appeared in the *Lux Radio Theater* version of Universal's 1952 romance film *Because of You*. Allyson played Christine, an ex-con on parole and working as a Long Beach veteran's hospital nurse's aid when she falls in love with Jeff Chandler and hesitates to reveal her past. Christine had been essayed by Loretta Young in the film. At the end of the show, Allyson laughs as she jokes with Chandler about him playing an Indian in the Fox Western *Broken Arrow* (1950).

On December 8, Allyson underwent an appendectomy at St. John's Hospital. On February 28, 1954, she was back on the *Edgar Bergen Show with Charlie McCarthy* radio show. Charlie imagines them starring together in a movie in which she plays Mary Glockenspieler, a girl behind the counter in a music store, and customer Charlie wants sheet music to wrap his dead fish in. Mary sings the Ben Ryan song "Heart of My Heart" to him, supported by Ray Noble and his orchestra and imitating Al Jolson's singing style. She laughs when Charlie blows a line, when she blows a line, and when he walks over one of her lines, and seems to do some ad-libbing. Allyson uses a Southern accent when Mary is a waitress in a Southern diner, and a Brooklyn accent when she works in a laundromat. The skit references *The Glenn Miller Story* and features Dick Powell as himself.

Her next film was director Jean Negulesco's Technicolor drama *Woman's World* (1954), produced by Charles Brackett and shot from May 10 to mid–June 1954 on locations in New York and at 20th Century–Fox. It had been in development at Fox since 1952; other actresses considered for the role of Katie (ultimately played by Allyson) included Jeanne Crain, Joanne Dru, Susan Hayward and Gloria Grahame. The screenplay was by Claude Binyon, Mary Loos and Richard Sale, based on a story by Mona Williams, with additional dialogue by Howard Lindsay and Russel Crouse. In New York, Gifford (Clifton Webb), president of Gifford Motors, plans to fill the general manager position by interviewing the three candidates' wives. Allyson is second-billed as Katie Baxter, the wife of Bill Baxter (Cornel Wilde). Hair stylist Helen Turpin duplicates Allyson's MGM standard hair style. Wardrobe director Charles LeMaire presents Katie's clothes as character, with a dowdy purple knee-length, round-collared, long-sleeved evening dress with a large ribbon on the chest, matching hat and white flower at the waist. This gauche number is said to be her favorite from Kansas City where the Baxters originate. Katie's lack of style is contrasted with the glamor and style of clothes worn by her rivals, Liz (Lauren Bacall) from Philadelphia and Carol (Arlene Dahl) from Dallas. Katie gets a makeover, with the help of Liz, wearing a crème low-cut sleeveless floor-length evening gown, though its tassels hint at her previous bad taste. The role has Allyson dance with Tony Andrews (Elliott Reid) and indulge in a lot of silliness, which includes having hiccups when drunk, dropping a champagne glass and tea on herself, holding cotton wool pieces over her eyes, getting locked in a ship's bathroom where she is splashed by water through the porthole and being hit on the head by the window frame, and wearing an evening dress that is too big for her. The hiccup scene is perhaps the actress' best because she is so good at doing it and ends with the implication of vomiting off-camera. Allyson makes Katie funny in contrast to the more serious roles of Liz and Carol, who have their own domestic crises. Katie gets a funny line to Tony after a faux pas during a tour of the city: "If you get near a river, would you please stop? I'd like to jump in."

The film was released on September 28, 1954, with the taglines "The Worldly Story of Three Deadly Females and the Men in Their Lives!" and "The Year's Most Star-Brilliant Cast!" It was praised by *Variety* and by Tony Thomas and Aubrey Solomon in *The Films of 20th Century-Fox*. The film was a box office success.

Allyson knew Lauren Bacall as calm and collected but saw her as otherwise when making the film. In a scene where Bacall had to pick up a champagne glass, turn and survey the room, Bacall's hand was shaking and she admitted to being nervous.

A 1955 *Motion Picture Herald* poll listed Allyson as one of the one actors who had earned the most money that year. The only other woman on the list was Grace Kelly.

Her next film was Paramount's Technicolor war actioner *Strategic Air Command* (1955), shot (starting in late March) on locations in Texas, Colorado, Florida and California and at Paramount. The working title was *Air Command*. The screenplay was by Valentine Davies and Beirne Lay, Jr., based on Lay's story. The director was Anthony Mann. It centered on Lt. Col. Robert "Dutch" Holland (James Stewart), an ex-pilot and baseball player who is recalled into the Air Force and assumes an increasingly important role in Cold War deterrence. Allyson, second-billed, played Dutch's wife Sally. She has the MGM signature hairstyle and is gowned by Edith Head. Sally is another devoted military wife; when she is said to be pregnant, there is no obvious physical sign of her condition. Her best scene is perhaps when Sally cries and expresses her unhappiness over Dutch's decision to re-enlist; she is later ashamed about having done so.

The film was released on March 25, 1955, with the tagline "Soar to New Heights of Adventure!" It was praised by *Variety,* who wrote that Allyson was warm and appealing, and by Bosley Crowther in *The New York Times,* who said she was effective. Allyson attended the film's premiere party at the Storz Mansion in Omaha, Nebraska, home of Offutt Air Force Base and of Strategic Air Command Headquarters. The film was a box office success and Oscar-nominated for Best Writing, Motion Picture Story.

In 1957, Allyson's participation in the film later prompted a joke by Maine Senator Margaret Chase Smith, who objected to James Stewart being made a brigadier general in the Air Force Reserve. Smith suggested that Allyson also be made a brigadier general because she was the female lead in the film.

On April 2, it was announced that she would play opposite Jose Ferrer in *The Shrike,* the film adaptation of the Broadway play that ran at the Cort Theatre from January 15 to May 31, 1952. The actress' role of Ferrer's vicious wife marked a change for her since she had been identified with more demure and homely assignments. Allyson was quoted as saying that she was fed up being sweet.

On May 14, Allyson received the Women's Home Companion Readers Favorite Movie Actress award for 1954. In silent newsreel footage of the event, she is presented her award by Jack Kimball on the Hollywood set of the Dick Powell–produced and –directed historical adventure *The Conqueror* (1956), standing with John Wayne, who was chosen as Favorite Male Actor.

The Conqueror was shot on location in St. George, Utah, from May to August. Allyson had decided to visit Powell after they had been communicating by telephone, concerned for his safety after reading in the newspaper that a gale had wrecked the set. Powell was happy to have her come as he was lonely and wanted his wife to bring the children. So

Allyson drove the 450 miles, only to arrive to find chaos and doubting how her husband could say he was lonely since most of the town were acting as extras, including Indians from a nearby reservation. The Utah heat hovered between 110 and 120 degrees and everyone's nerves were so frayed that she realized that the company was close to rebellion. Powell broke the tension, sitting high in the air on his camera, singing "I Only Have Eyes for You" off-key, which made everyone laugh before he asked them to continue working. After the day's shooting, he and Allyson relaxed over a cold drink with stars John Wayne, Susan Hayward and Agnes Moorehead.

Also on May 14, it was announced that Allyson would co-star with Alan Ladd as husband and wife in Warners' *The McConnell Story.* It was to be based on the war exploits of Capt. Joseph McConnell, a jet ace who shot down 16 Communist planes in Korea.

The Universal black-and-white drama *The Shrike* (1955) was produced by Aaron Rosenberg and shot from September 20 to early November on locations in New York and at Universal. (In October 1952, it was announced that Ida Lupino would co-star with Ferrer and that Lupino and her then-husband Collier Young would produce for RKO.) The Ketti Frings screenplay was based on the Pulitzer Prize–winning play by Joseph A. Kramm. Jose Ferrer, the play's producer, directed the film version. Ferrer also played Jim Downs, a successful theatrical director driven to failure by the supposed machinations of his vengeful wife of nine years, Ann (Allyson). (The role was played by Judith Evelyn on Broadway.) Joan St. Oegger once again duplicated the MGM Allyson hairstyle. Costumes by Jay A. Morley, Jr., include a slinky nightgown, a mink coat and a dark-colored high-necked long-sleeved knee-length dress with matching turban and white fox piece.

Film historians consider Ann to be one of the actress' most controversial parts because it was thought to be such a departure in type. A doctor theorizes that she is a shrike, an innocent-looking bird with a sharp beak that is intentionally destructive and impales its victim on a thorn. He says she has ambivalent feelings of love and hate for Jim. She supposedly feels excluded from his work which keeps him away from home and is jealous of those he comes into contact with, including other women. Ann loves Jim too much so that she becomes obsessive and resentful, trying to destroy the work which also destroys the man. The more damaged he is, the more damaged Ann becomes. She is lonely, frustrated, bitter, and full of rage, turning him into a helpless child which she hates him for. A modern viewing perhaps allows for a less judgmental view of her. The worst thing that Ann is accused of—deliberately keeping Jim in the hospital mental ward against his wishes—is in fact a decision that is not hers. Rather it is made by his doctors since Jim has been admitted after a suicide attempt that seems to be more related to his depression after not finding work and the end of his relationship with Charlotte Moore (Joy Page). Ann believes the doctors know best and Jim's refusal to go home with her no doubt adds to his predicament. She is shown to be a devoted wife who sacrifices her own acting ambitions to have her life revolve around Jim, giving up a role when Jim doesn't like her in it. Ann creates a scrapbook to record all the press on him, reads plays, gives dramaturgical assistance, and even puts her own money into one production. When he doesn't like her directorial suggestions, she leaves the rehearsal room. When Jim cannot get work in the theater, Ann says her father could get him a job in his store in Bridgeport to keep busy while he waits for something to come along. When he is released from hospital, she offers to stay with her father so that he can be at her apartment alone. And though perhaps she oversteps by giving up the apartment he took after leaving her, Ann does have his belongings moved back to her apartment.

The woman does express some harsh judgments though she considers Jim a brilliant man in many ways. He doesn't always know what's good for him, is a weakling and dependent, and his suicide attempt comes from a guilty conscience from what he has done to her. It is understandable that Ann should resent Charlotte as the woman Jim dates after leaving his wife. And it is understandable that Ann should ask Jim to promise to never see Charlotte again. Ann also reflects on her own behavior, saying she is ashamed for demanding that about Charlotte and also for being "sadistic" in refusing to accompany him to London to see a play he is interested in doing on Broadway. He claims the trip will be the honeymoon they never had but Ann sees it as her just being a tagalong on a business trip.

Allyson makes Ann funny, particularly when she aggressively pushes Dr. Barrow (Isabel Bonner) out of her way in the hospital emergency room to talk to Jim, and is snide to Katharine Meade (Jacqueline de Wit) at a play rehearsal with "I know you're nervous. Returning to Broadway after 20 years is enough of a problem without my adding to it." Her best scene is perhaps when she talks to Dr. Bellman (Kendell Clark) who theorizes about her being the shrike. Director Ferrer holds Allyson in a medium closeup as she listens and then the actress has Ann defend herself with anger while she cries. Regrettably, a comic music cue from Frank Skinner underscores Ann's supposed wicked acts. There is also a continuity inconsistency with the actress' hair in the final scene outside the hospital.

The film was released on July 7, 1955, with the tagline "Destined to be the most talked about Motion Picture of the Year!" It was praised by A.H. Weiler in *The New York Times,* who wrote that Allyson generally

Print ad for *The Shrike* (1955).

conveyed the impression that she would not consciously hurt a fly. Clive Hirschhorn in *The Universal Story* wrote that she was far too charming and un-psychotic to make much impact. The film was not a box office success. It was remade as an *ITV Play of the Week* broadcast on television on June 28, 1960, with Margaret Johnston as Ann, and as a West German made-for-TV movie, *Unter Kuratel,* broadcast on July 9, 1970.

Allyson said she was dying to play a dramatic, villainous role and begged for the part. Powell and her advisers felt it was wrong, fearing it would alienate her fanbase—the actress seemed to be doing right the way she was going so why change it? She cited Powell's experience of doing *Murder, My Sweet* and Allyson too wanted a challenge. After years playing the perfect wife, she wanted to be an imperfect one. The actress saw Ann as a monster of a wife, one of the least attractive in the history of the theater. And maybe she would even get an Academy Award. Allyson was eternally grateful to Ferrer for thinking of her and loved the role and working with him. However, preview audiences said Allyson would never put her husband in an insane asylum and leave him there so the ending was reshot. Ann went back to the asylum so she could be good. The original ending had Ann get Jim out of the asylum where he was going to continue to be her victim and be doomed. The second ending had Ann express her regret and say she was going to make it up to him for all the abuse he has suffered.

In his book *José Ferrer: Success and Survival,* Mike Peros quoted Ferrer, who felt Allyson would do an exceptional job. Screenwriter Frings also supported the casting, believing her to be a fine actress, especially after viewing *The Glenn Miller Story.* The role of Ann was softened from the way it was written and performed on stage, with Ann now beginning as a nice girl who slowly becomes jealous and clinging. It was thought that the director needed Allyson as box office insurance for what was considered downbeat material. Peros said that Allyson was unhappy that the ending had to be reshot on the orders of Universal and implored Ferrer not to, but the director felt he had no choice.

Allyson wanted Powell to find a movie vehicle in which to direct her; she regarded him as one of Hollywood's foremost talents. He was waiting for the right role but she felt he didn't realize that even a minor part would be acceptable just so the actress could work with him.

Powell dreamed of a simpler life on a farm far from Hollywood where he could have a cow and raise corn. Allyson had always dreamed of having animals to play with—goats and rabbits and chickens—and she could milk the cow. He showed her Mandeville Canyon with an isolated estate of 68 acres beyond a mile-long driveway and past a lake over a bridge. Around the main house (made of stone) were guest houses, stables, corrals and buildings for the live-in help. This was to be their new home. Powell again gutted the house and rebuilt, adding a special wing for the children with a separate dining room for them and a suite for their nannies, and a private bathroom suite for Allyson that included a dressing room with a connecting door. The Powells had a live-in staff, including a laundress and foreman who were married to each other, a gardener and assistant gardener, an upstairs maid and downstairs maid, a governess, a cook, a secretary for Allyson, a chauffeur and Frank the butler. There was a man to look after the lake and check the fish and, after a swimming pool was added, a pool man. Mandeville became such a busy complex with workers and visitors that one day Allyson got confused and invited two workers who had come to fix the bathroom to have coffee with her. Powell accused his wife of being overfriendly with the help but she couldn't bring herself to demand "Who are you?" and "What do you want?," preferring to say, "How nice of you to come." Soon Allyson had her animals—30 Black Angus cattle in the fields, 5000 chickens in the hen yard, a dog, 30 sheep grazing, turkeys and pheasants, and horses for riding. Every time Allyson tried to learn to ride, the horse either broke into a gallop without her prompting or rode under a low branch to swipe her off its back. One day Allyson tried to ride Pammy's Welsh pony. The stable helper did not properly tighten the harness lines and, when she tried to throw herself into the saddle, she ended up sliding under the belly of the horse. She never tried to ride it again.

Getting a good governess was a problem. The first slept in the trees and was fired. The second had food fetishes and insisted on growing her own veggies in her room and was fired. The third quit when she discovered the family's travel plans were not extensive enough to suit her. The fourth became known as Awful Nanny. At first Allyson was impressed: The governess rewarded Pammy for being good by putting gold stars on her collar and took the girl for walks. But then Allyson learned Nanny would lock Ricky in a closet for biting her, and would re-serve uneaten food the next day. Allyson was too frightened to confront Nanny so she conspired with Pammy to dispose of the spoiled food down the toilet. It was Frances Bergen who finally brought about Nanny's downfall. Powell and Allyson had gone on a trip and asked Bergen to check in on the children. Bergen found Pammy screaming for her mommy but wouldn't say why. When the Powells got home, she wouldn't tell them either. Allyson went to Nanny, who refused to discuss her discipline. Allyson fired her. A week later, the Powells visited the home of a prominent Hollywood family and there she was, smiling at them with her sinister little smile, bringing in the children to say goodnight. Allyson wondered if Awful Nanny would be less awful in the new household, but she doubted it.

Mandeville also brought more of the extended family together. Allyson's half-brother Arthur Peters lived in a guest house as he attended medical school to become a doctor. Powell's daughter Ellen joined them and now Allyson said she was a better mother to her than before. The girl had grown into a sad person with a lot of disappointment in her life and Allyson was her Pollyanna, trying to keep everything happy and upbeat. Allyson's mother Clara also came to live nearby after Powell gave her husband a job in transportation and maintenance. Powell had created Four Star Productions for television and added a heliport in a pasture near the lake at Mandeville to enable him to take a helicopter to the studio. Another sign of Powell's success was that they could afford the luxury of screenings at home. A huge screen at the end of the living room would be pulled down and a movie that had yet to be released would be shown. The kids loved watching movies this way but never seemed to want to view any of their mother's movies. Her day finally came when they wanted *The Reformer and The Redhead* for the birthday party. She assumed the kids wanted to see their parents acting in a movie together but they were more interested in the lions.

Hedda Hopper visited for an interview and angered the actress when she asked which of the children playing around on the lawn was hers. But Allyson wouldn't let Hopper see how angry she was and answered sweetly that they were all hers. Hopper continued, saying she wanted to know which one was adopted. Allyson saw her children's upturned faces and laughed, replying, "You know something. I can't remember." But while the actress saw this as her shining hour, it made her even more of an enemy to Hopper, who claimed that Allyson wore falsies. The actress laughed over this and wondered if Hopper knew about falsies because *she* wore them.

One day James Cagney, a regular visitor, was there when Ricky appeared in soaked cowboy clothes: The boy had fallen into the deep lake. Allyson was grateful she had taught the children to swim before they moved into Mandeville. Another potential drowning occurred with Candice Bergen, the daughter of her friend Frances. Candice and Pammy would swim in the pool and, one day as their mothers sat

A Powell family publicity portrait: (from left) Dick Powell, Ricky, Allyson and Pammy.

talking, Allyson noticed that Candice was gone. The actress dove into the deep end where the girl was floundering underwater and got her out.

Evenings saw visits from Ronald Colman, George Murphy, Jane Wyman (now divorced from Ronald Reagan) and Reagan with new girlfriend Nancy Davis. Powell had bought a yacht, the *Sapphire Sea,* and took the children while Allyson cooled her heels on shore. One night she died a thousand deaths when it was reported that they were adrift in the ocean in a great storm. Powell's gift to her one year was new linoleum for a room she never entered—the kitchen—in a color she detested but said was beautiful. There was also Fourth of July and Easter celebrations, and Halloween when Allyson would accompany the children trick or treating in a costume that rivaled theirs. One year when she was dressed as a tramp, they came to Gregory Peck's house. Allyson stood back as the children scooped candy and bubble gum from bowls into their large paper bags. Peck saw she was not dipping in and started tossing items into her paper bag until Allyson lifted her battered hat. Recognizing her, Peck roared with laughter. Her experience at Robert Mitchum's house was not so pleasant. He was having dinner on a tray in front of the fireplace and, when he told the children to help themselves, Ricky took a baked potato that was swimming in butter and sour cream. Allyson was mortified when he popped it into his bag and tried to fish out the greasy mess before slinking out of the house. The actress in her tramp costume was not recognized by the star.

Ricky wanted to run away from home, thinking no one was treating him right or listening or buying him what he wanted. Allyson helped her son pack his belongings, including his dog Tinker Bell, onto his wagon and watched him trudge along the drive, the boy repeatedly looking back. After he was out of sight, she waited 20 minutes until she could no longer bear it and ran to Frank the butler to get the car and find Ricky. She so wanted to get in the car with Frank but didn't. Ricky was found a full mile away at the end of the driveway, outside their gate at Mandeville Canyon Road. Frank drove the boy and his belongings back to the house and soon Ricky perked up and was running around and playing happily with Tinker Bell.

The most lavish sit-down dinner party Allyson ever gave was for the German star Curt Jurgens, to introduce him to the movie colony. There were 150 guests. Joan Crawford arrived with four escorts though there was a place card for one. Allyson wanted to swat her but instead smiled sweetly and rearranged the seating. Another party had her guests trapped by rain for three days; they had to be accommodated or washed down the mountain. They held barbeques on the inside porch, watched television, and entertained themselves and each other by night. Allyson and Judy Garland acted the clowns, doing duets and purposely wrecking each other's important songs. Van Johnson and Allyson did a hammy portrayal of her life with Powell , he playing her about to cry and she being the tough husband laying down the law.

Merle Oberon invited the Powells to dinner. She was known to be one of the most elegant and proper hostesses and her invitations were like royal commands. Allyson wore a white satin sheath floor-length dress but, as they were leaving the house, she noticed their Black Angus cows swimming in the pool. Powell appeared in his black tie and dinner jacket and, with the help of the servants, they used sticks to prod the cows up planks out of the water and back into the fields. The Powells were now wet and covered in dirt and he then had to fix the fence that the cows had damaged. The couple then changed clothes and, when they arrived at Oberon's, everyone was in the drawing room for after-dinner coffee and liqueurs. Allyson's breathless explanation why they were late was received with a deafening silence and every pair of eyes trained on them. She had the impression that no one believed the story and they were more inclined to accept the idea that the couple had fought. Oberon did not invite them again.

Allyson blamed Howard Hughes for the emerging strain in her marriage. Powell had made *The Conqueror* for RKO, which was run by Hughes, and the two men met in the dead of night, rather than in the day during standard business hours. This was to accommodate Hughes' eccentricities since he was going deaf and preferred the quiet of nighttime. Allyson begged to go along for one of these clandestine meetings but Powell refused, saying Hughes would not have liked her being there. She complained of being left alone at night though her husband reminded her there was a houseful of servants. After the film was made, Hughes continued to be important in Powell's life and in Allyson's by osmosis. But she continued to resent the amount of time her husband spent away from her in conference with Hughes and working on Hughes' projects.

One day Powell came home and said all the servants had the night off because Hughes was coming to the house. But Allyson could not meet him. She would have to wait in her room until Powell said it was okay to come out. Powell allowed her to sit with him until the buzzer on the security gate entrance to the property sounded to indicate that Hughes had arrived. Powell turned all the lights off except for one inside the house and unlocked the door. Allyson now refused to go to her room. She and Powell argued until four well-dressed men appeared and proceeded to check out the rooms as if expecting an assassin to jump out. One of them went to the door, motioned and in came the very tall and thin Hughes, dressed like a gardener in tattered clothes. Powell introduced him to Allyson and, as she shook his hand, noted his quiet, high-pitched voice. The actress then excused herself to feel her way up to her room in total darkness. She reclined upon her bed and waited, falling asleep. By the time she awoke hours later, Hughes had left and Powell was angry that she had touched him when they were introduced. (Hughes was terrified of germs and didn't like to be touched.) Hughes had wanted Powell to run RKO but he had declined the offer, which was just as well as this would have given her even less time with her husband.

Allyson joined Powell when he was the mystery guest on the November 7 episode of the CBS-TV game show *What's My Line?* The show was shot in New York and directed by Franklin Heller. The actress came out from backstage wearing a long-sleeved dress with fox neck-piece and muff. She was directed by moderator John Charles Daly to say hello to the panel before leaving with Powell.

The Warner Bros. Warnercolor war drama *The McConnell Story* (1955) was produced by Henry Blanke and shot from November 24, 1954, to late January 1955 on locations in Louisiana, Massachusetts, Washington, Maine, Alaska, Arizona, Texas, California and at Warner Bros. The Ted Sherdeman–Sam Rolfe screenplay, based on a story by Sherdeman, told the story of Capt. Joseph C. "Mac" McConnell (Alan Ladd), a Korean War fighter pilot hero who returns home to test-fly the new Sabre jets despite the unease of his wife Pearl "Butch" Brown (Allyson). The actress' hair is again done in her MGM signature style. Her wardrobe by Howard Shoup includes some hair ribbons, maternity outfits and many large chest bows. Another devoted housewife, Butch is seen handling children as well as making a dress, hanging clothes on a line, and gushing over the kitchen of a new house. Allyson has popcorn accidentally spilled on her by Mac at a boxing match, drops popcorn in a shocked reaction to his marriage proposal, and pushes the desk lamp of Sykes (Frank Faylen) out of her line of vision. The actress and Ladd are convincing in showing a couple smitten with each other. Her best scene is perhaps when Butch tells Col. Whitman (James Whitmore) she blames him for encouraging Mac to leave a desk job to fly again. Here Allyson underplays her anger and makes Butch vulnerable. Butch not wanting Mac to fly may be viewed as being unsupportive or as wifely concern. She eventually apologizes for her attitude, saying she is worried about him, as well as being jealous of the planes and his feeling for them. Director Gordon Douglas supplies one odd shot of the actress' face, seen behind window blinds at night as she cries and watches Mac walk away.

The film was released on September 29, 1955, with the tagline "The real thing! The true story of America's first triple jet ace!" Allyson reported that she and Ladd had a romance during the shooting, but it remained platonic because they did not want to be unfaithful to their spouses. She had been warned about working with Ladd, since his wife Sue was also Ladd's manager and never left him alone on set or on location. This was also because Sue felt Ladd had to be photographed carefully, even to the detriment of his leading lady. Allyson, unworried about how she was photographed, let the cameramen handle that. The actress had also been told that Ladd was cold and distant, but she would not let that bother as long as he did his job.

According to Beverly Linet's book *Ladd—The Life, The Legend, The Legacy,* the actor had reservations about Allyson. She was Hollywood's crown princess and certainly the biggest box office draw he had worked with in a decade. While reserved and somewhat awed by her, Ladd was pleased to have a leading lady who could look up to *him* while wearing high heels, since he usually had to stand on a box or have his co-star stand in a ditch due to his small size. Linet claims that Allyson found him to be very quiet and rather sad, his poor morale said to have been due to a less than tranquil home life, with prenuptial frenzy over the upcoming wedding of his stepdaughter Carol Lee. Ladd had also recently been in a car incident which left his forehead with a gash which he was self-conscious about despite the makeup department assuring him they could conceal it. Sue claimed his facial scar was from a fall in the shower and Allyson fought the urge to say something funny.

Allyson soon learned that all the warnings she had been given were unnecessary. Ladd was the man described by Linet: withdrawn and somber. Allyson tried to make him laugh by clowning around on the set, because the man certainly looked like he needed cheering up. Ladd seemed to regard her as some sort of strange creature but soon found the actress' exuberance contagious. When she was passing him one day at rehearsal, Allyson stumbled over her own feet—maybe by accident, maybe for fun—and he grabbed her. Ladd said, "Hey, small fry. One accident-prone person in a movie is enough" and laughed for the first time since Allyson had met him. After the rehearsal resumed, he showed up at her dressing room asking if he could come in. She replied, "Only if you stumble in," and they laughed together. When the couple got to talking, Allyson noticed how alike they were. While Ladd was playing a flyer, he hated flying and so did she.

It was a happy set and he found her a joy to work with. Allyson said he was the same, always professional and prepared and a wonderful actor. They never had any problems with their scenes and, when she would tell Ladd how good he was, the man couldn't accept it. He could be a very funny man with a wry sense of humor and they always found something to laugh about. But even as his mood changed, Allyson sensed an underlying sadness in him. In the past, Ladd felt uncomfortable in love scenes and kissing—but he didn't object to those with her. He was impatient to get to work in the morning, let down when shooting ended for the day, and invariably disappointed on the days the actress was not on call. Ladd found excuses to spend as much time as possible with her between setups. They talked about everything—their families, the way the film was going, acting—but nonetheless she felt he was a very private person and never discussed the past. Together they drove everyone else on the set out of their minds since they were both crazy about music and had it blasting, which helped keep anyone from overhearing them. The music would be turned off when Sue appeared. She was friendly with Allyson in the first weeks of shooting but when Sue left, Ladd could not keep his eyes off his co-star and the infatuation did not escape the notice of cast and crew. Rumors of a hot romance began to spread and blind items appeared in several Hollywood columns.

Aware of the gossip, they talked about the situation, she suggesting that maybe it would be better only to talk together on camera. But then decided that was silly. The pair were friends and had done nothing to be ashamed of. Sue heard the gossip but said nothing. When Sue came onto the set, cast and crew would hold their breath but there were no fireworks. Ladd was so disturbed by his feelings for Allyson that he had difficulty sleeping but he never became ill or had any accidents. The man even began looking forward to Carol Lee's wedding, to which Allyson and Dick Powell were invited.

At the Powell home, nothing had changed or improved. Powell was still on the telephone, preoccupied with his work, and out late. The actress quipped that she had to show the children pictures of their father so they wouldn't forget him. But Powell's absence allowed her to spend more time with Ladd. The actor would make some excuse to Sue so that he and Allyson could dine in their dressing rooms after shooting. Ladd had his wife to thank for doing the film as she chose the ones he did, much the same as Powell did for the actress. Ladd said he had a superstition and never read a script until he was signed for it, but her excuse was that she was just lazy. The couple laughed at the idea that neither had won Academy Awards because they needed new script readers. One difference the couple had was that while Allyson felt Powell wasn't giving her enough attention, Ladd felt Sue was giving him too much; she needed to know where he was at all times. But Ladd had a refuge: the Rancho Santa Fe where he could be alone. Now that Sue perhaps *should* have been paying more attention, she was preoccupied with the wedding of Carol Lee to actor Richard Anderson, set to take place at the Ladds' Holmby Hills house.

Allyson bore a haunting resemblance to the first Mrs. Ladd, Midge, who was his first great love. This was a marriage Hollywood wanted kept secret so that the actor could maintain the Hollywood fantasy of romantic availability, much like Powell's marriage where his wife was also kept secret. Allyson and Ladd were both good at picking up accents and would carry on hilarious conversations, each of them using a different dialect and pretending not to understand the other. They played the game of "What if?" a lot, speculating what would have happened if the pair had met when they were younger and created a whole life together in their reveries. Ladd asked her repeatedly how she could always be so cheerful and she replied that she was not. Sometimes she would sit and brood, or read her favorite cynic Oscar Wilde. Ladd told her that now that he had found her, he would never have to feel lonely again. He would know that somewhere there was one person who had seen the world as he saw it. She knew the same thing applied to her and that wherever Ladd was, she would always feel an invisible tie to him. They clung to every minute they could have together. He asked how it would feel to wake up next to her but she said he would not like it because she slept in flannel pajamas. He told her she had taken the place of sleeping pills: Since he had been working with her, he didn't need anything to put him to sleep. She laughingly said she was honored but he was serious as falling asleep was a problem for him. He said maybe there *was* something to this "happiness" that people were always yammering about. And he hadn't had a single accident either. She said she better check him over for any bumps, cut or bruises and pretended to be a monkey grooming another monkey. He grabbed her and pretended he was going to give her the spanking of her life. They were like puppies, wrestling, growling at each other, then marching off the best of buddies, arms around each other. Even on the set they walked that way, knowing perfectly well that they were setting tongues wagging. They didn't give a damn. When they were alone, Ladd sang to her, breaking into some Gilbert and Sullivan. She told him she liked to sing "Clair de Lune" with lyrics she had written for it and calling the song "I Remember." Ladd wanted her to record it for him but she knew it wouldn't be wise.

Allyson felt safe telling him about her hardships and heartbreaks and when they looked at each it was with deeply felt sympathy. He was the first person who really understood her and they gave each other concern and tenderness without any kind of pressure. The actress believed she was falling in love with Ladd. One time, Ladd kissed her and she didn't fight back. It felt like they were married, with that special awareness two people develop when they felt that they belonged together. Allyson suggested they both tell their mates that it was just a warm loving friendship that would not turn into a clandestine love affair. By now there was more gossip, which made Sue call Powell to say that Ladd was in love with his wife. Powell's reply: "Isn't everybody?"

To demonstrate that there was nothing to the gossip items, the four went to Trader Vic's for dinner. Powell talked about his favorite subject, *The Conqueror*, and Ladd and Allyson talked about their film. Somebody brought up the latest divorce story to hit the newspapers, which led to a general discussion of marriage. Sue said how terrible it was that a couple could break up over an outsider. Allyson bit her tongue but it just popped out that she did not believe anyone could take a husband away from his wife or a wife away from her husband unless they wanted to go.

The actress and Powell were invited to the Ladds for a Christmas party but Ladd did not come out of his room. Sue said he was not feeling well. When Allyson asked if she could go in and see him, Sue said no. The actress realized it had been a mistake for her to go to the Ladds. At a restaurant she and Powell argued about his daughter Ellen but Louella Parsons assumed the argument was about Ladd and printed the story under the heading "Little Spat."

On January 11 or in March (sources differ) 1956, the Powells attended a Sammy Davis, Jr., concert at Ciro's. It was his comeback after he had lost his left eye in a car crash. (He wore a silk eye patch for the show.) Davis saw tears rolling down Allyson's cheeks as she stood and applauded.

Carol Lee's January 22 wedding day loomed and Allyson was nervous about going. But she knew that if she *didn't* go, there would be more talk. Sue felt the same way about inviting the Powells to what was expected to be the biggest Hollywood wedding of the season. Ladd had warned Allyson that Sue was very jealous so the actress must not look at him when he escorted Carol Lee up the aisle or when Ladd came back down the aisle. Also, he felt that if Allyson did look at him, he would not be able to hide his feelings about her. So when it came time for the father of the bride to walk his daughter down the aisle, Allyson didn't look up. But during his walk back with Sue, Allyson did look up too soon and right into Ladd's eyes. The expression on his face tore her apart with its love and conflict. Sue was looking at her too, and hers was a stab of steel. Allyson wanted to run but was aware that every move she made was being audited by the guests as well as the press. She managed to smile and make polite conversation and dance with Powell under the outdoor lanterns. Ladd couldn't take his eyes off her—and Sue noticed. The two women graciously smiled at each other and Sue resisted the temptation to shove her rival into the swimming pool. Sue decided to confront the actress once Carol Lee and Richard were off on their honeymoon. The Powells escaped to the safety of home.

Judy Garland called to ask about the hot romance. The latest was that Sue had stayed away from the set but now would bring Ladd his lunch. This was Sue's segue to confrontation. One day she cornered Allyson in her dressing room. The actress was with her secretary, who had brought her lunch. Sue accused Allyson of trying to steal her husband. The actress assured her that there was nothing going on. She loved Ladd dearly but they were just friends. She added that Sue was a very lucky lady having him and thought she would be very foolish to spoil it. The women stood looking at each other, then Sue replied that wasn't the way she heard it and stalked out.

Powell received a phone call from Sue that night, telling him that right this minute Ladd and Allyson were in a restaurant having dinner together. That was strange as Powell was presently looking at his wife. When Powell asked if he should put Allyson on the phone, Sue hung up. Powell wanted to talk about this, calling her "June" and not one of his nicknames, so she knew he was serious. Powell asked if she loved Alan Ladd and Allyson replied yes but not in the same way she loved him. He then asked if she was going to walk out on him and Allyson replied no, not if he wanted her. She was not having an affair, at least not in the way that people said. Allyson loved her husband but he was always going away and never came home from the office on time and hadn't any time for her. Powell rocked his wife against his shoulder. He trusted her and understood how she felt, but the man was also trying to build something for the future. Someday they would have all the time together Allyson wanted and they would be young enough to enjoy it. Powell described the ultimate dream house he wanted to design and build at Newport Beach and this time she would be completely in charge of the décor. Allyson said that would be fine and her husband took her hand and led his wife to the bedroom where they made love. The couple still felt the same passion for each other and Powell told her to remember that he would never let her go. But she had to be careful not to make any mistakes.

When Ladd heard about Sue's call to Powell, he packed his clothes and moved out of the house. Louella Parsons had been at the wedding and saw the looks between Ladd and Allyson. Now she heard about the separation and telephoned Sue for the scoop, then filed the story for her January 28, 1955, column. Sue denied that they had separated. Ladd phoned Allyson to tell her he had moved out and the actress told him she had told Powell they were in love. But Allyson didn't want a divorce. Maybe if things were different—if there was no Pammy or Ricky and no Sue—but there was. She was sad for Ladd and the actress hoped she hadn't hurt him too much. Ladd didn't feel hurt. Rather, Allyson had brought a little sunshine into his life and he would just have to work it out somehow. Ladd hoped he hadn't hurt *her* and she said he had not. And Allyson would always love him in a special way.

The gossip columnists reported that Sue rushed to Santa Fe to join her husband on a second honeymoon and she said the word *divorce* had never been mentioned. Ladd played the role of the repentent husband admirably but Beverly Linet writes that his smile looked forced in the photographs, and that the light was gone from his eyes.

After *The McConnell Story* wrapped, Allyson and Powell went on a skiing vacation in Sun Valley, Idaho, then attended a big formal party thrown by Grace Kelly. After Powell left the table to socialize, Allyson (slightly tipsy) thought she saw him coming back and turned on a welcoming smile. But it was not Powell but Alan Ladd and Sue heading for their seats. It was a terrible moment. Sue and Ladd had noticed the Powells at the party and now Sue said something to him and he looked a little sick. They immediately turned and walked out of the party. Allyson never saw Ladd again. She always regretted that they couldn't have maintained a friendship or at least have worked together again. The actress always remembered him as one of the kindest, gentlest and sweetest men she had ever known.

Allyson tried to get over Ladd and to seem carefree, but a lot of laughter was now gone from her life. One day Ladd sent a gift, a record of "Autumn Leaves." She played it over and over, and missed him. They had telephone conversations—sometimes hurried, sometimes long and loving. Ladd said he missed her and was back to having insomnia and accidents. Allyson heard rumors about him drinking but she refrained from scolding the man and they cheered each up by doing their funny accents. When Powell answered the phone, he and Ladd would have long conversations and Allyson didn't pry into what was said. Sometimes her husband would be there when she talked to Ladd and they would have a three-way conversation. Ladd would call late at night and she would start by sitting on the floor of her dressing room and then lie on her stomach when she got tired. They still played "What if?" but both knew it had worked out the way it had to. He said she was lucky to have a man like Powell who was wise and full of understanding.

Allyson was a guest on the March 21, 1955, episode of the NBC-TV talk show *Sheilah Graham in Hollywood*. A source claims that on March 30, the actress attended the 27th Annual Academy Awards but Allyson wrote that she watched them on TV at home. This year was of particular interest for her as Judy Garland was nominated for the Best Actress Award for *A Star Is Born* (1954).

The leading contender in the Best Actress race, Garland was in the hospital after giving birth to her son Joey. Allyson visited her the day of the ceremonies, sure her friend was going to win, and helped make the room beautiful for the television cameras that would come to film Garland's predicted acceptance speech. By the time Allyson left, hairdressers and makeup experts had arrived and were busily working their magic as Garland sat up in bed. But the Academy announced Grace Kelly for *The Country Girl* as the winner. Allyson hated the Academy that year because Judy should have won that Oscar. Powell said that it was dangerous for his wife to be driving on the highway alone at all hours to be with Judy, but Allyson felt she couldn't abandon her. Finally he put his foot down and said there would be no more late-night drives. Allyson talked on the telephone with her for hours, but still felt she had let her friend down.

The Powells and Alan Ladd were guests on the August 10 episode of NBC's talk show *Tonight!*, shot at the Hudson Theatre in New York and directed by Dwight Hemion. The Powells were also guests on the September 2 episode of CBS's news documentary series *Person to Person*, directed by Franklin J. Schaffner. Host Edward R. Murrow talked with the couple at their home; they discussed their lives and careers, in particular Powell's singing career and the projects they have worked on together. Their two children made a brief appearance.

6

You Can't Run Away from It

Allyson's next film was Columbia's Technicolor musical comedy *You Can't Run Away from It* (1956), produced and directed by Powell and shot from November 8 to December 30. The working titles were *It Happened One Night* and *Night Bus*. It was a remake of the Columbia romantic comedy *It Happened One Night* (1934) which had already been reworked as the musical comedy *Eve Knew Her Apples* (1945). The screenplay was by Claude Binyon and Robert Riskin, based on the short story by Samuel Hopkins Adams. In September 1954, it was announced that Constance Towers would star, then in November 1954 the *Los Angeles Times* reported that Allyson would co-star with Robert Mitchum. Heiress Ellie Andrews (Allyson) flees from San Diego to get back to her husband, a man her father does not approve of. The actress is top-billed above the title and plays the leading role that was enacted by Claudette Colbert in the original. Her hair by Helen Hunt is done in the standard MGM style and costumes by Jean Louis include sunglasses, a pair of men's pajamas, and a wedding gown. She performs three musical numbers all with music by Gene de Paul and lyrics by Johnny Mercer. The actress sings part of "Howdy Friends and Neighbors" with Jack Lemmon, Stubby Kaye and the chorus, which is reprised and danced by her; "Temporarily" with Lemmon after the lyrics are first recited; and "Thumbin' a Ride," also with Lemmon. Vocal arrangements are by Norman Luboff. In addition, she dances in a new scene with a scarecrow (choreographed by Robert Sidney) and in front of a bull. The "Thumbin' a Ride" number is notable for the hitchhiker hailing and a shot of Ellie's legs, which may be that of a body double since the coverage is only of a woman's lower body. The role also sees the actress play a lot of slapstick that is in the original including turning over a tray of food, jumping into the sea and swimming (it's apparent that she is being doubled), being squished by Peter in a bus double seat, and Fred sleeping on her in another bus seat. The new screenplay adds to the scene where Peter

Allyson and Jack Lemmon in *You Can't Run Away from It* (1956).

carries Ellie across a river over his shoulder by including her swatting a bee and then falling into the water; Ellie's clothes being wet leads to her wearing the scarecrow clothes. Allyson uses a Texas accent in one scene and does some screaming when Ellie and Peter try to conceal her identity from detectives. While the actress is not the society woman that Colbert presented, she is funny. She gets a funny line when Peter offers her a carrot: "Don't point that thing at me," which is also something taken from the original film. Jack Lemmon plays the role of Peter.

The film was released on October 31, 1956. It was praised by Clive Hirschhorn in *The Columbia Story*. Allyson reported that Time magazine's review was titled "The film was tilted *You Can't Run Away from It*, but I tried."

Powell wanted her to change his wife's makeup because he felt she hadn't been well made-up in the past. There were long hours of experimentation and a new type of makeup made the director feel that his star now blossomed like a rose. He also wanted a change of hairstyle and showed her sketches of a modified Claudette Colbert–style do, which Allyson liked. The couple said that they enjoyed working together and could not have done it without the other.

In his book on Lemmon, Michael Freedland quoted Allyson saying he was the one of the most professional people she had ever worked with, and that he had a marvelous sense of humor. The nicest thing was that Lemmon always showed respect for everyone else, and would never expect anyone to do anything he was not prepared to do himself. Powell was worried about the effect the actor would have on his wife, frightened that their proximity would take a romantic turn. Powell had the idea that the couple would not kiss in the film. But they did end up doing so, and the director got along well with Lemmon.

On January 10, 1956, it was announced that the company formed by the Powells, Pamrick Productions, would adapt the Robert Wilder novel *And Ride a Tiger* into a film. The actress would co-star and Powell would produce and direct with the film distributed by RKO. In the meantime, she returned to MGM to play the top-billed role in the Metrocolor musical comedy *The Opposite Sex* (1956) for producer Joe Pasternak, shot from February 6 to May 23 on location in New York and at MGM. The screenplay was by Fay Kanin and Michael Kanin, adapted from the Clare Boothe Luce play. It was a remake of the MGM comedy *The Women* (1939) with Norma Shearer. In Manhattan, once-popular radio singer Kay (Allyson) is at the end of a ten-year marriage to theater producer Steve Hilliard (Leslie Nielsen), who strayed off the marital reservation for gold-digging chorus girl Crystal (Joan Collins). Allyson is a brunette here; her costumes by Helen Rose include a jungle red low-cut single-strapped floor-length glittery evening gown with train. Grace Kelly, Esther Williams and Eleanor Parker had all been contenders for the role of Kay.

Aside from singing a variation of the traditional folk song "The Yellow Rose of Texas" with Ann Miller and Agnes Moorehead, Allyson has three musical numbers: "The Young Man with a Horn" (music by George Stoll, lyrics by Ralph Freed) has vocals first heard on a record, then Allyson sings and dances. The vocal appears to be recycled from her recording of the same song used in *Two Girls and a Sailor* (1944). Her singing of "A Perfect Love" (music by Nicholas Brodszky, lyrics by Sammy Cahn) was dubbed by Jo Ann Greer. "Now Baby Now" (Brodszky and Cahn) has her singing and dancing, though the actress' vocal performance reveals her voice's weakening since the prior decade. The latter is the best of the three numbers, staged by Robert Sidney with vocal supervisor Robert Tucker. Allyson is revealed sitting on a lavender double bass and wears a turquoise sweater with bejeweled collar and cuffs and matching pants. She dances with tuxedoed double bass players and chorus boys in front of a metal scaffolding set.

There's some slapstick when Kay fights off the advances of Buck Winston (Jeff Richards) in a canoe and jumps into a lake to swim away from him, and when she tries to break up the catfight between Gloria and Sylvia. Kay also gets to slap Crystal so hard that one of Crystal's earrings flies off. There are several times when her face looks severe which may have been avoided with better lighting or makeup. The actress' best dramatic scene is perhaps when Kay is on the telephone to hear how Steve has married Crystal; she transitions from being romantic to stillness and a controlled sadness. Director David Miller notably uses an old portrait of Allyson for a Kay record cover.

The film was released on October 26 with the taglines "FAST, FRANK, FUNNY!," "M-G-M's FUN-FILLED GIRLIE SHOW—WITH MUSIC!," "A SCREENFUL OF FUN!," "M-G-M PRESENTS THE BARE FACTS ABOUT...*THE OPPOSITE SEX*" and "LISTEN IN ON THE LOW-DOWN ON DAMES (WITH MUSIC!)." On the one-sheet poster. the heads of Allyson, Ann Sheridan, Dolores Gray and Ann Miller are attached to multiple backsides of Collins, with Allyson's image suffering the most from this unfortunate procedure by the re-touching department. The film was praised by *Variety*; Bosley Crowther in *The New York Times* wrote that Allyson did an excellent job. The film was not a box office success. It was remade as the telemovies *Women in New York* (1977) and *Stage on Screen: The Women* (2002), and the feature *The Women* (2008).

Allyson has group scenes and a one-on-one scene with Joan Blondell who plays Edith. Allyson reported that the latter scene was very awkward since Blondell had called Powell to say his wife had tried to keep her out of the film. Allyson said this was not true; she didn't even know that Blondell wanted to be in it. Allyson thought Blondell was great in the film. Blondell was also reportedly insecure because she had not been in a film since 1951's *The Blue Veil,* having only worked on TV in the meantime. In his book *Joan Blondell: A Life Between Takes,* Matthew Kennedy wrotes that Blondell asked her daughter Ellen (Allyson's stepdaughter) to get her a role in the film.

In the scene where Kay slaps Crystal, Allyson reported the director had told her that Collins would pull back from the slap so she should swing as hard as she could. But he had told Collins not to move because Allyson would pull the slap. So the slap made Collins' earrings go flying and Allyson's handprint was visible on Collins' reddened cheek. Allyson said Collins didn't speak to her for days. Collins wrote about the incident in her autobiography *Past Imperfect.* She describes Allyson as petite, delicate and ladylike. But the little lady with the tiny hands had a punch like Muhammad Ali. When something flew and hit the floor with a loud clatter, she feared it was her teeth. The slap made her head ring and then Collins lost her hearing and stars danced before her eyes. She staggered to a chair and collapsed, David Miller screamed *cut,* and Allyson burst into tears and collapsed into another chair. Makeup men and dressers rushed in with smelling salts and succor. Collins put her hands tentatively to her mouth and felt she still had a full set of teeth while the wardrobe lady retrieved the long rhinestone earrings from the floor. Any more shooting was out of the question; it would take two or three days for the perfect imprint of Allyson's hand to vanish. Allyson was desperately sorry and it took longer to calm her down than Collins. When the footage was screened, it had complete authenticity and a re-shoot was unnecessary with Collins' reddened cheek barely visible.

Jay David wrote in his book Inside *Joan Collins: A Biography* that the scene was scheduled as one of the first to be filmed for its publicity appeal. The feuds and battles on the set of *The Women* were legendary and made news for weeks during the filming so there was potential for verbal and physical mayhem among the new group of women. Members of the publicity department prowled the set for days but it turned out that all the women liked one another, boosting each other in private and praising each other on the set. Nevertheless there was hope and a plan afoot for the slapping scene. On the day, a huge crowd assembled to watch, including members of the print media. David Miller told Allyson that they were going to use the first take, no matter what happened.

Jay wrote that the slap knocked Collins out cold and she fell to the floor with a black eye while Allyson burst into tears and ran to her dressing room. Collins was a long time coming to, but when she did, Allyson approached her diffidently and they sat and cried together.

Allyson reported that Ann Sheridan was lovely but since she was friends with Joan Blondell, Allyson kept away from them when they were together. Blondell also asked that Allyson not be on set to read lines off-camera for her in their scene together. Allyson insisted that she do it, and later Blondell thanked her for it.

The Powells celebrated their ten-year anniversary by taking their children fishing in the Mandeville lake. The couple had also had a new honeymoon aboard a yacht off Catalina Island. On December 2, 1956, Allyson appeared on the Jack Benny radio show Christmas Special, produced by the United States Armed Forces Radio and Television Service. Christmas shoppersg Benny and Mary Livingston run into Allyson, who says she hasn't seen Livingston since the last summer in London when they shopped together. Allyson received a card from Benny saying he was going to send her a present that never arrived. She promotes *You Can't Run Away from It*. Benny says Dick Powell had promised him the lead role but changed his mind, thinking that his name above the title would make people think it was a warning. Allyson recalls seeing Benny's show at the London Palladium where the audience gave a standing ovation only when the queen walked in.

Allyson claimed she was offered the leading role in *The Three Faces of Eve* (1957) but Powell talked her out of it, believing she would be miscast. Joanne Woodward took the role of the woman suffering from Multiple Personality Disorder and won the Best Actress Academy Award. On February 23, the Powells attended the 13th Golden Globe Awards and presented the Best Performance by an Actor in a Motion Picture—Drama award to Ernest Borgnine for *Marty* (1955).

Allyson returned to TV's *Talk of the Town* for the May 13, 1956, episode, directed by John Moffitt. On the show, Robert Young presented her with the Mother of the Year Award. Her next film was the Universal color romance *Interlude* (1957), produced by Ross Hunter and shot from June 18 to mid–August on locations in Germany and the Geiselgasteig Studios in Munich. (One source claims that interiors were also shot at Universal.) It was a remake of Universal's *When Tomorrow Comes* (1939). The new screenplay was by Daniel Fuchs and Franklin Coen, adapted by Inez Cocke from a Dwight Taylor screenplay and a James M. Cain story. In director Douglas Sirk's film, American Helen

Banning (Allyson) travels to Munich in search of life experience and has a romance with a married symphony conductor, Tonio Fischer (Rossano Brazzi). The actress is top-billed in the leading role, which was essayed by Irene Dunne in the original. Her costumes by Jay A. Morley, Jr., are mostly whites and pastels that include one ugly three-ruffled knee-length sleeveless dress but also a metallic blue dress and mustard yellow coat. The role sees Allyson dance with Dr. Morley Dwyer (Keith Andes), wade into a lake and struggle with Renie Fischer (Marianne Cook), who pushes her underwater. The actress makes Helen funny and sweet. Her best scene is perhaps when Helen tells Tonio that she has to be with him. Allyson also has scenes with her friend Frances Bergen, who plays Gertrude.

The film was released on September 18, 1957, with the taglines "Must It Happen Once to Everyone?," "...The Bitter-Sweet Love Story of a Young Girl and a Married Man" and "a story of love ... for lovers!" The story was again re-told in the British romance *Interlude* (1968).

After finishing the film, Allyson had a wonderful time seeing Buckingham Palace, the Eiffel Tower, the Swiss Alps and the Coliseum. London she found to be hectic and fun. She missed her telephone calls to Alan Ladd but her friend Sharman Douglas helped her get over the blues with a round of parties, including one where she met Princess Margaret, and a party for her at the Les Ambassadeurs. Seeing her off at Heathrow Airport, Sharman said she hated to see her go. Allyson suggested Sharman get on the plane with her and Sharman did, though she only had a nightgown under her coat.

On September 26, it was announced that Allyson would co-star with German actor O.W. Fischer in *My Man Godfrey*, a remake of the 1936 Universal comedy. The Ross Hunter production was set to start filming early in the New Year. The partnership of Allyson and Fischer continued the studio's tactic of teaming Hollywood and European stars *à la* Allyson paired with Rossano Brazzi in *Interlude*. The new policy increased the appeal of films in the foreign market and helped satisfy the desire of American audiences for new screen personalities.

On October 18, it was announced that the actress would play a nun in Universal's *No Power on Earth*, based on the Jay Anthony story "Late Have I Loved Thee." Filming was to take place in the spring in the Philippines. This film was never made.

Allyson separated from Powell in February 1957 after 11 years of marriage.

The Universal color comedy *My Man Godfrey* (1957) was shot from late January to April 27, 1957, with the working title *Her Man Godfrey*. Before Allyson got the part, Doris Day was considered. Filming was disrupted on February 19 when O.W. Fischer was fired after shooting for two weeks. The disagreement over his interpretation of the role of Godfrey resulted in Universal suing the actor for "failing, neglecting and refusing to perform." David Niven was brought in as a replacement. Production was again disrupted on March 3 because Allyson was diagnosed with bronchial pneumonia that sent her to the University of California Medical Center for treatment. She had been ill at home since February 27. Director Henry Koster shot scenes that did not require her for two days; she was back to work the next week. Sheridan Morley writes in *The Other Side of the Moon: The life of David Niven* that Koster resigned after a week of working with Fischer; Koster found him to be utterly humorless; his idea of comedy was to guffaw or ho-ho at the end of every line. The studio then told Koster they had fired the actor and hired Niven. The director was pleased, as he had worked with Niven on the fantasy comedy *The Bishop's Wife* (1947). Allyson said she suggested Niven because he was very popular in the U.S. and had a twinkle in his eye.

The new screenplay was by Everett Freeman, Peter Berneis and William Bowers based on the old Morrie Ryskind–Eric Hatch screenplay (based in turn on the novel by Hatch). Irene (Allyson), spoiled daughter of a rich American family, hires a vagrant, Godfrey (Niven), as a butler. Allyson, top-billed, is back to being a blonde. Costumes by Bill Thomas include a silver-white knee-length full-skirted dress with a shimmery bare-shoulder top that recalls a Travis Banton gown worn by Carole Lombard in the first film, as does a black sheer evening gown. The role sees Allyson handle mastiff, scream and cry. The actress also writhes around a sofa with stomach pains, falls back after kissing Godfrey, and has two catfights with Cordelia (Martha Hyer). Allyson is funny when she pushes the cigar of Lt. O'Connor (Dabbs Greer) away from her and when posing dramatically against a wall to get Godfrey's attention at a party. Allyson is scrappy and aggressive in comparison to Lombard, who was daffy and soft. Allyson may have been trying for a different interpretation, but her acting like a teenager is charmless. The actress' best scene is perhaps when Irene cries as she tells Godfrey that she wants to give him her love but he rejects her. For once in the film, Allyson is vulnerable. Director Koster ends the scene with her back to the camera as she sobs.

The film was released on October 11, 1957, with the tagline "She wanted her breakfast in bed—but not alone." Allyson was photographed with Dick Powell attending a Hollywood screening on October 18. The movie was praised by *Variety* and lambasted by Bosley Crowther in *The New York Times*.

On the set, Allyson found Niven always very businesslike but friendly, making it a good place to be. He was never any trouble (which was why the studios liked him) and he delivered his performances as quickly and pleasantly as he could. That was more than could be said of a lot of actors at that time. When Niven visited her home, he was a very different man, curious about all kind of non-work things.

Koster wrote in his memoir (co-authored by Irene Kahn Atkins) that O.W. Fischer was one of the craziest men he had ever worked with. The situation began with foreboding when Koster, Allyson and Fischer's agent Paul Kohner went to the Los Angeles International Airport to fetch him on January 12 when he arrived from Germany. Because someone knew that he liked cats, a white angora was placed in the bungalow rented for him at the Bel Air Hotel. Fischer wanted it removed because he would not be a traitor to his own cats by loving this one.

Allyson reported on March 19 that she and Powell had straightened out their problems and were back together. She appeared in NBC's two-hour *General Motors 50th Anniversary Show*, shot in New York and directed by Charles S. Dubin, which aired on September 17. The actress appeared as Emily Webb in the "Our Town" segment for which Powell got her paid $50,000 for three minutes work. The show was nominated for the Best Live Camera Work and Best Single Program of the Year Emmy Awards.

When Allyson visited Louis B. Mayer in the hospital, the man was still pressing her to be a good girl, especially now that she had children. Family was still important to him. He died on October 29.

Allyson was profiled in two parts in *The Saturday Evening Post*; the articles were entitled "Let's Be Frank About Me." She talked about her origins, her struggles, her psychiatric bouts and her separation from Powell. At this time, her father and her brother Henry lived in Los Angeles but she didn't know where and she didn't care. Allyson denied being ambitious, ruthless and opportunistic and admitted to being small and rather plain, someone who lisped a little and stuttered when she was tired and sometimes on the phone. Only until recently did she have a neurotic fear of failure: She was always running away from reality.

Allyson attended *The 30th Academy Awards* ceremony held on March 26, 1958, at the Pantages Theater in Hollywood and televised by NBC. She presented the Best Special Effects award to Water Rossi for director Dick Powell's action-adventure film *The Enemy Below* (1957). She embarrassed herself when announcing the winner, getting so excited that she called the film *The Enema Below*. This brought down the house and Allyson claims they went to an extreme closeup where you could see her face, which was getting redder and redder. Around this time, Judy Garland declared bankruptcy. Allyson said that in those days there was a stigma attached to such a thing, but she advised Garland to do it because it was no disgrace.

Her next film was the Universal black-and-white war romance *A Stranger in My Arms* (1959) which was shot from late November 1958 to early January 1959. (The film had been previously announced to be produced by the Powells for their production company but after RKO ceased functioning as a financier of films, the project transferred over to producer Ross Hunter at Universal.) The screenplay was by Peter Berneis, based on the Robert Wilder novel *And Ride a Tiger* (which was the film's working title). The director was Helmut Kautner. After Christina Beasley's (top-billed Allyson) husband Donald (Peter Graves) is killed in the Korean War, she is romanced by Air Force pilot Pike Yarnell (Jeff Chandler), who was with Donald when he died. Allyson sports a new, shorter hairstyle by Larry Germain which has bangs and a part on the other side. Gowns are by Bill Thomas. Christina is a rather humorless part and we never see the Allyson smile, because the character is a grieving widow. The actress' best scene is perhaps when Christina confronts Mrs. Beasley (Mary Astor) about why Donald married her. The scene doesn't give Allyson anything that extraordinary to do but she benefits from playing opposite Astor, who is magnificent.

It premiered on February 4, 1959, in Atlanta, Georgia; Birmingham, Alabama, and Nashville, Tennessee, and was then given a wide release on March 3. The taglines were "Another Emotional Shocker from the Passion-Dipped Pen of Robert Wilder, Author of *Written on the Wind*!" and "I'm trying to keep my hands off you ... but I can't.... I can't!" It was lambasted by Bosley Crowther in *The New York Times*.

Allyson's new hairstyle was a smattering of the close-cropped Italian-style cut with a few hints of pageboy and improvised waves and twists. It was worked out on a trial basis with her hairdresser and took less time to get in shape than any other hairdo she had ever had. That meant the actress could squeeze in at least another 30 minutes sleep in the morning before the studio call. Her fear of horses came back for the film, which was solved by the use of a mechanical stuffed horse.

She went back to television for the 90-minute special *Bing Crosby's*

"HOW LONG WILL YOU REMAIN
FAITHFUL TO A MEMORY...
WHEN WILL YOU BE
A WOMAN AGAIN...?"

Print ad for *A Stranger in My Arms* (1959).

White Christmas USO All Star Show which was broadcast on ABC, CBS and NBC on December 1. The show was shot in Hollywood and New York with a combination of live and studio performances. It was directed by Bob Hultgren, Norm Abbott and Alan Handley. It is only available in an abbreviated form, but Allyson is featured: She appears in the introduction where the performer's name themselves in alphabetical order, and then as a host for three acts, speaking in rhyme to a drumbeat. Her hairstyle is back to its signature side-part and she wears a dark knee-length short-sleeved round-collared dress with a sheer top. She and Powell wish the troops a Merry Christmas and introduce Marge and Gower Champion. Powell comes back to flirt with Cyd Charisse. Her song "Call Me Cyd" is followed by his "Call Me Dick" and then Allyson says, "Call the police!" before they introduce Tony Martin, Frankie Laine and Jimmy Rodgers. Allyson comes back with Charisse and Kim Novak, standing behind a screen and throwing clothes over it to indicate that they are undressing before stepping out fully clothed to introduce "Goldie, Fields and Glide" which is Jack Benny, George Burns and James Stewart.

Powell met Kim Novak before his wife did and told Allyson that Novak was the same type and had the same voice as her. Allyson thought this meant Novak was a girl-next-door and not the blonde, curvy and misty creature of loveliness. Allyson told Powell if Novak was a girl next door, then she was the boy next door.

Allyson was given as an example of someone who had become a success in Hollywood without worrying about her figure, weight and health. She felt those things had nothing to do with it. The actress certainly had the cards stacked against her but believed what mattered was what you do with what you had rather than how you looked or sounded. Allyson's advice to newcomers was to be yourself because you were your own best advertisement.

Subdividers were trying to persuade the Powells to break up Mandeville Canyon but she was opposed because she loved privacy. She had just finished remodeling the entire residence. At *The 31st Annual Academy Awards,* held at Hollywood's Pantages Theater on April 6, 1959, and broadcast on NBC, the Powells presented the Musical Scoring Awards to Dimitri Tiomkin for the drama *The Old Man and the Sea* (1958) as Best Scoring of a Dramatic or Comedy Picture and Andre Previn for the musical comedy *Gigi* (1958) for Best Scoring of a Musical Picture. On April 8, it was announced that she would host a filmed drama series to be televised by CBS on Mondays from 10:30 to 11:00 p.m. beginning in the fall. It would be produced by Four Star and sponsored by E.I. duPont de Nemours & Co. The actress would appear in dramatic roles on some of the episodes.

Powell's idea was to present his wife as one of his company's new talents and the public was going to love seeing her every week. She thought he was crazy and was terrified, but Powell was sure Allyson could handle it. She was happy to be working with her husband and to be able to have lunch with him.

First she was back on TV's *What's My Line?* as a mystery guest on the September 13 episode. She wears a light-colored short-sleeved dress with sheer top. To disguise her voice, she goes deeper as if doing Tallulah Bankhead, which gets laughs from the audience and which makes her cover her face to laugh. The show's moderator John Charles Daly explains that Allyson's TV series is to debut the following week.

She appeared in the documentary *Premier Khrushchev in the USA* (1959) which included the Soviet leader visiting the set of the musical comedy *Can-Can* (1960) and a luncheon at 20th Century–Fox. The film was released on September 19. The actress can be seen in the luncheon scene, next to Dick Powell at a table among the actors seated in the audience when Khrushchev makes a speech.

The black-and-white TV anthology series *The June Allyson Show* aka *The DuPont Show with June Allyson*, produced by Four Star and Pamric Productions, was shot at Republic in Hollywood. For each episode, hostess Allyson provided a prologue and epilogue, the latter including a description of the next week's episode. She was dressed in fashions by Orbach's.

Allyson appears and narrates the show's first episode, broadcast on September 21, "Those We Love," written by Arthur Ross and directed by Jack Smight. Ruth (Allyson) and her mother-in-law Naomi (Ann Harding) live together after the death of Ruth's husband. Allyson, top-billed, wears gowns by Howard Shoup. Her best scene is perhaps when Ruth demonstrates her discomfort with the proposal of David (Mark Richman) by physically struggling against him. The episode was praised by Jack Gould in *The New York Times*. Harding commented that it was a pleasure to work with Allyson.

Interviewed in the October 3 *TV Guide*, Allyson said she planned to take advantage of the variety of roles that the program would allow her to play. This included a girl next door and a conniving socialite who deserts her husband. The episode "Summer's Ending" (October 12) was written by Irwin and Gwen Gielgud and directed by Richard Dunlap.

Allyson plays the leading role of Sharon Foster, a San Francisco married woman who, while on vacation, is attracted to Seattle divorce lawyer Paul Martin (Powell). On the November 16 broadcast, the hostess reported that since so many of her Hollywood friends have written books, she has spent a full year working extremely hard to write a poem. The actress recites two lines, "Be ye wild/Be ye mild/Nothing touches like a child," then says, "Well, back to the typewriter." "Child Lost," written by Dave and Andy Lewis and directed by Water Grauman, centered on Vivian, the nurse of a four-year-old (Ronnie Howard) who disappears from her care. The role sees her run, be funny, have a burst of anger, and deliver a monologue in closeup as she looks out a window, about how her past carelessness allowed a child to be crippled by a stallion.

In "Night Out" (November 23), the hostess reveals that her husband has nights out bowling but, because the man never wins, he then grouses all night long. "The Girl" (November 30) stars Jane Powell, whom Allyson says is her favorite people. "The Wall Between" (December 7) has the actress talk about her trip to Europe taken a few years ago. On "The Crossing" (December 14), the background for the introduction is a dressed set for the first time, after having been a simple black background. In "Edge of Fury" (January 4, 1960), Allyson says she has been reading a wonderful book dealing with the trials and tribulation of the early years of married life. She knew a couple who almost broke up because the husband accidently broke his wife's favorite vase and finally found a way to patch up their differences: a bottle of glue. After their car is wrecked, Janet (Allyson) and her husband David (Dan O'Herlihy) are stranded in a seemingly abandoned desert town. Allyson's hair and clothes get dirty from the running and falling in their attempt to flee this nuclear testing site. At this point, the series began crediting Don Loper for the actress' gowns and décor, replacing Howard Shoup.

In "The Trench Coat" (January 11, 1960), the hostess wears a light-colored low-cut floor-length sparkly costume ball dress and mask, with long light-colored gloves and a sheer wrap. The skirt is so full that the underskirts crunch when it touches the floor carpet and the sofa when she sits. Allyson loves costume balls as it is wonderful to hide behind a mask and pretend she is somebody or something else. "The Way Home" (January 18) has her recall her high school days and the senior prom.

"So Dim the Light" (February 1), written by Stirling Silliphant and directed by Don Taylor, told the story of film star Nancy Evans, blinded in a car accident, who is given a guide dog that will assist in her new life. The actress plays the leading role which has some irony since she is no longer the film star the actress portrays. Called "America's darling," Nancy was a star for 20 years, which is longer than the real Allyson was in films. Nancy wears fur coats and sunglasses, though the latter is also appropriate for a blind person. She trains with the symbolic guide dog Stuart Douglas (Robert Culp) before getting a German Shepherd. She plays blind with a fixed stare. Despite her eyes being covered, the actress makes Nancy's small victories touching.

In "Trial by Fear" (February 8), she reported that two of her dearest friends are getting married in the next month and they have asked her to help them select a honeymoon spot. One option is an ocean voyage on a tramp steamer but she fears losing her friends if they get seasick. But the important thing is that they're in love and they would be just as happy if they never went anywhere. In "Piano Man" (February 29), Allyson says that some of her favorite people are the piano men who play requests in clubs and restaurants that always seem to know your favorite song. But she wonders who plays their favorite song for them. A piano man is someone that you see and hear between eight and midnight but what do they do in the daytime?

On March 2, it was reported that the future of the show was in doubt as CBS would rearrange their broadcast schedule, moving the news show *Face the Nation* to Allyson's Monday evening time slot. In response, DuPont announced they might switch the show to another network. But DuPont decided to continue with CBS, with the show now running on Thursdays. The switch to Thursdays did not occur until January 2, 1961.

Allyson was a presenter at *The 17th Golden Globe Awards* held on March 16 at the Cocoanut Grove Nightclub in the Ambassador Hotel in Hollywood, and broadcast on KTV as a TV special.

In the *June Allyson Show* episode "Sister Mary Slugger" (March 14), Allyson reports that she has found a sure cure for the later summer doldrums and the best way to feel like a kid again: get out to the nearest playground and watch the youngsters playing baseball. The episode centers on Sister Mary Ann (Allyson), a Catholic nun at St. Alphonsus School who becomes the boys' baseball team's new coach. She dresses in a nun's habit, plays baseball, hits hoodlums with a bat off-camera and receives a black eye. The actress makes Mary Ann funny.

Powell, host of "The Blue Goose" (March 21), reports that Allyson has the flu. She returned for "Once Upon a Knight" (March 28) and is seen primping in a mirror. She reports that it's almost impossible to get an objective viewpoint on the effect we have on other people. There are some people she met once that she will never forget and some she has met dozen of times and still doesn't know who they are. In "Surprise Party" (April 18), Allyson mentions a dear friend who believes that it isn't the present that counts but the thought, and has decided to give a big surprise. One hand will hold a large box with no present but a lovely thought and the other hand will have a small box with a present. "The Doctor and the Redhead" (April 25) has Allyson report that she takes health pills but doesn't know why because the actress already has so much energy.

In "Intermission" (May 2), Allyson says that, despite doctors saying there is nothing better than getting away from it all once in a while, she likes it so much at home that there is nothing to get away from. The episode is written by Archibald Joyce (based on the James Hilton story) and is directed by Don Taylor. New York lawyer Hugh (Russell Johnson), stranded at a remote hotel after a plane flight is delayed, romances Ann (Allyson), a mysterious fellow passenger. The character of Ann is supernatural, supposedly haunting the hotel where the stranded passengers are taken but also appearing on the flight with Hugh to suggest that she is from his imagination. Ann's wealth is suggested by her mink coat and the role sees Allyson handle a dog, dance with Johnson and run in the snow. She gets a self-referential moment when Ann looks at her own portrait at the hotel, presented in a painting with pigtails and standing with her hands on her hips. The actress plays Ann in a naturalistic style but with unusual halting breathiness in one scene to perhaps suggest that she is a supernatural being.

She was back as a mystery guest on *What's My Line?*'s May 22 episode. Allyson whistles rather than speaks her answers to the panelist's questions this time. Moderator John Charles Daly explains that whistling yes or no is acceptable because her voice is readily recognizable. Panelist Bennett Cerf guesses the actress' identity with few clues. He claims if you live near a person, you know their whistle as well as their voice—though Cerf admits to also knowing that she was in New York at the time. Allyson gets misty when Daly describes her as pretty as a picture, cute as a button and as nice as they ever made the fairer sex. Allyson had brought her daughter Pam with her to New York.

The second season of *The June Allyson Show* has briefer introductions that mostly lack anecdotes from the actress. The season begins with the episode "The Lie" (September 29), directed by Paul Henreid. Cliff White (Mark Damon), a handsome young beach bum, who worms his way into a family on vacation, but all is not what it seems. "The Dance Man" (October 6) shows the hostess with shorter hair and a gown by Roxane of Samuel Winston. "The Test" (October 20), Ruth Taylor (Allyson), the boss' secretary at New York's jewelry firm Silberg & Company, refuses to take a lie detector test after diamonds go missing. She is eventually wired to the polygraph machine. The actress plays the role ambiguously which fits the situation where Ruth has not stolen the diamonds but has a criminal record for forgery in her past.

Also broadcast on October 20 was the episode of CBS's Western TV series *Zane Grey Theatre* "Cry Hope! Cry Hate!" The show was too made by Four Star and Pamric Productions and shot at Republic studios. The episode was written by Margaret Armen and directed by Abner Biberman. Allyson played Stella, a woman with a reputation who returns home to her father to raise her son. Also in 1960, Allyson received a star on the Hollywood Walk of Fame at 1537 Vine Street for her contributions to the film industry.

The *June Allyson Show* episode "The Woman Who" (November 3), directed by Paul Henreid, presented Allyson as Louise Robertson, wife of a Senate candidate (Van Johnson). The actress wears an ensemble by Bill Blass of Maurice Rentrier which includes a mink coat. The role has her play drums, lead a conga line, smoke and imitates the Southern accent of Judge Tyler (Charles Watts). It is interesting to contrast Allyson's natural acting style with that of Johnson, who reads as artificial. "The Desperate Challenge" (December 15) centered on Carol Evans (Allyson), a schoolteacher cornered in an isolated cabin by two men.

"The Defense Is Restless" (January 9, 1961) told the story of Joanne Burnham (Allyson) and Stewart Church (John Lasell), lawyers who question their engagement to each other when they represent opposing sides in the divorce of mutual friends. The actress does a Chinese accent and is amusing when she gives back kitchen appliances that were presents to Stewart. Joanne as a professional woman is described as an ice maiden in contrast to the vamp Bobbi Gilbert (Roxanne Arlen), who wears a low-cut dress, has a facial beauty spot and talks like Marilyn Monroe. Allyson has a funny response to Stewart's line "I'm sure the court will find it obvious that Miss Gilbert is incapable of being a homewrecker": "Oh, I don't know. I think she's got a pretty good average." The actress' gowns are by Pauline Trigère.

"An Affair in Athens" (January 23) told the story of Betty Allen (Allyson), an American hired as the secretary to Theseus Kamares (Michael David) and tutor to his stepson Alexis (Rene Kroper). Her hair is now back to her signature MGM style. While the actress makes Betty funny, she has nothing else of note to perform, apart from underplaying against the overplaying of the other actors.

Powell was not happy at Mandeville and sold the house without consulting her. She could see that he was restless and never understood the man's hunger for money. If someone commented that they liked the house, Powell would ask if they wanted to buy it. Allyson thought he was just trying to be funny and her husband would reply that depended on the offer. The actress loved the house and said she would never move but could foresee Powell's actions. One morning he walked out of their bedroom only to come dashing back saying the man was only happy in a house where he could wear shorts and not run into a maid. Also, he felt the house had become too much responsibility and it was interfering with his career. He couldn't produce and direct and act and wonder what was happening in the barns. She suggested getting rid of the cattle and the horses, quit farming and just let the house be their home. But if Powell did that, with 68 acres, their taxes would zoom. He had the idea to sell some of the land to create a subdivision so the couple could stay in the house but decided to sell everything instead.

He found a new place they were to call Alpine, after the Beverly Hills street on which it was located. It was a long house with lots of showcase curved glass enclosing plants and a showcase patio. Allyson hated it on sight; she thought it looked like a prison. It didn't help matters when Powell said she could not bring her beloved specifically made braided rugs, the old English hunt table in the shape of a horseshoe and most of their comfortable British furniture. Alpine was a contemporary house and needed contemporary furniture. Her soft peach bedroom was a garish yellow. Chintz and printed patterns were out and solids with straight lines were the rule. Allyson clung to the one soft touch Powell did not dare throw out of the living room: the crocheted throw that his mother had made. She kept it on the sofa in front of the fireplace and it softened the effect of the orange rug.

The actress believed the sacrifices she had to make in the house's décor started their new life with bad feelings. Then her husband said he was finally ready to build their ultimate dream house, the retirement house on land in Newport, though Powell was delegating more rather than retiring from his business. She missed his love and tenderness and felt lonely, worse now that Allyson was trapped in this new modern museum. The telephone had become the object that destroyed every intimate moment. In restaurants, one would be brought to their table and her husband even had one installed at their dining table at home. When a call came, Allyson would stalk out of the room and her husband would eventually follow her to her room. One time she deliberately picked a fight knowing that it would end with the couple making love, just so the actress could have time with him. Soon he stopped following her and Allyson's anger would smolder all evening. When Powell had to travel to Dallas, he wouldn't allow her to go with him, repeating a promise to take her to Mexico that the man never kept. He said she was needed in the house as there was still much to do. Otherwise Allyson could read scripts to find something she liked. But instead the actress threatened not to be there when he got back. Her women friends thought the actress was crazy—Powell took care of everything and wasn't seeing other women. But it had become a hollow marriage for her.

When he had to go to Europe, it was the last straw. She was furious and he didn't do anything to soothe her or kid her out of it. So Allyson gulped and said that if her husband intended to be away from home that much, it was silly for them to stay married. The actress was shocked when he agreed, if that was what she wanted. He told her to get a lawyer to arrange the divorce as the man didn't have the time to do it. Powell had to pack for his trip; he asked her to save her other complaints until he got back. Allyson found out that the best divorce lawyer in town was Jerry Giesler and called him.

Giesler invited her to lunch. The actress didn't know what she wanted in the divorce and the lawyer was shocked that she had scant knowledge of her earnings during her years of marriage. Allyson remembered she had started at $125 a week at MGM and then got a raise to $150. Then Powell took over her finances, and while he said the actress would go on to earn over a million, she paid little attention. Her husband invested her money with his and they were going to retire someday and sail around on their boat. Giesler thought the boat was an asset and could be sold but Allyson knew Powell could not live without it. Giesler got in touch with Powell's lawyer and worked out a deal. Powell sent word through his lawyers that the divorce would not be contested. She was unaware of the property settlement until she saw a cartoon in the newspaper: A husband told his wife, "I don't know why they're worrying about the national debt. Dick Powell just settled four million dollars on June Allyson." That was an exaggeration because, with the aid of transatlantic phones and cables, the lawyers worked out the agreement that she would get $2.5 million. The children would stay with her and their father could see them as often as he wanted.

When Powell flew back, Allyson met him at the airport with the children. She kissed him as if nothing had happened, the children clung to his hands, and he smiled benignly. Allyson and Powell went home and made love half the night, after which the man told her that was what she would be missing. The next morning, he packed his belongings into a car in full view of the reporters stationed outside. The actress fought the urge to tell him not to go because this is what Allyson had said she wanted. She knew Powell's pride demanded his wife back down and plead with him to stay, and she might have, if he made the slight concession. But Powell didn't say that anything would be different in their battered relationship, so she retreated into the house. Suddenly Allyson rushed back and asked where he would go. "Newport Beach," he said, and then he drove off. The actress couldn't believe what she had thrown away and thought, to now keep busy and sane, she must go on a self-improvement kick.

7

Divorce

On January 17, the divorce suit was filed by Giesler in Santa Monica Superior Court. Powell tried to save face by telling the newspapers that he knew nothing of his wife's decision except what he read. Giesler countered that was a lie since Powell had signed the settlement agreement. Allyson charged extreme cruelty in the suit, which included a 46-page section listing community property. On the same day, it was reported that nine-year-old Ricky Powell found himself clinging to the side of a narrow ledge halfway up a 100-foot cliff in suburban Bel Air. The boy and a friend went climbing and Ricky couldn't get down. His friend summoned help, with a state trooper and two firemen rescuing the boy. On January 18, the Powells were photographed at their Beverly Hills home with Powell saying, "If people will only leave us alone, maybe we'll be able to work out our situation."

Suffering from a heart condition, Giesler was admitted to Mt. Sinai Hospital but still arranged for the divorce trial to be heard on January 31. At the trial, Allyson felt she was not a good actress in her big courtroom scene since Judge Allen T. Lynch could not understand why the divorce was necessary. Powell never struck her, and the worst that could be said is that he sometimes criticized and laughed at her and never came home for dinner. The newspapers were amused at these quibbles and headlined a story "THE MAN WHO DID NOT COME TO DINNER." Lynch suggested she think about it but Allyson felt the die was cast and the judge granted the interlocutory decree ending the 15-year marriage.

She stumbled out of court and drove home, feeling heartsick and brushing away tears. Powell had not come to court to shout "Stop this divorce!"; the actress found him at home, sitting in front of the fireplace having a sandwich and a glass of milk. He asked his ex-wife if she was satisfied and Allyson asked what he was doing here as they were just divorced. Powell only agreed to it for her sake and suggested if they co-habited, the legal action would be null and void. Suddenly life was very sweet again and they made love. She honestly hoped Powell would stay with her but he would not, feeling the couple would be the laughingstock of Hollywood if they came back together so quickly. Powell said when the time was right, they would call a press conference and announce their reconciliation and in the meantime they could have this liaison. Allyson thought it was a crazy idea but that's the way it was! The interlocutory decree would take a year to be finalized and they had all that time to play house. But finally he called a press conference in his suite of offices at Republic and the couple sat holding hands and acting like newlyweds, she wearing a new diamond ring and a new diamond pendant. Allyson said the divorce shouldn't have happened and Powell nodded in agreement. What made her see the light was the children, who kept telling them that they were both idiots. He joked that the real truth was that the man missed her stew. His wife was generally a lousy cook but stew was the one thing she made well. The Powells then had their delayed second honeymoon with the family sailing his boat to Mexico.

Her television show resumed broadcasting. The *June Allyson Show* Season 2 episode "Without Fear" (February 6) centered on David Baldwin (Dennis Joel) a 14-year-old who lives on a military base and has a troubled relationship with his dad, the taciturn, brutal Colonel Baldwin (Edward Binns). Allyson plays the supporting role of Eleanor, the colonel's new wife, who wants to help iron out the differences between her stepson and his father. The actress gets a slapstick moment when the backwards running Cadet Wade Farrell (Ryan O'Neal) knocks her down and Eleanor drops the boxes she carries. The character also has a football aggressively knocked out of her hand by Colonel Baldwin. Allyson is convincing as she negotiates between the two antagonists.

"The Old Fashioned Way" (February 20) has the hostess with her dog Mr. Bumply in the introduction. The episode centers on fashion designer Elsa Wilson (Allyson) who, with the help of a nurse, juggles work and parenthood with ease until she has an evening alone with her new baby. The actress' hair returns to its old MGM style with side part in one scene, and she wears maternity clothes in the ensemble by Donald Brooks of Townley. The role has her handle a baby and do Tallulah Bankhead and British voices. Allyson makes Elsa funny when she looks up and down nurse Polly (Rebecca Welles) dressed in evening clothes when she leaves. Elsa also has a funny exchange when she tells Polly she wants to see the baby. Polly tells her that the baby is sleeping and Elsa replies, "I'd like to see her, not play cards with her."

The introduction of "The Moth" (February 27) again features Allyson with her dog. The story centers on Stephanie Cate (Allyson), an American visiting an orphanage in France. She finds herself drawn to seven-year-old Philippe (Michel Petite), who turns out to be the son she abandoned years ago. The role sees her speak French, dance with Joe Maross and cry. "The Man Who Wanted Everything Perfect" (March 13) centered on Andrew Harwell (Russell H. Nype) who has created a computer for his office's Department of Human Factor Engineering; it also advises him on the perfect woman to date. Allyson plays Ann Lawson, a secretary who is in love with Andrew. The actress makes Ann funny when she flirts; Andrew is unaware of the flirting, adding to her frustration. The fact that he is presented as a nerd whom, inexplicably, all other women in the company desire, adds to Ann's angst; the computer has rejected them all as unsuited for him. Allyson's gowns are credited to Karen Stark of Harvey Berin.

She was back as a mystery guest on *What's My Line?*'s April 2 episode. She uses a whispery voice to hide her identity, though it fails to do so. The actress bumps noses with moderator John Charles Daly when he states, "When our guest is required to dance, she would do it with utmost grace, charm and excellence."

Allyson was a guest on the April 19 episode of CBS-TV's New York–based game show *I've Got a Secret*. She attended Judy Garland's concert at New York's Carnegie Hall on April 23. Allyson commented that it was a special, unbelievable evening. The show began with the house lights dark and then a spotlight came on and the audience waited, wondering where Garland was. According to Allyson, when Garland appeared, you could almost feel her saying "Please like me." The audience went from complete silence to sounding like panicked crowds after a terrible earthquake; they gave Garland a standing ovation before she did anything.

On April 27, Allyson underwent a throat operation because of a polyp on her vocal cords. A second operation followed on May 23 and it was expected that Allyson would be released from St. John's Hospital in a few days. She was photographed in a wheelchair with a nurse leaving the hospital on May 25. The actress held a horn which she used to communicate with others until her voice returned.

On August 11, she was taken to Monterey Hospital suffering from abdominal pains. The Powells had come to Monterey the previous day to collect their children from summer camp. Her physician Dr. William Layton reported that the actress' condition was good but she would be kept in hospital for two or three days under observation. On August 12, Allyson had a kidney stone removed but she had to stay in hospital indefinitely on antibiotics because of some infection. On August 23, the actress was photographed leaving the hospital after having been bedridden for two and a half weeks.

She made a cameo appearance on *What's My Line?*'s September 17 broadcast, when Dick Powell was the mystery guest. When Allyson speaks, her voice change is presumably from the throat surgery. On January 3, 1962, Allyson's interlocutory divorce decree was declared void since the Powells had reconciled. Powell said they would be just picking up where they left off.

She made her first appearance on NBC's black and white *The Dick Powell Show* in the January 9 episode "A Time to Die." This was written by Aaron Spelling, directed by Marc Daniels and shot at Republic. Injured in a car crash, Los Angeles gangster Steve Burton (Powell) is told by mysterious people that he can select someone to die in his place.. Allyson plays Mrs. Stevens, a widow and the mother of Chris (11-year-old Ricky Powell), one of the people Steve can allow to die because he has a heart condition which makes him bed-bound. Allyson's hair is in a new shorter style with bangs. She makes the character funny despite the grim circumstances, when Mrs. Stevens flirts with Steve. The actress also transitions from defending her "selfish" decision to refuse the risky operation on her son to questioning whether the decision is the right one. In addition to Ricky, the show features 13-year-old daughter Pamela in a cameo.

In early September when the Powells were in New York, he became sick with a swelling in his neck. It was thought to be penicillin poisoning, a condition he had suffered from before, and he was rushed back to California and admitted to St. John's Hospital on September 13. Powell was diagnosed with cancer of the nymph glands in the neck and chest and treated in hospital for seven days. After convalescing at home, he began radiation treatment at the University of California Los Angeles Medical Center. Allyson had to get him bigger and bigger shirt neck sizes and there are conflicting reports about whether either Powell or Allyson knew that the cancer would be terminal. Some sources say he knew and didn't want his wife to know, and vice versa. Powell wanted to sell the Alpine house and move into their vacation house on Lido Isle, Newport Beach, while he supervised construction of their retirement house. His doctors recommended he not be moved as he fought the disease because the Newport property was too far from medical facilities.

They convinced Allyson to tell Powell she didn't want to move until he was completely well. A woman had bought the Alpine house and was keen to move in. The actress went to see her to try and get a delay, even offering to pay for a hotel stay, but the woman refused to wait.

Allyson had to quickly find somewhere else for them to live. She asked a few friends to help and Eva Gabor offered her house, but the actress couldn't accept the invitation. They settled into the Marie Antoinette apartments in Beverly Hills. Powell's illness was now well-known and the apartment was full of friends, many of whom stopped in almost every day. A standout in the crowd was Joan Blondell, who kept her former husband company during the long days and nights. Allyson was amused that Blondell brought food to tempt him, since this was something no chicken soup on Earth could help. When the actress overheard Blondell tell her son Norman that she should have never divorced Powell, the words cut Allyson like a knife.

She returned to *The Dick Powell Show* for the September 25 episode "Special Assignment." The episode was written by Bob O'Brien and Ben Starr and directed by Don Taylor. Powell's introductory comments suggest that the show was filmed a week before it was broadcast. Lawyer Paul Martin (Powell) is hired by dying Oklahoma millionaire Vernon Clay (Lloyd Nolan) to determine which of six candidates deserves to inherit his $30,000,000 fortune. Allyson, her hair a longer length, plays Jerri Brent, a singer living in a mental institution under doctors' care, traumatized because of the death of her husband (Vernon's son). She sings along to a record and talks on a telephone that is revealed to be unplugged. Playing crazy is a new role for the actress; her altered voice and glassy stare and physical restlessness adds to the characterization.

In October, the doctors told Allyson that there was no hope because his cancer was spreading to too many places. She told them not to tell her husband but just to let her make life as normal as possible. Allyson filled in for Powell as host of the *Dick Powell Show*'s October 16 episode "The Doomsday Boys."

On the night of November 1, Alan Ladd called from his ranch to have a long conversation with Powell. Ladd urged Powell to drive out there to be with him; Allyson did not ask if the invitation included her. Powell did not go, perhaps in no condition to leave the house, and the next day came the news that Ladd had been shot. He was found near death in a pool of his own blood, his gun beside him, a bullet hole next to the heart. A .38 caliber bullet had to be removed. Powell was beside himself with grief because he had not gone to Ladd as Ladd had begged him to do. The newspapers offered various scenarios but Ladd said it was the result of a silly accident when he had tripped over one of his dogs in the dark.

The Powells were with Richard Nixon on November 6 when it was announced that Republican nominee Nixon lost the Californian gubernatorial election to the Democrat Pat Brown. On December 10, it was announced that Powell had cancelled his appearances on his television show for the rest of the 1962–1963 season because of his cancer treatments. It is believed that footage of Powell as host was shot for episodes broadcast up to January 1, 1963.

In his last days, the Powells grew very close. She would sit beside his bed talking and laughing and keeping him company for hours. They never spoke about death but went over their lives together. They reminisced about Marilyn Monroe, Dwight D. and Mamie Eisenhower and the fun they had at Palm Springs and Firecliff. Powell talked about the retirement house, saying this time his wife would have the best dressing room yet, including the sunken tub she had always wanted. The actress insisted that the house be done in her favored New England style and she wanted all her braided rugs back.

On one of Powell's more lucid days, they decided to go to his boat at Newport Beach, accompanied by the nurse. He wanted to watch the opening of the Dodgers game on shipboard television and she thought that was a good sign the man was still interested. They were in the station wagon so Powell could lie down in the back when Joan Blondell arrived with food. Normally Allyson considered this thoughtful, but today she resented it. Blondell put the containers in the back of the car, then came to a window to talk to Powell. The actress didn't want to give up one minute of precious time with her husband, and when Blondell saw the look on her face, she headed for her car without speaking again. On the trip, they had to pull over to the side of the highway so the nurse could give him morphine. At the dock, he pulled himself up and got aboard, then sat on a deck chair, absorbing the sun and looking at the water. Powell looked so weak and said that someday he wanted his ashes scattered in the sea. He wasn't looking at his wife and she didn't look at him. Smiling, she replied, "Yes, a hundred years from now." Powell reminisced about Howard Hughes and his strange hobby playing God making miracles happen as when Powell had appendicitis. Allyson prayed that the real God would make Powell well and not call on Howard.

Slowly Powell became less mobile and finally he was receiving morphine every two hours. Allyson couldn't eat, though people tried to force her, and the scales said she had dropped below 90 pounds. Her friend Mamie Eisenhower wanted Allyson to go with her to the Maine Chance spa, where Mamie was going to reduce. But Allyson could imagine being envied by the other women who had to diet on carrot sticks while she ate fattening foods. Her weight didn't matter. Nothing mattered now except taking good care of her husband. He was fading away before Allyson's eyes, his lucid moments interspersed with confused states and periods of coma. Powell would hallucinate, once reminding her to get Bette Davis' clothes off the foot of the bed, and she went through the motions of doing it. He wanted a normal Christmas so the actress wrapped presents and made the children deliver them. He was pleased she had found things he could use, and not the usual wild ties. There were gadgets to make it easier for him to read by holding books and papers and things to make his sickroom more cheerful.

January 2 was the last day. As Powell seemed to be coming out of a coma, Allyson sat on the bed and cradled his head against her shoulder, he hanging onto her sweater. Suddenly she was aware that the room was full of people and she became angry. At the foot of the bed was Ellen, her face wet with tears. Powell opened his eyes and Allyson moved him a little so he could look at his daughter. The man took a deep breath and said he was sorry. Then he took another deep breath and he was gone. Allyson went to comfort Ellen, who was focused on how the actress' brother Arthur pulled a sheet over her dad's face. Allyson pulled it back, saying he couldn't breathe like that. She hugged his bedroom slippers. People spoke to her but it didn't register. Pammy tugged at her mother and moved her out of the room, asking when she last ate. Out of the corner of her eye she saw white-clad attendants carrying Powell's body away. The actress considered the event from the child's standpoint and hugged her. But Allyson could not cry.

Everyone gathered around the dining room table to confer about the funeral arrangements. They asked her what hymns she wanted played. People made suggestions and the actress told them all to shut up because nobody in the room knew the man the way she did and he hated hymns, only singing them to earn money. Allyson wanted them to play every song that Powell sang in his career—the songs he loved. There would be no eulogies or any fancy words said about him but rather the Lord's Prayer and the Ten Commandments because that was his religion. Some of the people said it would be sacrilegious to play popular music in church and wouldn't be allowed. But Andy Maree, the son of Morgan, Powell's friend and financial manager, said if this is what Allyson wants, this is what she is getting.

The memorial service was held on January 4 at Beverly Hills' All Saint Protestant Episcopal Church. The day of the funeral found the widow still dry-eyed and frozen-faced as she was led from place to place, only half-comprehending, half-responding. The number of attendees was estimated to be 300. The actress declined to duck in a side door and avoid the crowd because she wanted to be like anyone else. She was surrounded by those who had loved her husband and some who wanted her to know they were there if she needed them: Jimmy Stewart, Jack Benny, George Murphy, George Burns, Danny Thomas, "Buddy" Rogers, Edgar and Frances Bergen, Ronald Reagan, Jane Wyman, Jimmy Cagney (who gave her a "hang in there, kid" signal), Richard and Pat Nixon, Walter Pidgeon, Ann Blyth, Johnny and Bonnie Green, Barbara Stanwyck and Joan Blondell. There were also those who waited outside the chapel listening to the service on a loudspeaker.

Allyson hung onto the hands of her children, Pammy and Ricky, one on each side. During the ceremony, she kept her eyes glued to the cross. Pammy whispered maybe God needed him for a special job, which should have been a comforting thought. But the actress hated God for taking her husband before he could see his children grow up. They played Powell's signature songs "I Only Have Eyes for You," "42nd Street" and "Hollywood Hotel," and ended with "Don't Give Up the Ship." The Ten Commandments was recited by the assistant director of the church, Dr. Kermit Castellanos.

Allyson couldn't talk as she was led away to the Bergen house. The actress sat on the floor in front of the fire staring into it, listening to the sound of voices. Jane Dart appeared, lifted Allyson to her feet, and bundled her into the Darts' private airplane with Pammy, Ricky, Jane and Justin and heading for Palm Springs. And still she did not cry. The body was to be cremated in Forest Lawn Cemetery in Glendale.

Powell's death from lymph gland and lung cancer was attributed to his having been a smoker. However, his passing was followed by over 90 of the 220 actors and crew of *The Conqueror* who also developed or died of cancer, as well as an abnormally large number of the local populace. Even some of the children of the stars who spent time on location developed tumors; the Powell children and Allyson luckily did not. Some thought there was a connection to the Utah sand which had also been trucked back to the studio for retakes and closeups. The sand that was spread by many dust storms may have contained radioactivity from atomic tests that had taken place at the Yucca Flat in Nevada. Powell did have some concerns at the time but the government assured him the radiation level was safe.

It was reported on January 10 that Powell's will had been filed for probate in Los Angeles Superior Court and left the bulk of his estate (valued in excess of $1 million) to Allyson and their two children. A codicil to the will also left 6000 shares of Four Star Television stock to be divided between Norman S. Powell and Ellen Powell Hayward. The block of shares was valued in excess of $63,000. The will established two equal trust funds: one for Allyson from which she could extract principal at her discretion, and one for their children from which the actress could receive up to $25,000 a year. She also received all her late husband's personal effects outright and her share of personal property. Mr. and Mrs. Edgar Bergen were named guardians of the minor children in the event Allyson should die before they reached majority. A. Morgan Maree, Jr., business manager, was named executor and trustee.

Allyson learned that Powell had drawn up the will on October 9, 1959, and the actress felt sick when she realized that, while she was bitching about his lack of attention and threatening divorce, he arranged for her future. If only Allyson could bring him back to say she was sorry. The will also made her see for the first time how busy the man had been building an empire and providing for the family's future. There were oil wells and blocks of business property and plain undeveloped land, stocks and bonds, cattle and other production companies apart from Four Star. And now for the first time, the actress saw her movie earnings and what he had done to make the money grow. The will's lesson for the children was that Powell didn't want them to grow up as spoiled rich kids with a big allowance to live on. He wanted them to earn their own way until they finally inherited their money. She could almost hear him telling her again, "Give a man charity and he comes back for more. Give a man a shovel and he earns his own living."

Hedda Hopper took him to task for not leaving any money to the motion picture charities, which angered his wife. How dare Hopper tell the man what to do with his money after he *had* given to charities as well as provided thousands of jobs and helped countless numbers of people while he was alive. Allyson rang Hedda to say what she thought of her, to which the columnist replied, "You're a bitch." In her sweetest voice, the actress countered with, "Yes I know," and hung up.

The Darts got her out on the golf course and made Allyson keep going. One day she was standing around in a daze on the green and Rosalind Russell came over and put her arms around her. Russell said the actress was a wonderful, brave woman and then disappeared. But Allyson wasn't brave. She had no choice. The actress didn't even know what she was doing or her reason for existence any more. She remembered the telegram she had gotten from Lauren Bacall. Of all of the condolence cards and messages the actress had received, that telegram said it best. It was just three words: "Terrible. Terrible. Terrible." Allyson kept in her purse for a long time.

Morgan Maree had let his son Andy take over the business dealings and it was Andy who called her about the disposal of Powell's ashes. They were not allowed to scatter them over the ocean as the man had wanted because it was illegal though the actress wanted to do it anyway. However she was convinced it was better to keep them in a special place at Forest Lawn reserved for those who had contributed most to the film industry. They drove with the urn to Forest Lawn and saw that the special place was high and they would need a ladder. Allyson insisted on doing the climbing to place the urn in the niche and then spoke to her late husband, saying this was so terrible and that she missed him. The actress ran her fingers in farewell over the words she had had inscribed under his name below the niche: "God Is Love." So many images flashed through her mind and Allyson remembered how Powell and she laughed when Gloria DeHaven had told them she wanted on her tombstone, "Here Lies Gloria DeHaven—But Nothing's Definite."

The widow leaned on Andy all through those difficult days and was finally able to cry. And then couldn't stop for eight years. She cried at a letter she found that Ricky had written to his father after he had been dead a few weeks. There was more crying when the actress found a little box Powell had kept filled with collars and cuffs that had been cut off shirts to be put on other shirts if his fortunes changed downward. The world was ugly without her husband. She had been a princess and didn't know it, championed by a prince in a storybook that was now closed. Lauren Bacall had said when Bogie died, the main thing you learned was that when your husband dies you go too, and Allyson now agreed.

She was back on *The Dick Powell Show* (now titled *The Dick Powell Theatre*) as host for the episode "Project X" (January 3), wearing her hair with bangs.

One source claims that archival footage of the actress appears in the historical documentary *Hollywood: The Great Stars,* which was written and directed by Marshall Flaum and broadcast as a television special on ABC on February 20. However the viewed film does not feature her. Allyson did attend *The 20th Annual Golden Globe Awards,* held at the Cocoanut Grove Nightclub in Hollywood and telecast on KTTV on March 5. She accepted the award for *The Dick Powell Show* for Best TV Program.

She returned to act on *The Dick Powell Theatre* for the episode "The Third Side of the Coin" (March 26) hosted by John Wayne. The story centered on Peter Haber (John Forsythe), whose brother, publisher William (Hugh Marlowe), asks him to negotiate with Rosalind Cramer (Allyson), who is blackmailing him. Allyson again wears her hair in bangs and in a wavy style though in the climax it has a side part. The actress makes Rosalind funny with the line, "That little speech will cost you $25,000," after William says he is not in love with her and never wanted to marry her. She gets kissed on the eyes by Peter before being kissed on the mouth. Allyson hints at Rosalind's madness with a burst of anger and when she is very still after telling Peter about being stood up at the wedding altar when younger. Rosalind's climactic reveal is Allyson's best scene which sees her dressed in a gauche low-cut knee-length sleeveless dress with sparkly top and matching sparkly cap. She starts manically speaking fast, transitioning to still moments and then being physically frozen as if in a coma. Director Marc Daniels uses several extreme close-ups of her (which he also does for Forsythe and Marlowe). There appears to be a continuity goof in regards to her hair in Allyson's first scene.

She again hosted *The Dick Powell Theatre* for the April 23 episode "The Old Man and the City." At *The 15th Emmy Awards,* held at the Hollywood Palladium on May 26 and broadcast on NBC. Powell was awarded a posthumous Academy Television Trustee Award for his contributions to the industry. The trophy was accepted by Powell's Four Star partners Charles Boyer and David Niven, who carried it to Allyson's table to give it to her. A photograph of her holding the Emmy and weeping appeared in newspapers the next day. She was still raw with pain over the loss of her husband but was told that it was important to be there. Initially they wanted the actress to accept the award but Boyer and Niven decided this was too much to expect. Friends arranged for her to have an escort that evening, a nice medical man who was divorced from a well-known movie star. She found it comforting to be with him until later, at a restaurant, his ex-wife entered and walked by angrily, with head held high and without even a hello.

Allyson attended Four Star business meetings and insisted that Aaron Spelling be given the reins because he was a friend and had fresh ideas that could help the company survive and grow. But she was voted down and the management led the company downhill. The actress foresaw the disaster and sold her stock.

Allyson felt she was never going to do another movie so decided to concentrate on her children. She wanted to be a good mother, the kind that her husband would have been proud of. The apartment had the shadow of Powell everywhere and to get away from its sad memories, she rented Betty Hutton's former home. Allyson had been happy to follow Hutton doing *Panama Hattie* decades before but now she seemed to be following her into obscurity. Allyson was not happy in the house and maybe Hutton's bad luck was rubbing off on her. She sought solace in a few glasses of wine. John Wayne invited her to go on his yacht and the actress went, but being on a boat brought all her memories back and she was not a good guest. Wayne asked her to go again but Allyson declined.

Judy Garland helped, phoning and trying to keep her friend from brooding. Garland knew how the actress felt and said she had to get out of the house. Allyson didn't know where to go or what to do so Garland invited her to her house. The actress declined, saying she had to take care of her children. In his book *Rainbow's End: The Judy Garland Show,* Coyne Steven Sanders wrote that Garland spotted Allyson in a restaurant, went over to her table, and bawled her out for looking terrible.

On June 3, Garland, Aaron Spelling, Carolyn Jones and the actress dined at La Scala restaurant in Beverly Hills and then went to the office of Sid Luft, where they watched Liza Minnelli appear on *The Tonight Show.* Garland then invited her to be a guest on her television program. Allyson said she was not ready, Garland replied "You're ready!" and penciled her in. The actress thought she would not be a good guest as she didn't like the way she sang, but Garland did like it and insisted her friend sing on the show. Garland also said it was compulsory for Allyson to go to a party at Garland's house for her June 10 birthday, suggesting she go with her agent Stan Kamen, who had replaced Johnny Hyde when he died. Somehow in her confused state, the actress ended up with three escorts. Everyone made a fuss over her at the party although the escorts glared at each other. Sanders wrote that it was here that producer George Schlatter cornered Allyson and got her to agree to appear on Garland's TV show.

For a few months she sank back into the tunnel of isolation and unhappiness. In September, Garland and Carolyn Jones got her involved in a press conference to raise funds for the families of children killed in the bombing of a Birmingham, Alabama, church in.

The *Judy Garland Show* episode was shot on September 13 and broadcast on CBS on October 27. Scott Schechter in his book *Judy Garland: The Day-By-Day Chronicle of a Legend* reported that it was in rehearsal from September 9 to 12 with videotaping of the dress rehearsal on September 13 from 5.30 p.m. to 7:30 and then the final videotaping from 9 p.m. to 10:30 p.m. The show had multiple writers and special musical material by Mel Tormé. The director was Bill Hobin. For her introduction, Garland sings "Life Is Just a Bowl of Cherries" and, in front of a blown-up photograph of Allyson, has the line, "And here's June Allyson. She's a peach." The actress appears from behind the photograph and hugs Garland, then retreats. Next Allyson sings and dances "The Doodling Song" to a chorus of dancers who scribble on large rolls of paper, then she dances. The actress wears a light-colored knee-length long-sleeved dress with lace collar and sleeve ends. Her post-operative voice seems to reveal an even weaker singing voice and it is apparent that she sings to a playback rather than live. Allyson sits down with Garland, who says she is proud of her friend though Allyson admits to having missed one note, looked at the wrong camera and missed her mark when she entered. Together the women sing "Tea for Two" at extra speed. In the "Tea for Two" segment, the women talk about their days at MGM. They are both funny, Allyson laughs a lot about *Royal Wedding,* and they duet live on "Just Imagine" from *Good News* which is very touching because the friendship between them is obvious. They return wearing the same light-colored top with looped fringing at the elbow-length sleeves and hems and dark-colored sparkly pants. The pair are joined by the show's other guest Steve Lawrence, who was about to star on Broadway in a musical version of *What Makes Sammy Run.* Allyson saying Sammy is one of the meanest roles to play makes Lawrence behave meanly, yelling, "Watch it!" when she touches him. The actress also holds him back when he wants to punch Garland. Lawrence throws Garland into a dip and sings "I'm in the Mood for Love." Garland tells Allyson, "Don't stop him. I like it," to which she replies, "Who's stopping him? I want to go next!" Then Jerry Van Dyke and the women do an MGM movie musical medley. Van Dyke says they made people cry but when the actress asks if he really cried, he replies, "No, my folks did. I don't remember either one of you." In front of a set where images of themselves are on standing large strips of film in the background, Allyson sits and sings "Honey" from *Her Highness and the Bellboy.* She then appears with Garland (both wearing Egyptian headdresses) to sing "Cleopatterer" from *Till the Clouds Roll By.* The two move and dance together, with Garland at one point waving an arm in front of the actress. At another point, they break up laughing but keep going. Lawrence joins them to sing the title song of *Till the Clouds Roll By.* The show's choreography and musical numbers were staged by Ernest Flatt and the costumes were designed by Ray Aghayan.

Allyson had a wonderful time, laughing all the way as the women skipped along the curvy Yellow Brick Road which CBS had put between the stage and Garland's dressing room. She loved hamming it up on the show. As September 13 was Mel Tormé's birthday, a cake was prepared, and after the show the women carried it out. But Tormé's delight turned to displeasure when they lifted the cake and pushed it into his face, laughing hysterically. Mel would say they were drunk but the actress denied this. They did drink some wine but it was after the show. Garland's favorite wine was Blue Nun Liebfraumilch. It didn't take much to get either of them high since Judy was already on pills and Allyson was allergic to liquor.

Mel Tormé wrote in *The Other Side of the Rainbow: With Judy Garland on the Dawn Patrol* that the women behaved like the Bobbsey Twins the week of production, all girlish and giggling. Allyson was eager to keep the gaiety going so, when Garland broke out the Blue Nun, she matched her sip for sip. By dress rehearsal, they were hilarious with laughter and by show time, forget it! Lawrence observed all this in astonishment and Tormé assured him that the taping would go on. Garland knew all the songs and the dialogue and Allyson was so patently in awe of her that it was felt her unabashed worship could work to the show's advantage. Tormé says that the cake was not pushed into his face but dropped onto the floor by the women.

The show's art director Robert Kelly reported that the actress was so nervous that she was trembling. Wearing curlers at rehearsal, Allyson joked about how both she and Garland were short because the MGM executives kept beating them down. CBS executive Ethel Winant claims that unbeknownst to the women, the network was not keen on having the actress in the show. Her years as the #1 box office star were over and while she had sung in her movies, Allyson's vocals needed sweetening which the show could not provide. And they thought she was a drunk. Production consultant Bob Wynn agreed that Allyson was drunk during filming and they only got away with it because of Garland's disgusted looks to camera. Wynn also claims that the cake incident had Allyson falling into it and throwing pieces around. The stories of drinking on set made it to the press, with Garland saying that she and Allyson really didn't drink that much and that the cake-throwing incident was just silliness. Coyne Steven Sanders reported that the MGM medley was so disconnected that pieces of the dress rehearsal and the final version footage had to be intercut to achieve the semblance of a whole performance. He also wrote that Allyson had laryngitis for three days during rehearsal, Garland got it, and then Allyson sounded like a bell.

Allyson was a guest on the live October 3 episode of NBC-TV's variety series *The Perry Como Show,* shot in Pittsburgh's Civic Arena. The episode was directed by Dwight Hemion. Allyson's hair is short with bangs and she wears a light-colored knee-length sleeveless low-cut sparkly dress. She banters with Como and together they sing "Thou Swell," "Small Hotel" and "Blue Room." The actress dances the "Varsity Drag" with the Lee Theodore Dancers, then rejoins Como to sing "The Best Things in Life are Free." She is finally escorted away by Frank Gallop, who gives her a bunch of roses. Allyson reappears at the end of the show to say goodbye to Como.

On October 8, it was announced that she planned to marry Glenn Maxwell, a men's hair stylist, on October 12. She had known him for three years as he was the owner of two exclusive men's hairstyling shops in Newport Beach, California, and had been Powell's barber. On October 9, the couple took out a marriage license. On the 10th, Maxwell accompanied Allyson when she addressed high school students in Miami Beach about the perils of becoming a movie star. They were also photographed meeting her 15-year-old daughter Pamela at Miami Airport; Pamela flew in to take part in the wedding. The ceremony took place in the home of County Judge Boyd H. Anderson in Fort Lauderdale.

Allyson next appeared in "Who Killed Beau Sparrow?," the December 27 episode of the crime action CBS-TV series *Burke's Law.* Silent archival footage of the actress was featured in the documentary *Hollywood Without Make-Up* (1963), written by Royal Foster. Presumably the Allyson footage was shot by Ken Murray. host and producer of *Hollywood Without Make-Up.* She is seen at the Sun Valley winter resort, said to be vacationing at that location.

Allyson felt life was going downhill fast. Unable to cope with her loneliness, she had jumped into a bad marriage. Then Alan Ladd died on January 29, 1964, which was the last tie with the good life. The actress cried alone. She had last heard from Ladd via a note he wrote when Powell died. Allyson, torn with grief, could not go to Ladd's funeral. She felt it was not right to go anyway and did not want to stir up the Ladd family and the gossip columnists. The actress drank and constantly fought with husband Glenn. She wanted to die and so, when her doctors said that drinking and not eating would kill her, it was good news.

Allyson surfaced in public on August 6 or 7 at the county courts building in Santa Monica. She was there to testify on behalf of Carolyn Jones, who was divorcing Aaron Spelling, supporting Jones' contention that he stayed out late at night without explanation. On August 13, she filed suit in Superior Court to divorce her husband of ten months on grounds of mental cruelty. The pair had separated on August 3 and it was said that that there was a dispute over the site of a permanent residence and conflict of business interests.

At this time she reportedly began dating writer-director Dirk Summers, a relationship that would last until 1975 and ended because he refused to marry her. They were members of the nascent jet-set and frequently seen in Cap d'Antibes, Madrid, Rome and London. The pairing motivated her mother Clara to file a suit for custody of Allyson's children after Summers was named their legal guardian.

She returned to work as the co-host of the TV talk show *The Mike Douglas Show* for the episodes broadcast from September 21 to 25, 1964. The show was filmed in Hollywood. The actress was also a team captain on the TV game-show *The Match Game* for the episodes broadcast from October 5 to 9, 1964. The shows were filmed in New York and directed by Ira Skutch. She is said to have supported Barry Goldwater in the 1964 presidential election. Goldwater lost to incumbent President Lyndon B. Johnson.

On January 14, 1965, Allyson suffered a kidney stone attack in her dressing room at the Paper Mill Playhouse in Millburn, New Jersey, where the actress was due to go on stage in the Carolyn Green play *Janus*. She was taken to Overlook Hospital and by the next day she was in satisfactory condition. But her physician Anthony Coppola reported that Allyson would probably be hospitalized for several days. *Janus* had been produced on Broadway at the Plymouth Theatre, running from November 25, 1955, to June 30, 1956. Allyson presumably played the role of Jessica, originated by Margaret Sullavan.

The actress now delayed the divorce, taking Maxwell back. Their fighting resulted in a disturbing-the-peace action which was dismissed. Then she re-started divorce proceedings. The divorce was granted on April 20, after Allyson testified that her husband had struck her, issued bad checks for gambling debts, and called her vile names in front of her children.

8

David Ashrow

Allyson's brother Arthur was so concerned that he invited her to go to Sun Valley with his friends. The actress was about to board the Snowbound Special train when Arthur appeared with his best friend, Dr. David Ashrow. Ashrow was attractive and tall with kindly eyes that Allyson felt she could stand and look at all day and drink up all the understanding they offered. Arthur said Ashrow was always asking about her. Allyson felt a kinship with him as if they were alone together. When he held her hand, it was as if she gained strength from him and the man seemed like someone who could save her from herself. They talked a mile a minute and, when Ashrow admitted to specializing in children's surgical dental problems, the actress figured that was why he looked so kind. He didn't scare kids. But the man was married and suddenly his wife pulled him away, while Arthur pulled Allyson away on the other side.

Allyson's trip was cut short because of a kidney infection. She was admitted to Roosevelt Hospital on May 3; this was her third kidney stone attack in almost four years. She was released on May 6, appearing tan and cheerful, advising that surgery was not necessary for her condition at this time. She rested with friends Peggy Jack Strauss in New York.

On September 8, Allyson appeared in probate court to ask for an immediate division of Dick Powell's estate, an estimated $2,804,500 worth of assets. The actress wanted her community interest share (which represented half of the estate) rather than accept the trust arrangement Powell had made for her in his will. She appeared in the Harold J. Kennedy play *Goodbye Ghost* at the Little Theatre on the Square in Illinois. It is said that the show was scheduled to go to Broadway but the deal fell apart.

In December, she and Glenn Maxwell had dinner together. Allyson reportedly instigated the date where he threw his arms around her

Allyson and David Ashrow in a publicity portrait.

and said, "No hard feelings. Aren't we a couple of idiots?" On April 1, 1966, the actress remarried Maxwell in Las Vegas' Sands Hotel. She had been released that morning from Cedars of Lebanon Hospital in Hollywood after minor surgery. Allyson planned on going to London in June for *Goodbye Ghost*, the play in which she had been touring the country. Maxwell was its director. She returned to *Goodbye Ghost* for a production at the Tappan Zee Playhouse in New York, directed by Christopher Lewis. It ran from July 18 to 23, 1966. The show also featured Dick Powell, Jr. The actress was back on *The Mike Douglas Show* for the March 10, 1967, episode, shot in Cypress Gardens in Florida. She also made two appearances on the talk show *The Joey Bishop Show*.

Bob Newhart wrote the *New York Times* essay "June Allyson Never Kicked Anyone in the Shins," printed on July 23. As a movie star seen on TV, she was his ideal housewife but he never thought of her and sex. The actress never kicked anyone in the shins the way Newhart's wife did after he read Balzac to her the way Don Taylor read it to Allyson in an unnamed film.

It was reported that she appeared with Donald O'Connor in a Las Vegas nightclub act in 1967, though the dates are unknown. Allyson guested on the TV game show *Personality*, filmed in New York and aired on NBC on February 12, 1968.

The "High on a Rainbow" episode of NBC-TV's *The Name of the Game* (December 6, 1968) was written by Irv Pearlberg and Robert L. Collins, based on a story by Bill Davidson, and directed by Richard A. Colla. It told the story of retired FBI agent Dan Farrell (Robert Stack), going undercover to find the supplier of drugs being given to schoolchildren. The actress played the part of Joanne Robins.

Allyson did not return telephone calls and refused invitations to dinner, thinking that these people were just trying to be kind. She believed that no one wanted a depressed person around and she crawled further down the tunnel, dragging her bottle of wine like a security blanket. The children were older now and needed her less, and the actress felt her career had gone downhill. The public did not remember her. Sympathetic to Allyson was Judy Garland, but she was struggling with her own demon: drugs. Garland told Allyson that if she died, Allyson had to make sure they put her in a white casket and that everybody wore white and yellow. Allyson heard of Garland's death on June 22 and commented that Garland could not have avoided her fate. The talent was so overwhelming but she didn't recognize it or know it, and Garland couldn't have done anything differently.

If Allyson hadn't committed suicide already, it owed to lack of will, not desire—and she thought it might only be a matter of time.

The November issue of the magazine *Films in Review* featured a June Allyson career article by Christopher Young. In one of the photographs, the actress is wearing an uncharacteristic long hairdo (probably a wig) as she poses with Dick Powell, Jr.

In 1969, it was reported Allyson was scheduled to star in two Spanish Westerns. They did not materialize. On December 31, it was announced that she had agreed to appear in the long-running Jay Allen play *Forty Carats* which had opened on Broadway at the Morosco Theatre on December 26, 1968. Producer David Merrick wanted her to replace star Julie Harris as Ann Stanley, the 40-year-old divorcée who falls in love with a man considerably younger. The Broadway show's director Abe Burrows would prepare the actress.

January 5, 1970, was her opening night, the first time in 27 years the movie star was on a Broadway stage before a live audience. For the January 6 *New York Times* she was interviewed by Murray Schumach. It was only three weeks ago when Allyson was visiting friends in Oregon and Merrick phoned to offer her the part. She accepted even though doing live theater had always frightened her, making her throw up before each performance and sometimes afterwards. But the actress theorized that if she failed now, it would complete her self-destruction. Allyson began the project with dark and destructive thoughts but her professionalism took over and she never drank before going on. During rehearsals there was considerable nervousness all around because the actress was a bit plumper and had a problem with the character saying bad words. When she finally succeeded in doing the latter, Allyson guessed that she had begun a new career. She played the role for six months. The show seemed to please audiences and, despite the tortuous vomiting, the sound of the applause was sweet: Allyson could still make people laugh. The actress said she only missed a few shows in the run due to the flu, but another source claims that more often than not, she was out due to "illness."

On TV's *Talk of the Town* (January 18), Allyson performed a medley of show tunes. *Merv Griffin Show, Tonight Show Starring Johnny Carson* and *David Frost Show* appearances followed. She competed on the March 9 episode of the game show *The Movie Game.*

Eight days later, the actress divorced Glenn Maxwell again, though she had left him before then. This breakup was said to have been prompted by the terms of the Powell will where Allyson would receive $4000 monthly if not married and only $700 monthly if she was. After Zsa Zsa Gabor replaced her in *Forty Carats* in July, Allyson returned to Los Angeles and drinking.

Allyson was the subject of the October 3 episode of the reality-TV biography series *This Is Your Life.* Guests included Gloria DeHaven, Van Johnson, Margaret O'Brien, Joe Pasternak and Dick Powell, Jr.

The actress appeared in the made-for-TV movie *See the Man Run* (working title: *The Second Face*), broadcast on ABC on December 11. Written by Mann Rubin and directed by Corey Allen, the story centered on struggling actor Ben Taylor (Robert Culp), who inadvertently receives a telephone call from kidnappers making a ransom demand. Fourth-billed Allyson plays Helene Spencer, mother of a kidnapped 18-year-old girl. Costumes are by Grady Hunt. The role has the actress run, cry and recite a prayer. Helene is unintentionally funny when screaming "Call the police!" when they receive the ransom call. Fortunately, Allyson gets more to do than just play the hysterical wife as victim, since Helene is calm telling the police that she and Thomas (Eddie Albert) no longer want their help after the first ransom delivery goes wrong. The film was remade as the Indian comic thriller *Ramji Rao Speaking* (1989) and the Indian action crime comedy *Hera Pheri* (2000).

Allyson was asked to star in the first national tour of *No No Nanette* (music by Vincent Youmans, lyrics by Irving Caesar and Otto Harbach) that had run on Broadway from September 16, 1925, to June 19, 1926, at the Globe Theatre. On January 19, 1971, a revival had opened on Broadway at the 46th Street Theatre and stayed until February 3, 1973. The production was directed by Burt Shevelove, with dances and musical numbers staged by Donald Saddler. Again the actress accepted, hoping she would fail, and again her professionalism surfaced and Allyson toured for a year, starting December 21, 1971. She played Sue Smith, the wife of Jimmy (Dennis Day). The tour included performances in Cleveland, Cincinnati, Milwaukee, Detroit, San Francisco and Los Angeles. Again it was claimed that the actress missed shows due to "illness." She also apparently appeared in a production of *Goodbye Ghost* at the Pheasant Run Playhouse in St. Charles, Illinois, from January 14.

Allyson appeared in "The Twentieth Century Follies," the February 16 episode of the TV series *The ABC Comedy Hour*. The show was directed by Stan Harris. The actress sang and danced to the song "Ballin' the Jack" (music by Chris S. Smith, lyrics by Jim Burris). She returned to MGM for producer William Belasco's mystery romance *They Only Kill Their Masters* (1972), shot from late July to early September. The screenplay was by Lane Slate and the director was James Goldstone. Forty-year-old Abel (James Garner), a California small town police chief investigating a suspicious death: the victim's own dog presumably killed its owner. Allyson plays the supporting role of Mrs. Watkins, who has short blonde hair with bangs. It is a change of pace for the actress to play a lesbian murderer who also appears to work at the Eden Landing Dog & Cat Hospital. She gets to run, say "bitch" and be handcuffed. Her face is cut in her dialogue scene after Mrs. Watkins has scuffled with Abel, and Allyson gives some poignancy to the moment when she speaks over the body of her husband (Hal Holbrook).

The film was released on November 22 with the tagline "Was the murderer a man ... or man's best friend?" It was praised by Howard Thompson in *The New York Times* who said Allyson did beautifully. It was not a box office success.

Allyson and Peter Lawford had no scenes together but James Spada in his book writes that they talked on the first day of filming. Spada quotes director James Goldstone that there were jokes and light banter between them, and some of it got a little nasty.

Between performances of *No No Nanette*, Allyson was interviewed by Aljean Harmetz for a November 12 *New York Times* article

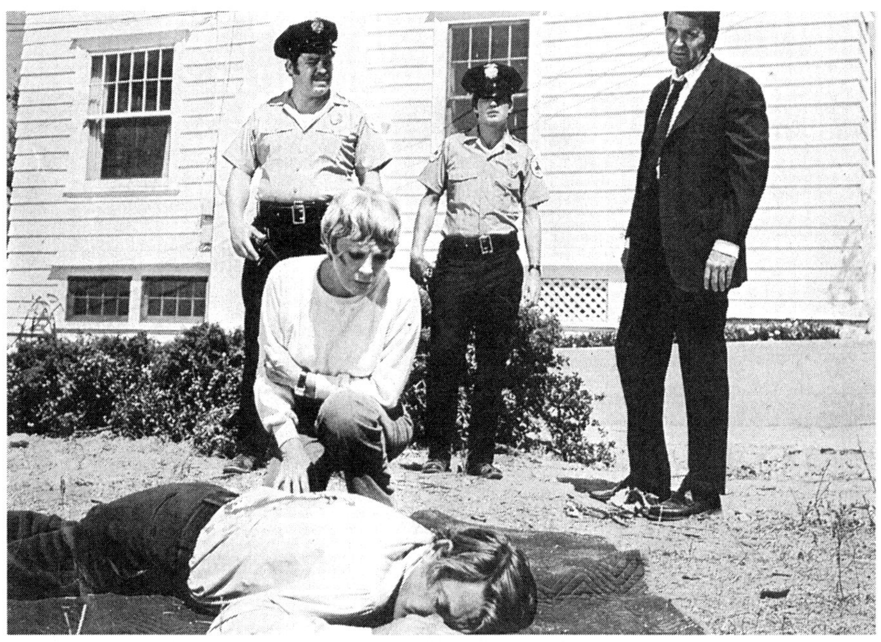

Lobby card for *They Only Kill Their Masters* (1972). Allyson kneels over Hal Holbrook as James Garner (right) and unidentified extras watch.

about the film. She always wanted to be a movie star, thinking it meant being famous, having breakfast in bed, and meeting handsome kings and princes who would be dying to marry you. Allyson didn't know you had to get up at 4 a.m. and work so hard. But the actress saw no shadows when she looked back and now exuded contentment.

After *No No Nanette,* Allyson returned to her home and solitude, still feeling deep inside that life was not worth living. She was deeply depressed and again sought comfort in wine. Most of the time, Allyson sat reading and drinking in her apartment or outside at the pool, gazing at the foliage. The day she visited Pammy at Marquette College, all her classmates made a fuss over her, saying they had seen *Little Women* and asking for career advice. Peggy and Jack Strauss were steadfast friends at a time when the actress needed someone most. They attempted to cheer her up and tried to make some sense of Allyson's life. Finding her drunk and bruised one time, they took her to a hospital. She leaned very strongly on her friend Carolyn Jones. Otherwise she lived like a hermit. Pammy decided what her mother needed was a babysitter, doing for her what Allyson had once done for Judy Garland. Nighttime brought terrors and the actress wouldn't go out yet couldn't bear to be alone. Robbie was a motherly black woman, hired by Pammy to stay overnight. Soon a second woman was hired for the daytime as well. When Allyson cried, Robbie comforted her with words like "I know you're suffering but just remember God never gives you more than you can handle." At other times Robbie held the actress on her lap like a child and rocked back and forth saying, "Hush now, child," until she quieted down.

Even with Robbie, Pammy still worried about her mother, and so did the actress' sister-in-law Carol Peters. Sometimes even Robbie was unable to stop the crying and at these times Carol came over to help. Allyson found life grim, scary and lonely but she didn't want to commit suicide because of what it would do to her mother, brother and children. Drinking became the solution but to keep the liquor down, the actress had to sit very quietly until her stomach settled.

If Allyson had to venture out, she didn't want to be recognized or speak to anyone so she wore wigs. She wore one while spending a few days with her brother and Carol, and stayed in her room if they had company. Her nephews slipped and mentioned that she was there, and someone asked to meet her. But Arthur or Carol said to make it another time as she was not feeling well. Allyson knew she was embarrassing them but was too deep in in her tunnel to really care.

The first man to lure her out of her tunnel was Jon Peterson, a dealer in antiques and an artist. He specialized in making very fine artificial floral arrangements, especially for the movies. She found herself laughing merrily at the stories of his set-designing adventures. With him, the actress felt safe enough to go to Tana's, his favorite restaurant, which soon became hers too. She had the wig and Ricky as added security blankets, as her son would arrange to suddenly appear at the restaurant and check up on her. Once Ricky learned to trust Peterson, he no longer needed to do this. Somehow Peterson and Allyson found themselves talking marriage. He understood her drinking problem and loved her anyway. But Peterson thought they should keep Robbie as he could not sit around holding her hand all night.

The actress felt good enough to ask Peterson to escort her to Arthur's surprise birthday party. Also at the party was the man with the kind eyes, David Ashrow. When Ashrow offered her his hand, Allyson clung to it. The pair talked and laughed about the ski trip where she ended up in the hospital. The actress joked that they didn't operate on her kidney, it couldn't be found; it must have stepped out for a drink. She wanted to keep the laughter going and made funny remarks about anything he mentioned. The pair was blocking a doorway while others were waiting. They also realized they should pay attention to their dates. Hers was hurt. Allyson heard Ashrow being told that he was making a fool of himself. She and Peterson left the party early but the actress had felt, thanks to Ashrow, something light up inside of her and nobody could take that away.

Soon she was back to her old routine, only leaving the tunnel to go to dinner with Peterson and visit her brother in Ventura. On one such visit, Arthur gave notice that a dear friend of his was coming to dinner and he wanted Allyson to join them. Of course she just wanted to stay in her room but Arthur said the man was going through a divorce and needed some companionship. The actress felt a divorced man was the worst kind but promised to join them and be polite. The actress made her appearance 15 minutes late, out of sheer nastiness. Allyson's mouth dropped open because the man was Ashrow; he was the friend going through a divorce. She put her hand out and said it was so nice to see him and then he was holding her hand. The pair was oblivious to anyone else, smiling at each other and talking until he was drafted to handle the steaks on the outside grill. To demonstrate his expertise, Ashrow flipped the steak into the air like a pancake and it landed on the concrete deck. He picked it up, blew on it and served her a piece. She started sawing away at it without much success until Arthur turned her knife over so that Allyson could cut with the sharp edge.

She gave Ashrow her unlisted telephone number and he called the next morning with an invitation to dinner. The actress declined; she wasn't ready to see anyone but Peterson, who understood her and made no demands. Allyson had tickets to a black tie children's charity dinner and had planned to go with Peterson. But now she asked Ashrow to be her date. He agreed but, by the time he arrived to collect her, the actress had drunk too much out of fear. She huddled on the bed with Robbie trying to get her to drink coffee. Allyson couldn't go to the dinner and told Robbie to tell Ashrow she was sick. He somehow persuaded Robbie to let him see her, and they sat up all night talking. When she cried, he held her tenderly. Allyson was beginning to care too much for him and had a strange sense of guilt because she should not love anyone but Dick Powell.

Allyson was a guest star in "Witness Within," the October 7 episode of ABC's mystery TV series *The Sixth Sense*. Written by Anthony Lawrence and Ed Waters and directed by Sutton Roley, the episode centered on Julie Desmond (Tippy Walker), who begins to have visions in which she is attacked by a man. Allyson played Julie's blind mother Ruth. Allyson was a presenter at *The 30th Annual Golden Globe Awards* (January 28, 1973) and a guest on the February 15 and March 15 installments of the musical comedy TV series *The Dean Martin Show.*

ABC's made-for-TV movie *Letters from Three Lovers* (October 3) was a sequel to the telemovie *The Letters,* broadcast back on March 6. Both had been developed as television pilots but neither was picked up. This one had three vignettes about letters whose delivery was delayed by a year, which changed the lives of the people to whom they were addressed. Allyson appears in the second vignette, "Dear Monica," written by Jerome Kass and directed by John Erman. She plays Monica, a wealthy married woman who has an affair with Bob (Robert Sterling) but his letter to her delays their second meeting. Allyson's hair is blonde-gray, worn in a full and reverse part style, and costumes are by Robert Harris and Madeline Sylus. The role is another departure for the actress, playing an unfaithful wife with the implied rationale that she is neglected by her husband Joshua (Barry Sullivan) and depressed over the death of her child. Monica smokes, dances with Bob and runs. She is convincing expressing Monica's femininity and sadness.

The actress was a presenter at *The 31st Annual Golden Globe Awards,* held on January 26, 1974, and returned to *The Merv Griffin Show* on May 16 for a salute to MGM.

She was a guest on the episode of the comedy music television show *ABC's Wide World of Entertainment,* "That's Entertainment: 50 Years of MGM," broadcast on May 29. This was written by John Vincent and directed by Mark Elliot. The show was shot at the Hollywood premiere of the musical documentary *That's Entertainment!* (1974) which featured the actress in clips from *Words and Music* singing "Thou Swell" and *Good News* doing "Varsity Drag." Written and directed by Jack Haley, Jr., the film featured special appearances from various MGM stars from yesteryear presenting their favorite musical moments from the studio's 50-year history. The TV special featured footage of her arriving at the Beverly Wilshire Hotel with hair seen in a longer blonde style (perhaps a wig). Allyson also appeared in the gathering of the MGM stars for a photograph in the hotel's Grand Ballroom. When the stars come on stage, we get a better look at her wearing a pink floor-length long-sleeve high-necked sparkly dress.

It appears that in November, she was in the Phoebe and Henry Ephron play *My Daughter, Your Son* at the Country Dinner Playhouse (city unknown). The play had run on Broadway at the Booth Theatre from

May 14 to June 21, 1969. Allyson starred in the new production with her son, Dick Powell, Jr.; it may have been part a 28-week national tour they reportedly did.

In 1974, a chapter was devoted to her in the James Robert Parish-Ronald L. Bowers book *The MGM Stock Company: The Golden Era* (Ian Allan Ltd.). Also released that year was Parish's *Hollywood's Great Love Teams* (Arlington House) which included a chapter on Van Johnson and Allyson.

After Allyson's old friend Pat Nixon had a stroke in July 1976, the actress visited her at San Clemente. Escorted by Ashrow, Allyson also attended a party ex-president Richard Nixon gave for the astronauts.

After a couple of dates, Ashrow and Allyson were in love. They had one difference that may have seemed unimportant to most people but very important to those contemplating marriage: She smoked and he didn't. Ashrow had helped with her feelings of guilt and disloyalty over Powell and the relationship also lessened the attitude of self-destruction.

The night Ashrow escorted her to the Thalian Ball (she was vice-president of the charity), Bing Crosby got up and sang "Besame Mucho." She remembered it as the song Powell used to sing to her. Allyson simply fell apart and, after just sitting there and crying, she left the table. In the rest room the actress was hardly able to see. Someone asked for her autograph and she shook her head no. A few days later, a gossip columnist wrote that Allyson was too tipsy to even sign an autograph book.

Allyson was scheduled to go on a celebrity luxury cruise during which the guests' movies would be run. She invited Ashrow to come along. One source claims the cruise occurred in 1977 but the chronology of Allyson's memoir suggests it was earlier. The couple had separate staterooms and decided to postpone any further discussion of marriage until after the cruise. Rita Hayworth was on the same cruise and one night she asked to join their table on the deck because she felt lonely and sad. They said yes, and Allyson felt close to Hayworth that night. The couple took her under their wing for the rest of the cruise.

Allyson moved from her Wilshire Boulevard apartment to Ashrow's house in Ventura to live together in sin. He taught her the basics of housekeeping and cooking because Ashrow felt the inside of the house was the woman's responsibility and the outside was the man's. Allyson was sure that he would help her with at least one tough inside job, the cleaning of the oven, but he declined. All day she worked with screwdriver and hammer and when he returned from his office, the oven, still encrusted with burnt grease and dough, was outside. Before Ashrow had a chance to say a word, the actress said, "Now it's an outside job." Every day he became dearer to her and eventually the subject of marriage arose again. But she still felt they couldn't make a success of it.

When Allyson felt apart again, her friend Gloria Luckenbill literally dragged her to a private hospital in a distant city. Gloria knew how much she loved Ashrow and was concerned over the actress' depression, hoping the hospital could provide a cure. It was 17 days of the worst hell she ever went through. Gloria stayed with her for several days for emotional support until Ashrow suddenly arrived, wanting to help. He remained nearby for two weeks. On the day of her release, when Allyson walked out of her room, there stood the man. The love and trust in his eyes did his proposing for him though he never actually proposed. Ashrow just asked where she would like to live.

The wedding, which took place on Saturday, October 30, in Palm Springs, was the third marriage for both. Their attendants were Pamela Powell, now national director of youth affairs for President Ford, and Dick Powell, Jr. Ashrow's best man was Dr. Arthur Peters. Also present were Rita Hayworth, Gloria DeHaven and Margaret O'Brien.

Allyson credited Ashrow with her stopping her drinking and smoking with practical reasoning. The drinking made the actress physically ill and the smoking made him ill (he had a heart condition). To quit, he took her to a medical center for a week, which worked.

While she loved the man, the house in Ventura was another matter. Allyson hated that it was painted green but more importantly hated how he had lived in it with his second wife. They went looking for another; she told the real estate dealer it had to have a feeling of charm (and be anything but Spanish). One day while having a picnic lunch in the Ojai area, they saw a house up on a mountain and explored the private road that ended with its own little lane. Even though it was in the Spanish style, the actress knew this was the one. It was the retirement home of the architect who built it. After being allowed to take a look, Allyson knew it was the home she had been looking for. They convinced the owner to sell and then she wanted some changes made, though Ashrow thought the house was great the way it was. His wife got her way. Soon the house was ready from them to live in. They name it Shangri-La and into this paradise came Tootsie the housekeeper.

The couple went backpacking and got caught in a cold rain. So instead of roasted hot dogs and marshmallows over a campfire, there was dehydrated mountaineer food cooked on his portable stove. They slept in sleeping bags, he having a clean and cozy one while the actress had an old army surplus bag patched together with black tape. When she needed to answer Nature's call, he handed her a flashlight and a shovel and said to walk about ten feet. That was her first and last backpacking trip.

Because her husband enjoyed meeting movie stars, Allyson introduced him to Cary Grant one night at a party and to Van Johnson when the Ashrows were in New York. Johnson invited them to dinner and she held her breath when the check came, remembering how the actor would never pay for her meal in the past. He said dramatically, "I wish we were back at Horn and Hardart," to which the actress replied equally dramatically, "A gentlemen never shows a lady the check." Van said he was not a gentleman. Ashrow looked at both of them and just shook his head.

Allyson judged the 1976 Miss USA Pageant. Her episode of the crime-action CBS-TV series *Switch*, "Eden's Gate," was broadcast on February 20, 1977. It was written by Robert Earll, based on a story by David Taylor, and directed by Gerald Mayer, with series stars Robert Wagner and Eddie Albert investigating a crooked health spa. The actress is given a special guest star credit and plays the supporting role of plastic surgeon Dr. Trampler. Her hair is worn with bangs and her costumes (by Burton Miller) include surgical whites. The doctor is meant to be a villain but the only thing of note Allyson has to do is cut a suture on the face of patient Andrea (Jayne Meadows).

The May 19 *New York Times* reported that the actress was one of the stars who had agreed to make a commercial to sell an energy program for the Jimmy Carter administration.

She was next in the made-for-TV movie *Curse of the Black Widow* aka *Love Trap*, broadcast on ABC on September 16. The teleplay was by Robert Blees and Earl Wallace, based on a story by Blees, and the director was Dan Curtis. Mark Higbie (Anthony Franciosa), a Los Angeles private detective, is on the trail of a murderer whose predominantly male victims are found mutilated inside silken cocoons. Allyson plays the part of Olga, the nanny of Laura Lockwood (Patty Duke Astin). Olga is said to know the two truths: that Laura's mother Mrs. Lockwood (June Lockhart) is kept locked away in an attic in her home, and that Laura is a split personality who can transform into a giant spider. The actress sports the same hairdo she wore in the *Switch* episode, with her hair here credited to Edie Panda. The role of Olga sees her handle a gun and end up hanged in her own cocoon. Allyson gets to give a lot of meaningful looks and gets one scene with the spider where she is seen from its point of view.

In her book with William J. Jankowski, *In the Presence of Greatness: My Sixty-Year Journey as an Actress*, Patty Duke wrote that she had a lifelong admiration for the actress, someone she quickly came to know and love. Allyson had a simple sweet elegance and came to do her job with no tantrums and a sense of humility. Allyson enjoyed hearing that Duke was a fan of hers and, by the end of the shoot, they were big fans of each other.

Allyson attended *An All Star Tribute to Elizabeth Taylor*, held at the Hollywood Burbank Studios on November 13 and broadcast on CBS on December 1. The show was directed by Dick McDonough. Allyson is seen in the audience sitting at a table with Esther Williams, and later introduced with Janet Leigh and Margaret O'Brien when *Little Women* is referenced. She wears a white and pink floor-length long-sleeved dress with her hair in bangs. Taylor thanks her in the climactic speech and says that seeing Allyson, Leigh and O'Brien again meant a lot to her.

Allyson returned to films for the 1978 Canadian action thriller *Blackout* aka *New York Escapees*, which was shot on locations in Canada and in New York from November 15 to December 20. The screenplay was by John C.W. Saxton based on an idea by John Dunning and Eddy Matalon, who was also the director. Four sadistic criminals escape from custody and take over a posh Manhattan apartment complex, terrorizing its occupants. Allyson plays the supporting role of Mrs. Grant. Her hair is shorter and she only has one costume from Blanche-Danielle Boileau. Mrs. Grant's husband (Fred Doederlein), dependent on a ventilator, is vulnerable when the power goes out and the couple suffers when the criminals get to their apartment. She is tied and gagged and we don't get to know her fate. The actress is convincing when pleading for the criminals to leave.

The film premiered in France on June 28 and opened in the U.S. on September 13 with the taglines "One City-Wide Blackout.... Deranged Killers on the Loose ... Twelve Hours of Sheer Terror!," "Psychopaths on the Loose...in a City Without Lights...No One is Safe!," "New York City: When the lights go out...the TERROR begins!," "The most incredible twelve hours of terror ever lived!" and "The night the power failed ... and the shock began!"

The made-for-TV movie *Three on a Date* was broadcast on ABC on February 17, 1978, with the taglines "You've just won a fabulous week in Hawaii with the blind date of your dreams" and "The love-romp that starts where *The Dating Game* stops." It was written by Michael Norell, Stanley Ralph Ross and an uncredited Bernie Kahn, based on a story by Dale McRaven and a book by Stephanie Buffington. The director was Bill Bixby. It told of the adventures and mishaps of four couples, winners on a TV game show, along with their young chaperone Stephanie Barrington (Forbesy Russell) on a Hawaiian holiday. Allyson plays the supporting role of Marge Emery, who is matched with Andrew (Ray Bolger). She gets to play slapstick when the nine tourists must squeeze into one taxi. Allyson has what is perhaps her first screen post-coital scene in bed with Bolger, and she gets one funny line: When the tourists are told that they have been secretly photographed, Marge says, "My son would absolutely drop dead. Do you think I could have a couple of 8×10s and some little ones for my wallet?" One gold outfit that is the same color as her hair and skin washes her out on screen.

Loni Anderson, who played Angela Ross, wrote in her memoir, *My Life in High Heels*, that actor John Bryner did impressions of the cast including a wicked one of Allyson that made the actress laugh with glee. She also told the funniest stories of the old studio days of Lana Turner and Dick Powell.

Allyson appeared in the comedy television special *Dean Martin Celebrity Roast: Jimmy Stewart*, broadcast on NBC. Shot at the MGM Grand Hotel in Las Vegas, the show was directed by Greg Garrison. Garrison cuts to her numerous times for her laughing reaction to various speakers. When it is her time to speak, she is seen wearing a white sparkly long-sleeved high-necked dress. The actress believes they *should* be honoring Stewart's wife Gloria, and Allyson is entitled to say this because she played Stewart's wife in movies. The actress is given a run of roast quips. She and Stewart were married so many times that when their old movies are re-run, Allyson gets alimony. In *The Glenn Miller Story*, the actress worried that Stewart might have an affair with a sexy band singer but who knew that Doris Day would turn out to be a virgin? On *The Stratton Story*, he received an honor that thrilled him more than an Academy Award: his picture on a bubble-gum card. In World War II, he was a bomber pilot and even today can still handle a B-36 and a B-47—not the airplanes, the vitamins. Allyson finishes by saying she never met a more talented star, a nicer man, or one that she loves more than Stewart.

Other guests on the dais zinged her. Wanda Paige said she doesn't know what Allyson was doing at the event with all the dirty old drunks.

She was always so sweet and pure and innocent and made Donny and Marie look like Bonnie and Clyde. Janet Leigh commented that the actress had trouble with love scenes with Stewart: In *The Glenn Miller Story,* by the time he got through playing "In the Mood," she wasn't. Don Rickles said Allyson was still lovely at 83—though she was only 60. When Stewart made his speech, he had Dean Martin deliver the zingers with the actress spared. The show featured a clip of them in *The Stratton Story.*

On May 22, Allyson was photographed at London's Heathrow Airport. She was there to appear in a charity concert paying tribute to Glenn Miller. She appeared in "High Roller," the pilot episode of the crime-mystery TV series *Vega$,* broadcast on ABC on November 3. Written by Michael Mann and directed by Richard Lang, the episode was shot on location in Vegas and at 20th Century–Fox. It saw Las Vegas private eye Dan Tanna (Robert Urich) probe the murder of teenage prostitute Marilyn Ochs (Elissa Lees). Allyson gets a special appearance credit and plays the supporting role of Marilyn's mother, Loretta.

She was a guest on the ABC-TV romantic comedy *The Love Boat* for the episode "The Minister and the Stripper/Her Own Two Feet/Tony's Family," broadcast on November 18. Allyson plays in the "Her Own Two Feet" segment, which was written by Ann Gibbs and Joel Kimmel and directed by Richard Kinon. Allyson's Audrey Wilder is blind but has refused to accept her condition and is dependent on her husband Bert (Van Johnson). When Audrey boards the ship, she is accidentally jostled by other passengers, which shows her anxiety. The episode is set around the time of Thanksgiving but Audrey believes she has nothing to be thankful for; that attitude changes and she begins being grateful to Bert. The plot gives her a beauty parlor appointment with no payoff, which is funny considering how severe the actress' face is photographed. Johnson appears to be wearing more makeup than she is. Allyson uses an indirect focus to play blind, and dances with the ship's captain (Gavin MacLeod) and Bert. Her sincere acting is in contrast to Johnson's overacting.

In 1978, the actress appeared in a print advertisement for Lebenthal & Co. municipal bonds. For her book *Ladd, the Life, the Legend, the Legacy of Alan Ladd* (Arbor House, 1979), Beverly Linet wrote that she was indebted to Allyson for frankly discussing—for the first time—an episode in her life which made her and Ladd the subjects of gossip and scandal.

The actress was a guest on the British historical documentary television series *The Hollywood Greats* for the episode entitled "The Golden

Years," broadcast by the BBC on August 30. The series profiled various Hollywood stars of yesteryear and more recent times. The episode was written by Barry Norman and directed by Judy Lindsay.

She was a guest on the action-adventure TV series *The Incredible Hulk* for the October 5 episode "Brain Child." Written by Nicholas Corea and directed by Reza S. Badiyi, the episode had Dr. David Banner (Bill Bixby) meeting Joleen (Robin Deardon), a 16-year-old genius pupil who has escaped from the Kirkland Institute to find her mother. Special guest star Allyson plays the supporting part of Dr. Kate Lowell, who works at the institute. She wears an unflattering pair of large black glasses and gets to deliver two unintentionally funny lines. When Joleen threatens to jump off a rooftop, Kate tells her, "This is not intelligent. Not intelligent at all." Mr. Arnold (Joseph Mascolo) asks Joleen to just think about what she is doing, what her loss would mean to the country, and that people like her are needed; Kate screams, "Oh, shut up, Mr. Arnold. Shut up!"

Allyson guested in "I'll Be Suing You," a March episode of the CBS-TV comedy series *House Calls,* written by Mark Egan and Mark Solomon and directed by Mel Ferber. The actress, billed as "guest star," plays the part of con artist Florence Alexander, who fakes an accident and visits Kensington General Hospital. This is a sizable narrative part although the only noteworthy thing she gets to do is sit in a wheelchair. Florence's change of heart about the con comes when she learns that the appearance of Dr. Charley Michaels (Wayne Rogers) in court puts a patient at risk. Costumes were provided by Darryl Martell.

Allyson appeared on the PBS special *G.I. Jive* aka *The G.I. Jive Years* and *G.I. Jive: A Salute to the Entertainers of World War II,* broadcast on March 15 or August 16 (sources differ), 1986. Inspired by the American Theatre Wing's Stage Door Canteen and videotaped at New York's Roseland Ballroom, it was written by Donald Driver and directed by William Cosel. Stills of special guest Allyson and Van Johnson are shown before the actress joins host Johnson on stage. They duet on a medley of "Thou Swell" and the Richard Rodgers-Lorenz Hart song "I Could Write a Book," (their vocals on the latter are shaky). Allyson's hair is short with bangs and she wears a black suit with white collar and sleeve ruffles. The actress, seated at a table by the stage, is seen many times applauding the other acts, and she introduces Cab Calloway.

In 1980, Allyson and David Ashrow did the play *My Daughter, Your Son* together (dates and location unknown); the director was Bob Moak. This was Ashrow's first acting role, having just retired from dentistry after open heart surgery. She had been asked to do the play again and, when Ashrow was helping her rehearse, she realized that he had talent. The producer agreed that the man was a competent actor and could appear as her co-star. Sometimes he strove a little too hard because Ashrow was a perfectionist. Determined to improve his appearance as well as know every line perfectly, he dyed his gray temples jet black. The dye bottle label said **Dark Brown** and when he tried to fix it, the dye job came out a ghastly red. He looked so dejected that she didn't have the heart to laugh but recommended her husband consult a stylist.

Allyson was still uptight about Powell. She would not have any picture that included him out where it could be seen. Ashrow made her get some pictures of Powell and the children and place them about. The children were entitled to see that their mother thought he was an important part of their lives. When old friends visited, they seemed to avoid the subject of Powell, so Ashrow would ask them to talk about him. Her husband's understanding and sensitivity enabled the actress to start talking freely about him again.

One day Ashrow asked about the wigs which she wore (because it was easier than taking care of her own hair and they gave her confidence). He wanted to see the real her and that night he and Ricky built a bonfire outside and a great ceremony took place. One by one they threw the wigs on the fire after a few words and a lot of laughter (Allyson joined in). The burning of the wigs was like giving up drinking, both acts of emancipation from dependency. Now Allyson was at peace. Most women never found happiness once but she had found it twice.

The actress appeared in the TV documentary *Did America Kill John Wayne?* which was broadcast on March 7. The program was a pilot for a possible syndicated series titled *The Great Mysteries of Hollywood*. It pondered the question of whether the fallout from the 1953 atomic bomb exploded over the Nevada desert caused the cancer that killed Wayne and Dick Powell.

She did the play *My Daughter, Your Son* at the Windmill Dinner Theatre in Houston, Texas, from September 15 to October 25, and guested on the Australian TV talk show *Parkinson* for the episode broadcast on September 26.

In 1981 or 1983 (sources differ), Allyson became the spokesperson for Depend undergarments. The marketing campaign was credited for reducing the social stigma of incontinence and it was the first time adult diapers were spoken about on television. The actress was approached because the company felt she would appeal to the right age group.

Allyson was hesitant until she learned her mother had stopped coming to family gatherings and withdrew from social events until she began to use the product. The actress agreed, wanting to help other people and give back to the world which had given wonderfully to her. The advertisement saw her reading a letter from someone who used Depend with confidence; the tagline was "Get back into life." She was proud to have done the campaign, though Allyson got some kidding, with people asking if she wore the diapers. Her response: "Don't joke about it because one day you may need them and then you'll have to call me." The actress also received hundreds of letters thanking her, more letters than when she was a movie star. Kids on the street recognized her as the Depend Lady.

Allyson was a guest on *The Dick Cavett Show* though the date of the 1982 broadcast is unknown. She comments on the forthcoming *Night of 100 Stars* so the interview was presumably done in early February or before. The actress wears a purple suit with a medallion necklace. One of her topics is Joan Crawford, who Cavett had promised not to ask questions about. Allyson never had more fun in an interview, apparent from her laughing a lot during it. The director credited as Richard Romagnola.

The actress appeared in *Night of 100 Stars* which was held at New York's Radio City Music Hall on February 14 and broadcast on ABC on March 8. The event celebrated the centennial of the Actors' Fund of America. It was written by Hildy Marks and directed by Clark Jones. Allyson (in a silver suit) and Van Johnson appear in the segment related to lovers of the silver screen, their entrance preceded by a clip from *Two Girls and a Sailor.* She joins all the other lovers in a lineup to sing the song "Love Makes the World Go Round." The actress is also seen in a clip from *The Stratton Story* in the segment devoted to James Stewart. The show won the Emmy for Outstanding Achievement in Music Direction and Outstanding Variety, Music or Comedy Program; it was also nominated for Outstanding Achievement in Music and Lyrics, Outstanding Directing in a Variety or Music Program and Outstanding Lighting Direction (Electronic). In March, she was back at the Windmill Dinner Theater with the play *My Daughter, Your Son.*

Allyson was interviewed by C. Gerald Fraser in the April 4 *New York Times.* She said she was happy living up on her hilltop and happily married. There was no emotional need to work, but she enjoyed doing it when there was a script she liked. The industry thought Allyson wanted to work, so she did get a lot of offers.

The NBC-TV movie *The Kid with the Broken Halo* (April 5) was written by George Kirgo and the director was Leslie Martinson. Fallen angel Andy LeBeau (Gary Coleman) is given one more chance to do good by helping out three mortals. Allyson, billed third, plays the supporting part of Dorothea Powell, a wealthy, grumpy former movie star. Dorothea is described as "the most glamourous movie star of all time," which is perhaps too much for Allyson to live up to. Stylist Julie Purcell alternates Allyson's bangs with a side part. Andy attempts to make Dorothea more sociable by hypnotizing neighbor Harry Tanenbaum (Mason Adams) to romance her and provide football tickets, which leads the recluse to reconcile with her estranged grandchildren. The actress makes Dorothea's misanthropy funny. The show was spun-off into the animated family television series *The Gary Coleman Show* (1982).

Allyson's autobiography, written with Frances Spatz Leighton, was published on May 1 by Putnam. It was praised by Janet Maslin in *The New York Times*, who wrote that Allyson presented herself as the same sunny, tomboyish figure she played on screen in Hollywood.

Allyson guested on the action-crime CBS-TV series *Simon & Simon* for the December 9 episode "The Last Time I Saw Michael," written by Philip DeGuere, Jr., and James Crocker and directed by Vincent McEveety. The Simon brothers, A.J. (Jameson Parker) and Rick (Gerald McRaney), help family friend Margaret Wells (Allyson) look for her husband, who is missing and presumed dead. Top-billed among the guest stars, she breaks a glass in her hand and play the piano (her hands are not shown). Margaret gets a funny line regarding the cigar smoking of Myron Fowler (Eddie Barth): "[The house] is ever so much nicer since you brought the air freshener with you." Allyson wears her hair in her signature MGM style, with costumes by Al Lehman. An uncredited makeup artist made her face pale. She has more energy than the lethargic styles of Parker and McRaney.

The actress was back on *The Love Boat* for the episode "Vicki's Dilemma/Discount Romance/Loser & Still Champ" (March 5, 1983). Allyson appeared in the segment "Discount Romance" which was written by Roy Battochio and directed by Jack Arnold. Salesman Jimmy Morrow (Red Buttons), the uncle of Gopher the ship's purser (Fred Grandy), romances Shirley Walsh (Allyson), who runs the ship's gift shop.

Allyson's father died on April 16 at the age of 90 and was buried at Ivy Lawn Memorial Park in Ventura County, California.

She was a guest on ABC-TV's crime-action-adventure series *Hart to Hart* for the episode "Always, Elizabeth" (May 15, 1984). The show was written by Lawrence Hertzog and directed by Ralph Senensky. The Harts' Beverly Hills house is visited by Elizabeth Tisdale (Allyson), who was the New York pen pal of the Hart cook Max (Lionel Stander). She is given a special guest star credit and wears clothes by Grady Hunt. Elizabeth is tied up when the Hart house is invaded. The most notable thing about the actress in the episode is how pale and thin she looks.

According to Martin Gottfried in his book, *Balancing Act: The Authorized Biography of Angela Lansbury,* Allyson was considered for the part of professional writer and amateur sleuth Jessica Fletcher in CBS-TV's crime mystery series *Murder, She Wrote.* The actress was a guest on the show for the episode "Hit, Run and Homicide" (November 25). In the episode, written by Gerald K. Siegel and directed by Alan Cooke, Jessica investigates a seemingly driver-less murderous car that suddenly appears in Cabot Cove. Allyson plays the supporting role of Katie Simmons, a guest from Memphis in the home of Daniel O'Brien (Van Johnson). Her hair is longer and worn in bangs with costumes by J. Allen Highfull and makeup by an uncredited artist who gives her more color. Katie makes no great contribution to the plot.

Although the date is unknown, it is said that Allyson was a guest on the TV documentary series *Lifestyles of the Rich and Famous.* On March 31, 1985, she attended the wrap party for the eighth season of *The Love Boat* at the Beverly Hilton Hotel.

She joined James Stewart at the Cannes Film Festival where *The Glenn Miller Story* was screened on May 17 (another source gives the date as June). The couple had reportedly visited eight countries promoting the film with the Cannes appearance the final stop; it was there that the actress received the Cannes Festival Distinguished Service Award. She was seen in the Spanish television series *De película* for the episode "Cannes 1985," broadcast on June 15.

Allyson was referenced in the cabaret act of Larry Adler, the mouth organist whose show at New York's Ballroom Theater ran in October. Adler had appeared in *Music for Millions* and recalled that the actress was the easiest crier in Hollywood: "She would cry seed catalogs." Allyson was a guest on NBC's comic science fiction TV series *Misfits of Science* for the episode "Steer Crazy" (November 1 or 29). The episode was written by James D. Parriott and directed by John Tracy. The team of misfit superheroes visit a farm to investigate the impact of a meteor which irradiated the cows grazing there. Allyson plays the supporting role of Bessie, one of the senior citizens who develops superhero strength after eating hamburgers. The role sees the actress lift weights,

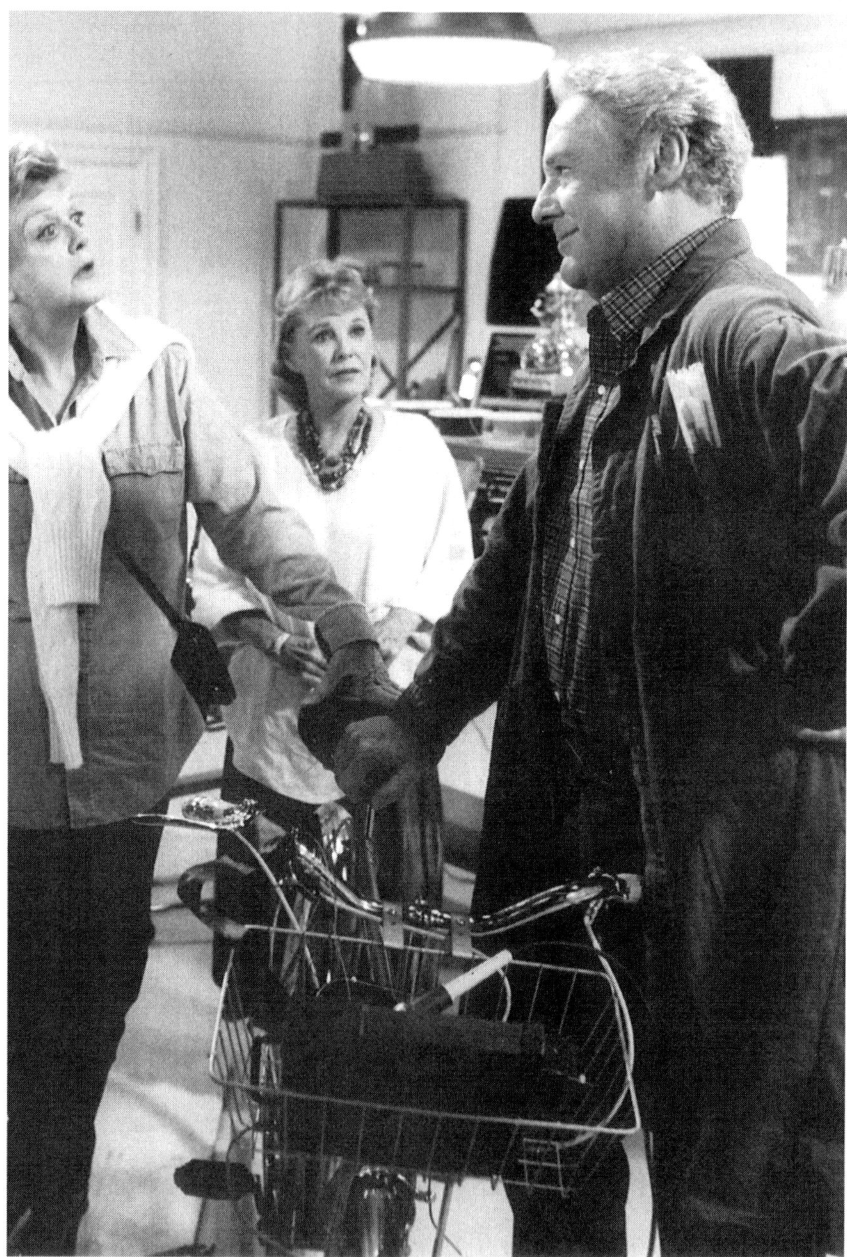

(From left) Angela Lansbury, Allyson and Van Johnson in the *Murder, She Wrote* episode "Hit, Run and Homicide."

bend the bars of a fence, dance with Jane Miller (Jennifer Holmes) and roller skate (her feet are not shown).

Allyson appeared in *The Annual Friars Club Tribute Presents a Salute to Gene Kelly,* broadcast on NBC on November 9, and *The 2nd Annual American Cinema Awards,* broadcast on NBC on November 22. She guested in *All Star Party for "Dutch" Reagan,* taped in Hollywood on December 1 and broadcast on CBS on December 8. The show honored Ronald Reagan, America's 40th president, the year he was sworn in for his second term of office. It was directed by Dick McDonough, who cuts to the actress in the audience once as she applauds Frank Sinatra after he sang. The show was Emmy-nominated for Outstanding Achievement in Music and Lyrics.

Allyson appeared on CBS-TV's comedy-crime-mystery series *Crazy Like a Fox* in the episode "Hearing is Believing" (January 15, 1986). Written by Julie Friedgen and directed by Paul Krasny, it centered on San Francisco lawyer Harrison Fox, Jr. (John Rubenstein), whose blind client Joanna Blake (Robin Dearden) overhears a murderous plan. The actress played the role of Neva.

Allyson was a presenter at *The 43rd Annual Golden Globe Awards 1986,* held at the Beverly Hilton Hotel and broadcast on January 24. In "Little Wolf," the February 1 episode of CBS-TV's science-fiction-action-adventure series *Airwolf,* Dominic Santini (Ernest Borgnine) and Stringfellow Hawke (Jan-Michael Vincent) become unwitting pawns in a potentially deadly custody battle between a grandmother and the ex-wife of a friend. Allyson gets special guest star billing and plays the supporting role of Martha Stewart, the grandmother. Her costumes include a particularly ugly black patterned dress with puffy long sleeves. She uses measured speech to play this villainess, and her best moment has Martha in a long closeup to give a crying reaction to the news of the death of her son. The episode was written by Robert Specht and directed by Bernard McEveety.

At *The 58th Annual Academy Awards,* held at the Dorothy Chandler Pavilion on March 24, she appeared as part of the tribute to MGM musicals which included the song "Once a Star, Always a Star" (music by David Shire, lyrics by Richard Maltby, Jr.). *The New York Times*' John J. O'Connor described Allyson in the number as frisky. The show was Emmy-nominated for Outstanding Directing in a Variety or Music Program.

She appeared in the ABC-TV documentary *Happy 100th Birthday, Hollywood,* broadcast on May 18, 1987. Directed by Jeff Margolis, it was a celebration of Hollywood featuring some of its biggest stars. Allyson is in the segment "Heroines of the Silver Screen," standing at a gazebo as a medley of songs is sung by an off-screen male chorus: "You Were Never Lovelier" (music by Jerome Kern, lyrics by Johnny Mercer) and two songs with Kern music and Dorothy Field lyrics, "The Way You Look Tonight" and "Lovely to Look At." Her hair is short with bangs and she wears a white high-necked gown.

She was a guest in "A Tribute to American Music: Cole Porter," an episode of the music documentary series *In Performance at the White House*. It was taped in the East Room of the White House on June 28, the day before its PBS telecast. John Corry in *The New York Times* wrote that she told an anecdote about meeting Porter. The actress' second book, *June Allyson's Feeling Great: A Daily Dozen Exercises for Creative Aging,* was released by Capra PR on December 1.

Director Henry Koster wrote in his 1987 book that he heard that she lived in seclusion. Koster believed Allyson had followed the path of many lady stars who had their glamorous and successful time, that was wiped out in the fog of growing a little more mature.

In 1988, President Reagan appointed Allyson to the Federal Council on Aging and she worked to normalize and raise public awareness about incontinence. The following year, she appeared in *America's All-Star Tribute to Elizabeth Taylor.* The event was held at the Desert Princess Resort in California and broadcast by ABC on March 9, 1989. Allyson was one of the MGM alumni signing Taylor's autograph book. She wears a white-patterned long-sleeved floor-length dress, talks about *Little Women*, and joins the other stars to sing "My Friend, Here's to You." The actress also stands with the cast to listen to Taylor's climactic speech of gratitude.

CBS's 1989 telefilm *Wilfrid's Special Christmas* was written by Elizabeth Swados and directed by Jesus Salvador Trevino. Matthew Lawrence starred as Wilfrid Gordon McDonald Partridge, a boy who visits a retirement home and makes friends with Miss Nancy (Allyson). The actress was a speaker at *The Film Society of Lincoln Center Annual Gala Tribute to James Stewart,* held on April 23, 1990, and broadcast on NBC. She also attended the after ceremonies at Tavern on the Green. Also in 1990, she and Ann Miller introduced an in-store video promo for MGM musicals, which provided a continuous-loop sampler of 12 musicals, as well as the actresses telling their own personal anecdotes and behind-the-scenes stories about many of the films.

Allyson, Jane Powell, Ginger Rogers and Esther Williams were guests on the August 29, 1991, episode of the CBS-TV talk show *Burt Reynolds Conversations With...* Allyson wears a white high-necked sweater with a colored jacket and her hair is in bangs. The show features a clip of her singing "Cleopatterer" from *Till the Clouds Roll By*; she is also seen in footage with Dick Powell in *Right Cross* and with Van Johnson in *Two Girls and a Sailor.* She reveals that she sang in a boys' choir as a child, and mentioned that Esther Williams gave her lessons in assertiveness: They had done several cruises together and one time they were having dinner and the actress couldn't make up her mind what she wanted. As the waiter stood over her shoulder and Allyson held everybody up, she asked what he would suggest. The waiter said the fish. When he left, Williams pointed out that the actress hated fish but Allyson wanted the waiter to be happy. She spoke of her admiration for Ginger Rogers and said that it was hard to keep from crying as they sat at the same table now. Asked for one-word answers, the actress described Peter Lawford as *fun*, Gene Kelly as a *master*, Lana Turner as *beauty*, Claudette Colbert as *mother*, Esther Williams as *friend*, Ginger Rogers as *idol*, and Jane Powell as *lovely friend*.

She was a guest on the ABC-TV action series *Pros and Cons* for the episode "It's the Pictures That Got Small" broadcast on October 19. The episode was directed by Win Phelps, and Allyson played the role of Gloria Hartford.

Allyson appeared in the TV documentary miniseries *MGM: When the Lion Roars*, broadcast on TNT on March 22, 1992. Interviews were done at the Santa Clarita Studios in Hollywood. The series surveyed the history of MGM from its creation and rise in the 1920s, its pinnacle in the '30s and '40s to its final days. The actress appeared in two of the three episodes, "Part Two: The Lion Reigns Supreme" and "Part Three: The Lion in Winter." The former covered the studio's history from 1936 to 1945 and she talked about publicity and the fan magazines. (She is also seen in clip from *Two Girls and a Sailor.*) In "The Lion in Winter," which covered the studio from 1945 to 1986, she talked about *Little Women*, Judy Garland, leaving MGM and the death of Louis B. Mayer. In clips, Allyson is seen in "Varsity Drag" from *Good News* and in scenes from *Little Women*. The show was praised by John J. O'Connor in *The New York Times* and won the Outstanding Informational Series Emmy Award.

On the September 7 episode of the TV talk show *Vicki!*, Allyson and Janet Leigh talked about *Little Women*. She wore a brown turtleneck sweater and pants, with a darker brown leather jacket and boots and a crucifix necklace. Allyson and Leigh sang a few lines from the Irving Berlin song "There's No Business Like Show Business" to show they are troopers, with the actress' voice hoarse. When Kim Hunter joined them, Allyson reported that she knew Hunter because Hunter's husband was in love with her. Host Vicki Lawrence brought out three packets of Depend for the actress to use as a footstool.

In February 1993, she and her husband filed a suit in Ventura County Municipal Court against comic Marty Ingels. Ingels pleaded no contest to making annoying telephone calls to them over money he claimed was owed for his agency commission for the commercials Allyson had done for Depend. The lawsuit said Ingels made 138 calls in a single eight-hour period. He was ordered to stay away from the couple.

On April 13, Allyson was one of the narrators of a backers' audition at Michael's Pub in New York for the show "Red, Red Rose," based on the life and works of the eighteenth-century Scottish poet Robert Burns, with music by Paul Johnson.

In August, the Ashrows were back in court claiming that Marty Ingels had violated the order to stay away from them. They now accused him of slander and emotional distress. The suit was settled with Ingels agreeing to perform 120 hours of community service working in a Los Angeles–area nursing home, where he entertained the residents. Extending an olive branch, he invited the actress to join him there, saying it would be the perfect truce, and what better thing for Depend? It is not known whether she accepted the offer.

*The New York Time*s of October 10 reported that Allyson would appear that season on the theme cruise of Delta Queen Steamboat Company's "1940's Remembered." In December, she christened the Holland America Maasdam, one of the flagships of the Holland America line, in tribute to her Dutch ancestry.

Debbie Reynolds, interviewed by Bob Morris in the March 20 *New York Times,* commented that she planned to extend the stage of her Debbie's Star Theater at the Debbie Reynolds Hotel and Casino for musicals to star her girlfriends, which included Allyson.

Allyson's mother Clara Josephine Provost Peters of Ventura County, California, died on April 23 at the age of 96. She was buried at the Ivy Lawn Memorial Park in Ventura County.

9

That's Entertainment! III

Allyson was one of the co-hosts of the documentary *That's Entertainment! III,* written and directed by Bud Freidgen and Michael J. Sheridan. She enters via the studio's original main gate, driven in a chauffeured car. Allyson is introduced with "Cleopatterer" from *Till the Clouds Roll By* and by Esther Williams, who describes her as one performer who exemplified the light-hearted spirit of the MGM musical. After "The Three B's" from *Best Foot Forward* is shown, the actress talks about the hundreds of performers like her brought to the studio every year hoping to get a break in the movies. After lessons in acting, posture and movement, singing and dancing, the next big step was a screen test for those who had star quality. She introduces clips of Kathryn Grayson, Ann Miller, Joan McCracken in *Good News,* the novelty act The Ross Sisters, and one from *On the Town.* Then the actress segues into the next host, Cyd Charisse. The film was released on May 6, 1994. It was praised by Todd McCarthy in *Variety,* Caryn James in *The New York Times* and Roger Ebert.

In the featurette *Behind the Screen,* directed by David Engel, she is seen filming her entrance into the studio with a slate dated May 1, 1993. Allyson was chosen to present the star development section because she epitomized the ingénue who was groomed to be a superstar. The filmmakers found her to be perfectly charming and the actress did a terrific job. She talks about Louis B. Mayer, the studio's concerns over her voice and teeth, her training, her image and Judy Garland.

In an article by Glenn Collins in the July 7 *New York Times,* the Kimberly-Clark Corporation reported that the actress, long the Depend spokeswoman, would introduce the men's product in a national television advertising campaign to begin July 25. On July 25 or 26, she attended the Video Software Dealers Association Convention held at the Las Vegas Convention.

Allyson provided a filmed tribute for the Debbie Reynolds episode

A still of Allyson shooting her *That's Entertainment! III* (1994) segment.

of the British biographical documentary TV series *This Is Your Life,* broadcast on Thames Television International on March 15, 1995. The show was filmed on location at Reynolds' Las Vegas hotel and directed by Brian Klein. The actress is on board the S.S. *Rotterdam* for a cruise to China and reports that she and Reynolds had danced around the studios together back in their MGM days. Reynolds would show Allyson how to do the steps and Allyson could never do them right. She envied Reynolds for dancing with Gene Kelly in *Singin' in the Rain.*

Next Allyson was a guest on the CBS-TV crime mystery series *Burke's Law* for the episode "Who Killed the Toy Maker?," broadcast on June 15. The show was written by James L. Conway and directed by Gilbert Shilton. Los Angeles police Chief Amos Burke (Gene Barry) and his detective son Peter (Peter Barton) investigate the death of Dean Winters (Adam West), a toy manufacturer killed by an exploding stuffed animal. She plays the supporting role of Shelly Knox, head of Funland Toys stuffed animal division, former lover of Dean and one of the suspects. The actress' wardrobe is by Eilish and hair is by Chris McBee. The only memorable scene is where Shelly sorts a pile of paper money on the floor and stuffs it into a piñata.

Allyson was in the made-for-television movie *Inside the Dream Factory* broadcast on TCM on November 1. It was written by Maureen Corley and Bob Waldman and directed by Mark Woods. The show had host Faye Dunaway wandering around the studio lots and chatting up old movie stars.

On October 26, 1996, Allyson attended the Long Island Cinema Arts Center Salute to Hollywood Legends gala held at the Huntington Hilton in Melville and received an accolade. This was a fund-raising black-tie event for the cinema with 600 people paying $250 each to see the stars, or $500 to sit at a dinner table with one of them. The actress was delighted that men said they still had a crush on her. In 1996, she became the first recipient of the Harvey Award, presented by the James M. Stewart Museum Foundation, in recognition of her positive contributions to the world of entertainment. With her husband, she supported fund-raising efforts for museums for Stewart and Judy Garland.

On March 23, 1997, Allyson appeared in the "Judy Garland: Beyond the Rainbow" episode of the A&E documentary series *Biography*. The show was written and directed by Peter Jones, based in part on the book *Judy Garland—World's Greatest Entertainer* by John Fricke. She talked about Garland's marriages to David Rose and Vincente Minnelli, *Royal Wedding*, the death of Garland's mother, Garland's self-doubt, losing the Academy Award for *A Star is Born*, Garland being bankrupt and battling with prescription drugs, and her death. The episode won the Outstanding Informational Series Emmy Award and was nominated for the Outstanding Informational Programming Award.

She attended the funeral of James Stewart, held in early July at the Beverly Hills Presbyterian Church. The actress appeared on the arm of Esther Williams, who had driven her there. She said that Stewart really died after the February 1994 death of his wife Gloria; he couldn't wait to join Gloria because they were so happy together and so perfect for each other. After Stewart's death, Allyson received letters from people about how sorry they were she had lost her "husband."

The actress participated in *Carnegie Hall Celebrates the Glorious MGM Musicals*, held on July 15 and 16. She was one of the stars who reminisced about musicals of the 1930s and '40s and introduced filmclips. Allyson told anecdotes about Peter Lawford. Allyson appeared in the *Biography* episode "Jimmy Stewart: His Wonderful Life," broadcast on December 22. She described Stewart as an icon and an institution, exactly the same on-screen and off-screen, and scenes are shown from *The Stratton Story* and *The Glenn Miller Story*.

She was the subject of the June 30, 1998, episode of the TCM talk show *Private Screenings*, directed by Tony Barbon. For her interview with Robert Osborne, she was dressed in a purple suit. Featured were clips from the actress' films, newsreel footage, portraits and film posters. Making movies was mostly fun but also hard work, and she believed her appeal was to both men and women. Women never had to fear that Allyson would be the other woman, and men thought she could be the kind of wife they wanted, one who would always have dinner ready, never complain too much and always be there for them. Her three favorite films were *The Glenn Miller Story, Little Women* and *Good News.* Allyson didn't particularly like her work in musicals, never able to dance as well as Ann Miller and Cyd Charisse or sing as well as Judy Garland and Kathryn Grayson. She was envious of the beauty of other MGM ladies but knew it wasn't always beauty that a man wanted—rather he wanted what is inside. The girl-next-door type the actress often played was now considered old-fashioned and corny but this thinking was wrong as there were still naïve nice people. She said that Esther Williams was one of the funniest people she had ever met and a wonderful friend. If Allyson went into Hollywood for an event, she would spend the night at Williams' where the pair would spend time talking and laughing. Van Johnson nicknamed her the Powell Heiress. The actress recalled being on a cruise with Osborne, where she was asked to give introductions to the movies being screened. Unable to read the cue cards he provided, Allyson had to wear the big eye glasses with black frames she never wanted to be seen in public in. The actress had teary eyes when talking about Dick Powell's death and did a funny impression of Margaret O'Brien's little girl voice.

Allyson never really learned to cook; her husband always knew when dinner was ready because the smoke alarm went off. Her key to life was to always look forward to good things and to never feel sorry for yourself because you could always do better. Also in June, she attended The 23rd Annual Judy Garland Festival held in Grand Rapids, Minnesota.

In 1998, the actress helped to establish the June Allyson Foundation for Public Awareness and Medical Research with the American Urogynecologic Society funded by Kimberly-Clark. The Foundation was non-profit; contributions by public, private and corporate supporters enabled it to award grants into researching the causes and management of pelvic floor disorders.

On March 25 and 26, 1999, she was back in New York as part of *Carnegie Hall Celebrates the Glorious MGM Musicals: An Encore Presentation.* She again reminisced about her MGM days. On October 6, the Official June Allyson Web Site was created with chapter links for

Biography, Richard, Career Highlights, Memorabilia, Photo Album, Did You Know and Joonangels.

The actress appeared in the *Biography* episode on Ann Miller, "I'm Still Here," on January 13, 2000. She returned to films in the comedy *A Girl, 3 Guys, and a Gun* (2000), shot around Ojai, California. Written and directed by Brent Florence, it centered on three small-town friends, Joey (Kenny Luper), Frank (Brent Florence) and Neil (Christian Leffler), looking to leave their troubles behind. They come up with a robbery scheme to fund their trip to the big city. Allyson has a cameo in a countryside scene in which she and her husband Ed (David Ashrow) are in a car that passes the stalled car of the three friends. Allyson has a few lines to say to Joey: "Say hello to your grandma for us, okay? Thank you. Bye." Allyson is seen behind Ashrow so she doesn't even get her own shot.

The film premiered at the Cinequest Film Festival on March 5 and was released on video on December 4, 2001. It was lambasted by Dennis Harvey in *Variety.* Brent Florence reported that the actress' casting arose from Ashrow being cast. She simply accompanied him on location on the day, perhaps because filming was to take place in their residential area, and the director asked if Allyson would like to be in the scene.

The comedy *Hanging Up* (2000), written by Nora Ephron based on the book by Delia Ephron, had a reference to Allyson. Los Angeles party planner Eve (Meg Ryan) has trouble remembering the name of a 1950s movie actress who was blonde with very thin hair, bland, short and kind of wide; she played wimps and was always suffering. On his deathbed, her father Lou (Walter Matthau) identifies her as Allyson. This reference originated in the Delia Ephron book.

Allyson reportedly made an uncredited cameo in the made-for-TV comedy *These Old Broads* which was broadcast on ABC on February 12, 2001. It was written by Carrie Fisher and Elaine Pope and directed by Matthew Diamond. It centered on Kate Westbourne (Shirley MacLaine), Piper Grayson (Debbie Reynolds) and Addie Holden (Joan Collins), stars of a 40-year-old movie. After its re-release, they are asked to do a new show. Allyson was offered the role of Miriam Hodges (Addie's mother) but reportedly backed out at the last minute. Carrie Fisher said Allyson really wanted to be one of the broads, and didn't want to be dowdy. Fisher assumed the veteran actress would want the opportunity to work again and was peeved when she withdrew. Allyson is said to have appeared as a guest at the hotel but she is not seen in the viewed film.

The actress was a guest on the CNN news talk-show *Larry King Live* on July 4. She discussed her career, Dick Powell, Judy Garland, Van Johnson, Peter Lawford, Ronald Reagan, Marilyn Monroe and James Stewart. Powell, she said, could do anything, and she never reached the pinnacle he did. Allyson never felt she was truly a star. The actress still wanted to work if a really good part came along. She didn't feel she had much talent, and felt that people gave her a break because they felt sorry for this person trying so hard. The one thing she felt she did well was learn her lines. She was never comfortable with fame. The dream of becoming a doctor was lived through her brother, whose career she financed.

Next was an appearance in the video documentary *Ronald Reagan: The Hollywood Years, the Presidential Years,* released on August 22. It was written by Jeff Miller and Steven Vosburgh and directed by Kent Hagan and Vosburgh.

On August 24, *The New York Times'* James Barron reported that composer Mark Adamo had contacted the actress about his opera of *Little Women.* He thanked her for her performance as Jo and, when she described the character to him, Adamo knew he was the only artist in the world to owe an opera to June Allyson.

Allyson attended the 27th Annual Judy Garland Festival, held in Grand Rapids, Minnesota, from June 20 to 22, 2002. In the Jane Ellen Wayne book *The Golden Girls of MGM: Greta Garbo, Joan Crawford, Lana Turner, Judy Garland, Ava Gardner, Grace Kelly and Others* (Carroll & Graf, 2002), Allyson was listed among the Others in the chapter "Famous But Not So Naughty." Wayne wrote that it was the husky voice in contrast to her pixyish image that gave Allyson an interesting quality.

The actress was referenced in John Wallowitch's cabaret act, which played at New York's Danny's Skylight Room in July and August 2003. One zany number lauded her courageous "public service": appearing in adult diaper ads.

It was reported that in 2003 she had hip-replacement surgery and afterwards her health began to deteriorate.

Allyson gave a new interview but was not seen in "Judy Garland: By Myself," an episode of the PBS biographical documentary series *American Masters* broadcast on February 25, 2004. Garland (voiced by Isabel Keating) tells her own story through recordings she made while preparing to write an autobiography. Allyson comments that Garland had more talent in one little finger than all the rest of them at MGM put together. People thought Garland was a tough lady but Allyson found her fragile, evidenced by the many times she broke. The actress also speaks about the Carnegie Hall concert of April 23, 1961.

She was in the video documentary *That's Entertainment! The Masters Behind the Musicals,* released on October 12. Directed by an uncredited Peter Fitzgerald, it centered on the fine musical directors, orchestrators, choreographers, directors and vocal coaches that MGM brought together to create their musicals. Allyson speaks about Charles Walters.

On July 8, 2006, Allyson, age 88, died at her home from pulmonary respiratory failure and acute bronchitis, according to an announcement made by her daughter Pamela. *New York Times* obituary writer Aljean Harmetz defined the actress as someone whose perky wholesomeness made her the perfect girlfriend in a series of MGM musicals during the 1940s and the perfect screen wife during the 1950s. She was survived by her daughter and her husband, David Ashrow. Allyson had a net worth of $10 million. She was cremated and the ashes given to the family. A burial plaque was placed at the Forest Lawn Memorial Park in Glendale, California.

After Allyson's death, Kimberly-Clark contributed $25,000 to the June Allyson Foundation for Public Awareness and Medical Research to support research advances in the care and treatment of women with urinary incontinence. On November 2, an event was held at the El Portal Theatre in North Hollywood, "Hollywood Salutes June Allyson with Legends of the Silver Screen." It featured Gloria DeHaven, Debbie Reynolds, Margaret O'Brien, Jane Withers, Marsha Hunt, Jane Russell and Allyson's children Ricky and Pamela. Topics for the evening included loving anecdotes of working and playing with the actress.

Allyson was included in the "In Memoriam" segment of the *13th Annual Screen Actors Guild Awards.* She was given the same recognition at *The 79th Annual Academy Awards.*

David Ashrow died on April 23, 2007, at the age of 86. He was cremated and his ashes given to family.

Allyson's association with Depend was the target of a joke by Joan Rivers on *The Late Show with David Letterman* on July 8, 2014, the anniversary of the actress' death. Rivers quipped that that she lost the Depend advertisement, which was one of the great commercials, and did her impression of Allyson saying "Hi, I'm June Allyson. While I'm talking to you, I'm taking a dump." This resulted in Letterman walking off the set; he returned after a commercial break.

Appendix

Theater

Note: The dates apply to Allyson's appearances, not to the run of the show.

Sing Out the News (September 24, 1938–January 7, 1939). Music Box Theatre, New York. Part: Chorus.

Very Warm for May (November 17, 1939–January 6, 1940). Alvin Theatre, New York. Part: June.

Higher and Higher (April 4–June 15, 1940). Part: Specialty Girl.

Panama Hattie (October 30, 1940–date unknown). 42nd Street Theatre, New York. Part: Dancing Girl and understudy for Florrie.

Best Foot Forward (October 1, 1941–July 4, 1942). Ethel Barrymore Theatre, New York. Part: Minerva.

Janus (dates unknown, 1964). Paper Mill Playhouse, New Jersey. Part: Jessica.

Goodbye Ghost (dates unknown, 1965). Little Theatre on the Square, Illinois; 1966 tour (including July 18 to 23), Tappan Zee Playhouse, New York.

Forty Carats (January 5–date unknown July 1970). Morosco Theatre, New York. Part: Ann Stanley.

No No Nanette (1971–1972, national tour dates include December 27, 1971, Hanna Theatre, Ohio; February 15–March 5, 1972, Shubert Theatre, Cincinnati; March 7–25, Palace Theatre in Milwaukee; March 28, Fisher Theatre, Michigan; May 4–date unknown, Curran Theatre, San Francisco, and May 16–date unknown, Ahmanson Theatre, Los Angeles). Part: Sue Smith.

Goodbye Ghost (From January 14, 1972, to Date Unknown). Pheasant Run Playhouse, Illinois.

My Daughter, Your Son (November 1974). Country Dinner Playhouse, State Unknown.

My Daughter, Your Son (September 15–October 25, 1981). Windmill Dinner Theatre, Texas.

My Daughter, Your Son (March 1982). Windmill Dinner Theatre, Texas.

Carnegie Hall Celebrates the Glorious MGM Musicals (July 15–16, 1997). New York. Part: Herself.

Carnegie Hall Celebrates the Glorious MGM Musicals: An Encore Presentation (March 25–26, 1999). New York. Part: Herself.

Films

Swing for Sale (1937). Part: Unknown.
Pixilated (1937). Part: Unknown.
Ups and Downs (1937). Part: June Daily.
Dime a Dance (1937). Part: Harriet.
Dates and Nuts (1937). Part: Wilma Brown.
Sing for Sweetie (1938). Part: Sally Newton.
The Prisoner of Swing (1938). Part: Princess.
The Knight Is Young (1938). Part: June.
Rollin' in Rhythm (1939). Part: Band Vocalist.
All Girl Revue (1940). Part: Mayor.
Girl Crazy (1943). Part: Specialty.
Best Foot Forward (1943). Part: Ethel.
Thousands Cheer (1943). Part: Herself.
Meet the People (1944). Part: Annie.
Two Girls and a Sailor (1944). Part: Patsy Deyo.
Music for Millions (1944). Part: Barbara Ainsworth.
Her Highness and the Bellboy (1945) Part: Leslie Odell.
The Sailor Takes a Wife (1945). Part: Mary.
Two Sisters from Boston (1946). Part: Martha Canford Chandler.
Till the Clouds Roll By (1946). Part: Mary/Jane.
The Secret Heart (1946). Part: Penny Adams.
High Barbaree (1947). Part: Nancy Frazer.
Good News (1947). Part: Connie Lane.
The Bride Goes Wild (1948). Part: Martha Terryton.
The Three Musketeers (1948). Part: Constance.
Words and Music (1948). Part: Unnamed.
Little Women (1949). Part: Jo.
The Stratton Story (1949). Part: Ethel.
The Reformer and the Redhead (1950). Part: Kathleen Maguire.
Right Cross (1950). Part: Pat O'Malley.
Too Young to Kiss (1951). Part: Cynthia Potter.
The Girl in White (1952). Part: Dr. Emily Dunning.
Battle Circus (1953). Part: Lt. Ruth McGara.
Remains to Be Seen (1953). Part: Jody Revere.
The Glenn Miller Story (1954). Part: Helen Burger.
Woman's World (1954). Part: Katie Baxter.
Strategic Air Command (1954). Part: Sally Holland.
The Shrike (1955). Part: Ann Downs.
The McConnell Story (1955). Part: Pearl "Butch" Brown.
You Can't Run Away from It (1956). Part: Ellen "Ellie" Andrews.
The Opposite Sex (1956) Part: Kay.
My Man Godfrey (1957). Part: Irene.
Interlude (1957). Part: Helen Banning.
A Stranger in My Arms (1959). Part: Christina Beasley.

Premier Khrushchev in the USA (1959). Part: Herself.
Hollywood Without Make-Up (1963). Part: Herself.
They Only Kill Their Masters (1972) Part: Mrs. Watkins.
Blackout (1978). Part: Mrs. Grant.
That's Entertainment! III (1994). Part: Herself.
That's Entertainment! III: Behind the Screen (1994). Part: Herself.
A Girl, 3 Guys, and a Gun (2000). Part: Ed's Wife.
Ronald Reagan: The Hollywood Years, the Presidential Years (2000). Part: Herself.
That's Entertainment! The Masters Behind the Musicals (2004). Part: Herself.

Television

The Arthur Murray Party (February 4, 1951). Part: Herself.
Olympic Fund Telethon (June 21-22, 1952). Part: Herself.
Talk of the Town (March 1, 1953). Part: Herself.
The 25th Academy Awards (March 19, 1953). Part: Herself.
What's My Line? (November 7, 1954). Part: Herself.
Sheilah Graham in Hollywood (March 21, 1955). Part: Herself.
Tonight! (August 10, 1955). Part: Herself.
Person to Person (September 2, 1955). Part: Herself.
Talk of the Town (May 13, 1956). Part: Herself.
General Motors 50th Anniversary Show (September 15, 1958). Part: Emily Webb.
The 30th Academy Awards (March 26, 1958). Part: Herself.
Bing Crosby's White Christmas USO All Star Show (December 1, 1958). Part: Herself.
The 31st Annual Academy Awards (April 6, 1959). Part: Herself.
What's My Line? (September 13, 1959). Part: Herself.
The June Allyson Show Season 1: "Those We Love" (September 21, 1959). Parts: Host/Ruth; "Dark Morning" (September 28, 1959). Part: Host; "The Opening Door" (October 5, 1959). Part: Host; "Summer's Ending" (October 12, 1959). Parts: Host/Sharon Foster; "The Tender Shoots" (October 19, 1959). Part: Host; "The Pledge" (October 26, 1959). Part: Host; "Love Is a Headache" (November 2, 1959). Part: Host. "Child Lost" (November 16, 1959). Part: Host/Vivian; "Night Out" (November 23, 1959). Part: Host; "The Girl" (November 30, 1959). Part: Host; "The Wall Between" (December 7, 1959). Part: Host. "The Crossing" (December 14, 1959). Part: Host; "No Place to Hide" (December 21, 1959). Part: Host; "Suspected" (December 28, 1959). Part: Host; "Edge of Fury" (January 4, 1960). Part: Host/Janet; "The Trench Coat" (January 11, 1960). Part: Host; "The Way Home" (January 18, 1960). Part: Host; "Moment of Fear" (January 25, 1960). Part: Host; "So Dim the Light" (February 1, 1960). Part: Host/Nancy Evans; "Trial by Fear" (February 8, 1960). Part: Host; "The Threat of Evil" (February 15, 1960). Part: Host;

"Escape" (February 22, 1960). Part: Host; "Piano Man" (February 29, 1960). Part: Host.

The 17th Golden Globe Awards (March 8 or 10, 1960). Part: Herself.

The June Allyson Show: "Sister Mary Slugger" (March 14, 1960). Part: Host/Sister Mary Ann; "Once Upon a Knight" (March 28, 1960). Part: Host; "Slip of the Tongue" (April 11, 1960). Part: Host; "Surprise Party" (April 18, 1960). Part: Host; "The Doctor and the Redhead" (April 25, 1960). Part: Host; "Intermission" (May 2, 1960). Part: Host/Anne.

What's My Line? (May 22, 1960). Part: Herself.

The June Allyson Show Season 2: "The Lie" (September 29, 1960). Parts: Host/ Janet Ramsey; "The Dance Man" (October 6, 1960). Part: Host; "Dark Fear" (October 13, 1960). Part: Host; "The Test" (October 20, 1960). Part: Host/ Ruth Taylor.

Zane Grey Theatre: "Cry Hope! Cry Hate!" (October 20, 1960). Part: Stella.

The June Allyson Show: "Play Acting" (October 27, 1960). Part: Host; "The Woman Who" (November 3, 1960). Parts: Host/Louise Robertson; "I Hit and Ran" (November 10, 1960). Part: Host. "Love on Credit" (November 17, 1960). Part: Host; "The Visitor" (November 24, 1960). Part: Host; "A Thief or Two" (December 1, 1960). Part: Host; "Emergency" (December 8, 1960). Part: Host; "The Desperate Challenge" (December 15, 1960). Part: Host/Carol Evans; "A Silent Panic" (December 22, 1960). Part: Host; "End of a Mission" (January 2, 1961). Part: Host; "The Defense Is Restless" (January 9, 1961). Parts: Host/Joanne Burnham; "The Guilty Heart" (January 16, 1961). Part: Host; "An Affair in Athens" (January 23, 1961). Parts: Host/Betty Allen; "The School of the Solider" (January 30, 1961). Part: Host; "Without Fear" (February 6, 1961). Parts: Host/ Eleanor Baldwin; "A Great Day for a Scoundrel" (February 13, 1961). Part: Host; "The Old Fashioned Way" (February 20, 1961). Parts: Host/Elsa Wilson; "The Moth" (February 27, 1961). Parts: Host/Stephanie Cate; "The Haven" (March 6, 1961). Part: Host; "The Man Who Wanted Everything Perfect" (March 13, 1961). Parts: Host/Ann Lawson; "The Country Mouse" (March 20, 1961). Part: Host; "Our Man in Rome" (March 27, 1961). Part: Host.

What's My Line? (April 2, 1961). Part: Herself.

The June Allyson Show: "Death of the Temple Bay" (April 3, 1961). Part: Host.

I've Got a Secret (April 19, 1961). Part: Herself.

What's My Line? (September 17, 1961). Part: Herself.

The Dick Powell Show: "A Time to Die" (January 9, 1962). Part: Mrs. Stevens.

The Dick Powell Show: "Special Assignment" (September 25, 1962). Part: Jerri Brent.

The Dick Powell Show: "The Doomsday Boys" (October 16, 1962). Part: Host.

The Dick Powell Theatre: "Project X" (January 3, 1963). Part: Host.

The 20th Annual Golden Globe Awards (March 5, 1963). Part: Herself.

The Dick Powell Theatre: "The Third Side of the Coin" (March 26, 1963). Part: Rosalind Cramer.

The Dick Powell Theatre: "The Old Man and the City" (April 23, 1963). Part: Host.

The 15th Emmy Awards (May 26, 1963). Part: Herself.

The Judy Garland Show (October 27, 1963). Part: Herself.
The Perry Como Show (October 3, 1963). Part: Herself.
Burke's Law: "Who Killed Beau Sparrow?" (December 27, 1963). Part: Jean Samson.
The Mike Douglas Show (September 21 to 25, 1964). Part: Co-Host.
The Match Game (October 5-9, 1964). Part: Team Captain.
The Tonight Show Starring Johnny Carson (January 6, 1965). Part: Herself.
You Don't Say (April 26, 1965). Part: Herself.
The Celebrity Game (June 3, 1965). Part: Herself.
You Don't Say (August 16, 1965). Part: Herself.
I'll Bet (August 30, 1965). Part: Herself.
The Mike Douglas Show (March 10, 1967). Part: Herself.
The Joey Bishop Show (May 23, 1967). Part: Herself.
The Joey Bishop Show (July 11, 1967). Part: Herself.
Personality (February 12, 1968). Part: Herself.
The Name of the Game: "High on a Rainbow" (December 6, 1968). Part: Joanne Robins.
Talk of the Town (January 18, 1970). Part: Herself.
The Merv Griffin Show (January 21, 1970). Part: Herself.
The Tonight Show Starring Johnny Carson (January 29, 1970). Part: Herself.
The David Frost Show (February 16, 1970). Part: Herself.
The Movie Game (March 9, 1970). Part: Herself.
The Mike Douglas Show (March 23, 1970). Part: Herself.
The Merv Griffin Show (May 3, 1970). Part: Herself.
The Tonight Show Starring Johnny Carson (June 14, 1970). Part: Herself.
The Mike Douglas Show (June 25, 1970). Part: Herself.
The Merv Griffin Show (August 24, 1970). Part: Herself.
The Mike Douglas Show (September 24, 1970). Part: Herself.
This Is Your Life: "June Allyson" (October 3, 1970). Part: Herself.
The Merv Griffin Show (October 4, 1970). Part: Herself.
The Tonight Show Starring Johnny Carson (November 26, 1970). Part: Herself.
See the Man Run (December 11, 1970). Part: Helene Spencer.
The Bob Braum Show (February 14, 1972). Part: Herself.
The ABC Comedy Hour: "The Twentieth Century Follies" (February 16, 1972). Part: Herself.
The Tonight Show Starring Johnny Carson (May 18, 1972). Part: Herself.
The Merv Griffin Show (June 1, 1972). Part: Herself.
The Tonight Show Starring Johnny Carson (July 28, 1972). Part: Herself.
The Hollywood Squares (Daytime) (August 7, 1972). Herself.
The Merv Griffin Show (August 23, 1972). Part: Herself.
The Sixth Sense: "Witness Within" (October 7, 1972). Part: Ruth.
The Hollywood Squares (Daytime) (November 27, 1972). Part: Herself.
The 30th Annual Golden Globe Awards (January 28, 1973). Part: Herself.
The Dean Martin Show (February 15, 1973). Part: Herself.
The Dean Martin Show (March 15, 1973). Part: Herself.
It's Your Bet (March 19, 1973). Part: Herself.

The Hollywood Squares (daytime) (September 10, 1973). Part: Herself.
Letters from Three Lovers (October 3, 1973). Part: Monica.
The 31st Annual Golden Globe Awards (January 26, 1974). Part: Herself.
The Merv Griffin Show (May 16, 1974). Part: Herself.
ABC's Wide World of Entertainment: "That's Entertainment: 50 Years of MGM" (May 29, 1974). Part: Herself.
The Bob Braum Show (August 14, 1974). Part: Herself.
The Gong Show (June 14, 1976). Part: Herself.
Switch: "Eden's Gate" (February 20, 1977). Part: Dr. Trampler.
Curse of the Black Widow (September 16, 1977). Part: Olga.
An All Star Tribute to Elizabeth Taylor (December 1, 1977). Part: Herself.
Three on a Date (February 17, 1978). Part: Marge Emery.
The Hollywood Squares (daytime) (April 17, 1978). Part: Herself.
Dean Martin Celebrity Roast: Jimmy Stewart (May 10, 1978). Part: Herself.
Vega$: "High Roller" (November 3, 1978). Part: Loretta.
The Love Boat: "The Minister and the Stripper/Her Own Two Feet/Tony's Family" (November 18, 1978). Part: Audrey Wilder.
All-Star Party for James Stewart (December 7, 1978). Part: Herself.
The Hollywood Greats: "The Golden Years" (August 30, 1979). Part: Herself.
The Incredible Hulk: "Brain Child" (October 5, 1979). Part: Dr. Kate Lowell.
Good Morning America (January 1, 1980). Part: Herself.
Good Morning America (January 24, 1980). Part: Herself.
House Calls: "I'll Be Suing You" (March 3 or 10, 1980). Part: Florence Alexander.
"G.I. Jive" (March 15, 1980). Part: Herself.
Over Easy (October 14, 1980). Part: Herself.
Did America Kill John Wayne? (March 7, 1981). Part: Herself.
Parkinson (September 28, 1981). Part: Herself.
The Dick Cavett Show (Date Unknown, 1981). Part: Herself.
Night of 100 Stars (March 8, 1982). Part: Herself.
The Kid with the Broken Halo (April 5, 1982). Part: Dorothea Powell.
The Irv Kupcinet Show (June 20, 1982). Part: Herself.
The Tonight Show with Johnny Carson (August 24, 1982). Part: Herself.
Hour Magazine (September 14, 1982). Part: Herself.
Simon & Simon: "The Last Time I Saw Michael" (December 9, 1982). Part: Margaret Wells.
The Love Boat: "Vicki's Dilemma/Discount Romance/Loser & Still Champ" (March 5, 1983). Part: Shirley Walsh.
Hart to Hart: "Always, Elizabeth" (May 15, 1984). Part: Elizabeth Tisdale.
Murder, She Wrote: "Hit, Run and Homicide" (November 25, 1984). Part: Katie Simmons.
De película: "Cannes 1985" (June 15, 1985). Part: Herself.
Wogan (June 7, 1985). Part: Herself.
Misfits of Science: "Steer Crazy" (November 1). Part: Bessie.
Des O'Connor Tonight (November 5, 1985). Part: Herself.
The Annual Friars Club Tribute Presents a Salute to Gene Kelly (November 9, 1985). Part: Herself.

The 2nd Annual American Cinema Awards (November 22, 1985). Part: Herself.
All Star Party For "Dutch" Reagan (December 8, 1985). Part: Herself.
Crazy Like a Fox: "Hearing is Believing" (January 15, 1986). Part: Neva.
The 43rd Annual Golden Globe Awards 1986 (January 24, 1986). Part: Herself.
Airwolf: "Little Wolf" (February 1, 1986). Part: Martha Stewart.
The 58th Annual Academy Awards (March 24, 1986). Part: Herself.
Wogan (September 19, 1986). Part: Herself.
Happy 100th Birthday, Hollywood (May 18, 1987). Part: Herself.
In Performance at the White House: "A Tribute to American Music: Cole Porter" (July 29, 1987). Part: Herself.
The 6th Annual American Cinema Awards (January 6, 1989). Part: Herself.
America's All-Star Tribute to Elizabeth Taylor (March 9, 1989). Part: Herself.
Wilfrid's Special Christmas (Date Unknown, 1989). Part: Miss Nancy.
The 7th Annual American Cinema Awards (January 7, 1990). Part: Herself.
*The Film Society of Lincoln Center Annual Gala Tribute to James Stewart (*April 23, 1990). Part: Herself.
The 35th Annual Thalians Gala (October 13, 1990). Part: Herself.
The 8th Annual American Cinema Awards (January 12, 1991). Part: Herself.
Burt Reynolds Conversations With... (August 29, 1991). Part: Herself.
Pros and Cons: "It's the Pictures That Got Small" (October 19, 1991). Part: Gloria Hartford.
MGM: When the Lion Roars (March 22, 1992). Part: Herself.
Vicki! (September 7, 1992). Part: Herself.
Reflections on the Silver Screen (July 2, 1994). Part: Herself.
This Is Your Life (March 15, 1995). Part: Herself.
Burke's Law: "Who Killed the Toy Maker?" (June 15, 1995). Shelly Knox.
Inside the Dream Factory (November 1, 1995). Part: Herself.
Biography: "Judy Garland: Beyond the Rainbow" (March 23, 1997). Part: Herself.
Private Screenings (June 30, 1998). Part: Herself.
Biography: "Ann Miller. I'm Still Here" (January 13, 2000). Part: Herself.
Larry King Live (July 4, 2001). Part: Herself.
Biography: "Dick Powell" (Date unknown, 2002). Part: Herself.
American Masters: "Judy Garland: by myself" (February 25, 2004). Part: Herself (audio only).

Radio

Command Performance (July 30, 1944).
Command Performance (September 13, 1944).
Mail Call (January 31, 1945).
Old Gold Comedy Theater (June 10, 1945).
Presenting Lily Mars on *Lux Radio Theatre* (March 11, 1946).
Mail Call (January 22, 1947).
Music for Millions on *Screen Director's Playhouse* (April 10, 1949).
Kitty Foyle on *Hallmark Playhouse* (April 21, 1949).

The Bride Goes Wild on *Screen Guild Theater* (May 19, 1949).
The Edgar Bergen Show with Charlie McCarthy (December 18, 1949)
Little Women on *The Screen Guild Theatre* (December 22, 1949).
The Stratton Story on *Lux Radio Theatre* (February 13, 1950).
Little Women on *Lux Radio Theatre* (March 13, 1950).
"Mrs. X Can't Find Mr. X." *Richard Diamond, Private Detective* (June 21, 1950).
The Bride Goes Wild on *Lux Radio Theatre* (June 26, 1950).
The Reformer and the Redhead on *Lux Radio Theatre* (June 25, 1951).
The Girl in White on *Lux Radio Theatre* (May 18, 1953).
Because of You on *Lux Radio Theatre* (November 2, 1953).
The Edgar Bergen Show with Charlie McCarthy (February 28, 1954).
Jack Benny Christmas Special (December 2, 1956).
Books
June Allyson (May 1, 1982). Putnam.
June Allyson's Feeling Great: A Daily Dozen Exercises for Creative Aging (December 1, 1987). Capra Press.

Bibliography

Adams, Val. "Du Pont May Move 2 C.B.S. Programs." *The New York Times.* March 23, 1960. Retrieved September 15, 2021, from http://www.nytimes.com.

______. "New Role for Actress." *The New York Times.* April 8, 1959. Retrieved September 10, 2021, from http://www.nytimes.com.

______. "2 C.B.S.-TV Shows Will Be Replaced." *The New York Times.* March 2, 1960. Retrieved September 15, 2021, from http://www.nytimes.com.

______. "2 DU PONT SERIES TO STAY AT C.B.S." *The New York Times.* March 29, 1960. Retrieved September 15, 2021, from http://www.nytimes.com.

Allyson, June, with Leighton, Frances Spatz. *June Allyson.* New York: G.P. Putnam's Sons, 1982.

Anderson, Loni, with Warren, Larkin. *My Life in High Heels.* New York: Morrow, 1995.

Arnold, Jeremy. "Article: Good News (1947)." *Turner Classic Movies.* April 23, 2004. Retrieved April 20, 2021, from http://www.tcm.com.

Astor, Mary. *A Life on Film.* New York: Delacorte Press, 1971.

______. *My Story.* Garden City, New York: Doubleday, 1959.

Atkinson, Brooks. "The Play: 'Best Foot Forward.'" *The New York Times.* October 2, 1941. Retrieved February 28, 2021, from http://www.nytimes.com.

______. "The Play: 'Sing Out the News.'" *The New York Times.* September 26, 1938. Retrieved February 20, 2021, from http://ww.nytimes.com.

______. "The Play: 'Very Warm for May.'" *The New York Times.* November 18, 1939. Retrieved February 21, 2021, from http://www.nytimes.com.

______. "The Play: Higher and Higher.'" *The New York Times.* April 5, 1940. Retrieved February 21, 2021, from http://www.nytimes.com.

______. "The Play: Panama Hattie.'" *The New York Times.* October 31, 1940. Retrieved February 21, 2021, from http://www.nytimes.com.

A.W. "At Loew's State." *The New York Times.* May 31, 1952. Retrieved June 22, 2021, from http://www.nytimes.com.

Bakish, David. *Jimmy Durante: His Show Business Career, with an Annotated Filmography and Discography.* Jefferson, NC: McFarland, 2007.

Barbour, Alan G. *Humphrey Bogart. Pyramid Illustrated History of the Movies.* New York: Pyramid, 1973.

Barrios, Richard. *Words and Music DVD Audio Commentary.* Warner Bros, 2007.

Barron, James. "Boldface Names ... Inspirational June." *The New York Times.* August 24, 2011. Retrieved December 19, 2021, from http://www.nytimes.com.

Barton, Ruth. *Hedy Lamarr: The Most Beautiful Woman in Film.* Lexington: University Press of Kentucky, 2010.

Basinger, Jeanine. *Anthony Mann.* Middletown, CT: Wesleyan University Press, 2007.

______. *Gene Kelly. Pyramid Illustrated History of the Movies.* New York: Pyramid, 1976.

______. "The Girls Next Door." *The New York Times.* November 24, 1996. Retrieved November 28, 2021, from http://www.nytimes.com.

______. *Lana Turner. Pyramid Illustrated History of the Movies.* New York: Pyramid, 1976.

______. *A Woman's View. How Hollywood Spoke to Women 1930–1960.* London: Chatto & Windus, 1993.
Beard, Lanford. "On the Scene: Why Was Joan Rivers Part of Another Walkout on 'Letterman'?" *Entertainment Weekly.* July 9, 2014. Retrieved January 11, 2022, from http://www.ew.com.
Becker, Christine. *It's the Pictures That Got Small: Hollywood Film Stars on 1950s Television.* Middletown, CT: Wesleyan University Press, 2009.
Bennett, Bruce. "Article: Film Comment: Executive Suite." *Turner Classic Movies.* October 29, 2020. Retreived July 18, 2021, from http://www.tcm.com.
Blair, Betsy. *The Memory of All That.* New York: Knopf, 2015.
Blau, Eleanor. "The Night is Filled with Stars for Actors' Fund Benefit Gala." *The New York Times.* February 15, 1982. Retrieved October 22, 2021, from http://www.nytimes.com.
Brady, Thomas F. "June Allyson Gets New Comedy Lead." *The New York Times.* July 6, 1949. Retrieved June 8, 2021, from http://www.nytimes.com.
______. "Lead In 'Red Head' For June Allyson." *The New York Times.* July 28, 1949. Retrieved June 8, 2021, from http://www.nytimes.com.
______. "Metro Buys Option on Schmitt Novel." *The New York Times.* November 5, 1947. Retrieved April 27, 2021, from http://www.nytimes.com.
______. "Metro Fills Casts For 2 Major Films..." *The New York Times.* April 9, 1948. Retrieved June 7, 2021, from http://www.nytimes.com.
______. "Metro Purchases Story by Mealand." *The New York Times.* June 13, 1948. Retrieved June 7, 2021, from http://www.nytimes.com.
Bret, David. *Elizabeth Taylor: The Lady, the Lover, the Legend - 1932–2011.* Edinburgh: Mainstream, 2011.
Brog. "The Glenn Miller Story." *Variety.* January 5, 1954. Retrieved July 9, 2021, from http://www.variety.com.
______. "Good News." *Variety.* December 2, 1947. Retrieved April 20, 2021, from http://www.archive.org/variety.com.
______. "The Sailor Takes a Wife." *Variety.* December 28, 1945. Retrieved April 4, 2021, from http://www.variety.com.
Brozan, Nadine. "Chronicle." *The New York Times.* April 9, 1993. Retrieved November 18, 2021, from http://www.nytimes.com.
______. "Chronicle." *The New York Times.* July 11, 1997. Retrieved December 1, 2021, from http://www.nytimes.com.
Callahan, Dan. *Barbara Stanwyck: The Miracle Woman.* Jackson: University Press of Mississippi, 2012.
Calta, Louis. "June Allyson ... Take Stage Role." *The New York Times.* December 31, 1969. Retrieved September 27, 2021, from http://www.nytimes.com.
Capra, Frank. *It Happened One Night.* Columbia/Frank Capra Productions, 1934.
Carr, Jay. "Article: Strategic Air Command." *Turner Classic Movies.* April 10, 2007. Retrieved Augut 3, 2021, from http://www.tcm.com.
Coe, Jonathan. *Jimmy Stewart. A Wonderful Life.* New York: Arcade, 1994.
Collins, Glenn. "The Media Business: Advertising." *The New York Times.* July 7, 1994. Retrieved November 23, 2021, from http://www.nytimes.com.
Collins, Joan. *Past Imperfect: An Autobiography.* New York: Berkley Books, 1985.
Corry, John. "White House Hears Songs by Cole Porter." *The New York Times.* July 29, 1987. Retrieved November 4, 2021, from http://www.nytimes.com.
Cox, Amy. "Article: Words and Music." *Turner Classic Movies.* July 27, 2005. Retrieved May 11, 2021, from http://www.tcm.com.
Crane, Cheryl, with De La Hoz, Cindy. *Lana: The Memories, the Myths, the Movies.* Philadelphia: Running Press, 2008.
Crowther, Bosley. "Drake and Rooney Play Rodgers and Hart in 'Words and Music.'" *The New York Times.* December 10, 1948. Retrieved May 11, 2021, from http://www.nytimes.com.

______. "'Executive Suite' Has Debut at Music Hall." *The New York Times.* May 7, 1954. Retrieved July 18, 2021, from http://www.nytimes.com.

______. "'Good News.'" *The New York Times.* December 5, 1947. Retrieved April 20, 2021, from http://www.nytimes.com.

______. "Lana Turner and Gene Kelly Top Cast of 'Three Musketeers.'" *The New York Times.* October 21, 1948. Retrieved May 4, 2021, from http://www.nytimes.com.

______. "Metro Fails to Spare Pathos in 'Little Women' Remake Seen at Music Hall." *The New York Times.* March 11, 1949. Retrieved May 17, 2021, from http://www.nytimes.com.

______. "'Music for Millions.'" *The New York Times.* December 22, 1944. Retrieved March 28, 2021, from http://www.nytimes.com.

______. "The Screen: 'Best Foot Forward.'" *The New York Times.* June 30, 1943. Retrieved March 12, 2021, from http://www.nytimes.com.

______. "The Screen: 'The Bride Goes Wild.'" *The New York Times.* June 4, 1948. Retrieved April 26, 2021, from http://www.nytimes.com.

______. "Screen: Into the Wide Blue Yonder; 'Air Command.'" *The New York Times.* April 21, 1955. Retrieved August 3, 2021, from http://www.nytimes.com.

______. "Screen: 'My Man Godfrey' Returns." *The New York Times.* October 12, 1957. Retrieved September 5, 2021, from http://www.nytimes.com.

______. "The Screen: 'The Opposite Sex.'" *The New York Times.* November 16, 1956. Retrieved August 28, 2021, from http://www.nytimes.com.

______. "The Screen: 'Stranger in My Arms.'" *The New York Times.* March 4, 1959. Retrieved September 10, 2021, from http://www.nytimes.com.

______. "The Screen in Review: Fox's 'Woman's World' Offered at Roxy." *The New York Times.* September 10, 1954. Retrieved July 27, 2021, from http://www.nytimes.com.

______. "The Screen in Review: 'The Glenn Miller Story.'" *The New York Times.* February 11, 1954. Retrieved July 9, 2021, from http://www.nytimes.com.

______. "The Screen in Review: 'Till Clouds Roll By.'" *The New York Times.* December 6, 1946. Retrieved April 11, 2021, from http://www.nytimes.com.

______. "The Screen in Review: 'Too Young to Kiss.'" *The New York Times.* November 23, 1951. Retrieved June 16, 2021, from http://www.nytimes.com.

______. "The Screen in Review: 'Two Sisters from Boston.'" *The New York Times.* June 7, 1946. Retrieved April 7, 2021, from http://www.nytimes.com.

______. "Still at Sea." *The New York Times.* June 6, 1947. Retrieved April 16, 2021, from http://www.nytimes.com.

______. "Two Girls and a Sailor." *The New York Times.* June 15, 1944. Retrieved March 24, 2021, from http://www.nytimes.com.

Daniel, Douglass K. *Tough as Nails: The Life and Films of Richard Brooks.* Madison: University of Wisconsin Press, 2011.

Darby, William. *Anthony Mann: The Film Career.* Jefferson, NC: McFarland, 2009.

David, Jay. *Inside Joan Collins. a Biography.* New York: Carroll & Graf, 1988.

Davis, Ronald L. *Just Making Movies: Company Directors on the Studio System.* Jackson: University Press of Mississippi, 2005.

______. *Van Johnson: MGM 's Golden Boy.* Jackson: University Press of Mississippi, 2001.

Delatiner, Barbara. "Long Island Guide." *The New York Times.* October 20, 1996. Retrieved November 28, 2021, from http://www.nytimes.com.

Dewey, Donald. *James Stewart.* London: Little, Brown, 1997.

Duke, Patty, and Jankowitz, William J. *In the Presence of Greatness: My Sixty-Year Journey as an Actress.* Albany, GA: BearManor Media, 2018.

Eames, John Douglas. *The MGM Story. the Complete History of Fifty Roaring Years.* London: Octopus, 1975.

______. *The Paramount Story. the Complete History of the Studio and Its 2,805 Films.* London: Octopus Books, 1985.

Ebert, Roger. "Reviews: They Only Kill Their Masters." November 22, 1972. Retrieved October 2, 2021, from http://www.rogerebert.com.

______. "That's Entertainment! III." July 22, 1994. Retrieved November 24, 2021, from http://www.rogerebert.com.
Eliot, Marc. *James Stewart: A Biography.* London: Aurum, 2006.
Ellenberger, Allan R. *Margaret O'Brien: A Career Chronicle and Biography.* Jefferson, NC: McFarland, 2000.
Ephron, Delia. *Hanging Up.* New York: Putnam, 1995.
Erickson, Glenn. "Article: Executive Suite." *Turner Classic Movies.* November 19, 2007. Retrieved July 18, 2021, from http://www.tcm.com.
Eyles, Allen. *Humphrey Bogart.* London: Sphere, 1990.
______. *James Stewart.* London: W.H. Allen, 1984.
Eyman, Scott. *Lion of Hollywood: The Life and Legend of Louis B. Mayer.* New York: Simon & Schuster, 2005.
Fishgall, Frank. *Pieces of Time: The Life of James Stewart.* New York: Scribner's, 1997.
Florence, Brett et al. *A Girl, 3 Guys, and a Gun* DVD audio commentary. Buena Vista Home Entertainment, 2005.
Fordin, Hugh. *M-G-M's Greatest Musicals: The Arthur Freed Unit.* New York: Da Capo Press, 1996.
______. *The Movies' Greatest Musicals: Produced in Hollywood USA by the Freed Unit.* New York: F. Ungar, 1984.
Fowler, Karin J. *David Niven: A Bio-Bibliography.* Westport, CT: Greenwood Press, 1995.
Fox, Margalit. "Marty Ingels, Actor Funny Onscreen and Outrageous Off, Dies at 79." *The New York Times.* October 22, 2015. Retrieved November 27, 2021, from http://www.nytimes.com.
Frankel, Mark. "Article: Executive Suite." *Turner Classic Movies.* July 28, 2003. Retrieved July 18, 2021, from http://www.tcm.com.
Fraser, C. Gerald. "Television..." *The New York Times.* April 4, 1982. Retrieved October 22, 2021, from http://www.nytimes.com.
Freedland, Michael. *Jack Lemmon.* London: Weidenfeld and Nicolson, 1985.
Fricke, John. *Girl Crazy DVD Audio Commentary.* Warner Home Video, 2007.
Fristoe, Roger. "Article: Girl Crazy (1943)." Turner Classic Movies. July 28, 2003. Retrieved March 8, 2021, from http://www.tcm.com.
______. "Article: Music for Millions." *Turner Classic Movies.* September 23, 2004. Retrieved March 28, 2021, from http://www.tcm.com.
Garrett, Gerard. *The Films of David Niven.* Secaucus, NJ: Citadel Press, 1976.
Gates, Marya E. "From the Warner Archive: Battle Circus, 1953 (dir. Richard Brooks)." *Cinema Fanatic.* September 15, year unknown. Retrieved June 28, 2021, from http://www.cinema-fanatic.com.
Gene. "Strategic Air Command." *Variety.* March 29, 1955. Retrieved August 3, 2021, from http://www.variety.com.
______. "You Can't Run Away from It." *Variety.* October 3, 1956. Retrieved September 2, 2021, from http://www.variety.com.
Gould, Jack. "TV: June Allyson Series." *The New York Times.* September 22, 1959. Retrieved September 12, 2021, from http://www.nytimes.com.
Gow, Gordon. *Hollywood in the Fifties.* New York: A.S. Barnes, 1971.
Grant, Lee. *Intimate Portrait: Elizabeth Taylor.* Feury/Grant Entertainment/Lifetime Productions, 2002.
Gussow, Mel. "The Sometimes Bumpy Ride of Being Joseph Mankiewicz." *The New York Times.* November 24, 1992. Retrieved November 17, 2021, from http://www.nytimes.com.
Halliday, Jon. *Sirk on Sirk: Conversations with Jon Halliday.* London: Faber & Faber, 1971.
Harmetz, Aljean. "June Allyson, Adoring Wife in MGM Films, Is Dead at 88." *The New York Times.* July 11, 2006. Retrieved January 5, 2022, from http://www.nytimes.com.

______. "M-G-M: Thanks For 52 Years of Shoeshines." *The New York Times.* February 3, 1981. Retrieved October 16, 2021, from http://www.nytimes.com.

Harvey, Dennis. "Solid Ones." *Variety.* May 8, 2000. Retrieved December 12, 2021, from http://www.variety.com.

Haskell, Molly. *From Reverence to Rape: The Treatment of Women in the Movies.* New York: Holt, Rinehart and Winston, 1974.

Heeley, David. *James Stewart: A Wonderful Life—Hosted by Johnny Carson.* Educational Broadcasting Corporation, 1987.

Herm. "The Stratton Story." *Variety.* April 20, 1949. Retrieved May 27, 2021, from http://www.variety.com.

Heymann, C. David. *Liz: An Intimate Biography of Elizabeth Taylor.* New York: Atria, 1995.

H.H.T. "Wartime Romance Flourishes in Korea." *The New York Times.* May 28, 1953. Retrieved June 28, 2021, from http://www.nytimes.com.

Hicks, L. Wayne. "1952 Olympics Telethon." *TVparty!* Undated. Retrieved July 4, 2021, from http://www.tvparty.com.

Higham, Charles, and Greenberg, Joel. *Hollywood in the Forties.* New York: A.S. Barnes, 1968.

Hirsch, Foster. *Elizabeth Taylor: Pyramid Illustrated History of the Movies.* New York: Pyramid Publications, 1973.

Hirschhorn, Clive. *The Columbia Story.* London: Pyramid, 1989.

______. *The Hollywood Musical.* New York: Crown, 1981.

______. *The Universal Story.* London: Octopus, 1983.

______. *The Warner Bros. Story: The Complete History of the Great Hollywood Studio, Every Warner Bros. Feature Film Described and Illustrated.* London: Octopus, 1979.

Hirsen, Steve. "Burt Reynolds' Conversation With: James Stewart, Mickey Rooney, Van Johnson & Ricardo Montalban." October 31, 1991. CBS Entertainment Productions/Burt Reynolds Productions.

Hischak, Thomas S. *The Jerome Kern Encyclopedia.* Lanham, Maryland: Scarecrow, 2013.

Holden, Stephen. "Cabaret: Larry Adler." *The New York Times.* October 20, 1985. Retrieved October 30, 2021, from http://www.nytimes.com.

______. "Cabaret Review: Mischievous Musical Jokes from a Cocktail Raconteur." *The New York Times.* July 16, 2003. Retrieved December 28, 2021, from http://www.nytimes.com.

______. "Music Review: Stars of Old Movie Musicals Bask in Their Own Light." *The New York Times.* July 17, 1997. Retrieved December 1, 2021, from http://www.nytimes.com.

Hollimon, Rod. "Article: The Three Musketeers (1948)." *Turner Classic Movies.* February 1, 2007. Retrieved May 4, 2021, from http://www.tcm.com.

Hulme, George. *Mel Torme: A Chronicle of His Recordings, Books and Films.* Jefferson, NC: McFarland, 2000.

Irvin, Sam. *Kay Thompson: From Funny Face to Eloise.* New York: Simon & Schuster, 2010.

James, Caryn. "Review/Film; Waste Not, Want Not: MGM's Outtakes Are a Movie." *The New York Times.* May 6, 1994. Retrieved November 23, 2021, from http://www.nytimes.com.

Johnston, Laurie. "Notes on People..." *The New York Times.* October 28, 1976. Retrieved October 7, 2021, from http://www.nytimes.com.

Juneau, James. *Judy Garland. Pyramid Illustrated History of the Movies.* New York: Pyramid, 1974.

Kael, Pauline. *5001 Nights at the Movies.* New York: Holt, Rinehart and Winston, 1982.

Kanfer, Stefan. *Ball of Fire: The Tumultuous Life and Comic Art of Lucille Ball.* New York: Knopf, 2003.

Karol, Michael. *Lucy A to Z: The Lucille Ball Encyclopedia.* New York: iUniverse Star, 2008.

Kashner, Sam. *The Bad and the Beautiful: A Chronicle of Hollywood in the Fifties*. London: Time Warner, 2003.
Kear, Lynn. *Agnes Moorehead: A Bio-Bibliography*. Westport, CT: Greenwood, 1992.
Keck, William. "Scandal's History for 'These Old Broads.'" *Los Angeles Times*. February 12, 2001. Retrieved December 15, 2021, from http://www.latimes.com.
Kelley, Kitty. *Elizabeth Taylor: The Last Star*. New York: Simon & Schuster, 1981.
Kellow, Brian. *Ethel Merman: A Life*. New York: Penguin, 2008.
Kennedy, Matthew. *Joan Blondell: A Life Between Takes*. University Press of Mississippi, 2014.
Ketcham, Diane. "Long Island Journal." *The New York Times*. November 3, 1996. Retrieved November 28, 2021, from http://www.nytimes.com.
Koster, Henry, and Atkins, Irene Kahn. *Henry Koster*. Metuchen, NJ: Scarecrow Press, 1987.
Krebs, Alvin. "Notes on People ..." *The New York Times*. November 2, 1976. Retrieved October 7, 2021, from http://www.nytimes.com.
La Cava, Gregory. *My Man Godfrey*. Universal/Gregory la Cava Productions, 1936.
Lamarr, Hedy. *Ecstasy and Me: My Life as a Woman*. New York: Bartholomew House, 1966.
Landazuri, Margarita. "Article: Her Highness and the Bellboy." *Turner Classic Movies*. February 4, 2008. Retrieved March 31, 2021, from http://www.tcm.com.
______. "Article: The Opposite Sex." *Turner Classic Movies*. August 22, 2005. Retrieved August 28, 2021, from http://www.tcm.com.
______. "Article: The Secret Heart." *Turner Classic Movies*. February 24, 2005. Retrieved April 13, 2021, from http://www.tcm.com.
______. "Article: Too Young to Kiss." *Turner Classic Movies*. December 7, 2007. Retrieved June 16, 2021, from http://www.tcm.com.
______. "Article: Two Girls and a Sailor." *Turner Classic Movies*. August 26, 2003. Retrieved March 24, 2021, from http://www.tcm.com.
Leigh, Janet. *There Really Was a Hollywood*. New York: Berkley, 1985.
Leonard, John. "John Leonard's TV Notes." *New York Magazine*. August 14, 1995. Retrieved November 27, 2021, from http://www.books.google.com.au.
Levoit, Violet. "Article: The Sailor Takes a Wife." *Turner Classic Movies*. February 14, 2014. Retrieved April 4, 2021, from http://www.tcm.com.
Linet, Beverly. *Ladd: The Life, the Legend, the Legacy of Alan Ladd*. New York: Arbor House, 1979.
______. *Star-Crossed: The Story of Robert Walker and Jennifer Jones*. New York: Putnam, 1986.
LoBianco, Lorraine. "Article: 'My Man Godfrey.'" *Turner Classic Movies*. March 8, 2014. Retrieved September 5, 2021, from http://www.tcm.com.
Lovell, Glenn. *Escape Artist: The Life and Films of John Sturges*. Madison: University of Wisconsin Press, 2008.
Macksoud, Meredith C., et al. *Arthur Kennedy, Man of Characters: A Stage and Cinema Biography*. Jefferson, NC: McFarland, 2003.
Madsen, Axel. *Stanwyck*. New York: HarperCollins Publishers, 1994.
Mann, William J. *How to Be a Movie Star: Elizabeth Taylor in Hollywood*. New York: Houghton Mifflin Harcourt Publishing, 2009.
Marill, Alvin H. *Movies Made for Television: The TeleFeature and the Mini-Series, 1964–1986*. New York: Zoetrope, 1987.
Maslin, Janet. "Film View; Hollywood Leaves Its Imprint on Its Chroniclers." *The New York Times*. July 11, 1982. Retrieved October 22, 2021, from http://www.nytimes.com.
Mateas, Liz. "Article: They Only Kill Their Masters." *Turner Classic Movies*. May 27, 2008. Retrieved October 2, 2021, from http:///tcm.com.
McCarthy, Todd. "That's Entertainment! III." *Variety*. April 25, 1994. Retrieved November 24, 2021, from http://www.variety.com.

McDowell, Edwin. "A Directory of Cruises Worldwide." *The New York Times.* October 10, 1993. Retrieved November 18, 2021, from http://www.nytimes.com.
McGee, Scott. "Article: Meet the People." *Turner Classic Movies.* September 29, 2006. Retrieved March 20, 2021, from http://www.tcm.com.
Meredith C. Macksoud, Craig R. Smith, Jackie Lohrke · 2002
Merman, Ethel, and Eels, George. *Merman.* New York: Simon & Schuster, 1978.
Merrill, Gary. *Bette, Rita, and the Rest of My Life.* Lance Tapley, 1988.
Meyerson, Harold, and Harburg, Ernest. *Who Put the Rainbow in the Wizard of Oz: Yip Harburg, Lyricist.* Ann Arbor: University of Michigan Press, 1993.
Miller, Frank. "Article: 'Battle Circus.'" *Turner Classic Movies.* October 20, 2009. Retrieved June 28, 2021, from http://www.tcm.com.
______. "Article: 'Best Foot Forward.'" *Turner Classic Movies.* July 26, 2004. Retrieved February 26, 2021, from http://www.tcm.com.
______. "Article: 'Little Women' (1949)." *Turner Classic Movies.* July 28, 2003. Retrieved May 17, 2021, from http://www.tcm.com.
Milner, Jay Dunston. *Confessions of a Maddog: A Romp Through the High-flying Texas Music and Literary Era of the Fifties to the Seventies.* Denton: University of North Texas Press, 1998.
Mitgang, Herbert. "'100 Stars and More to Benefit Actors' Fund." *The New York Times.* January 6, 1982. Retrieved October 22, 2021, from http://www.nytimes.com.
Morella, Joe, and Epstein, Edward Z. *Rita: The Life of Rita Hayworth.* New York: Delacorte, 1983.
Morley, Sheridan. *Elizabeth Taylor.* London: Pavilion, 1989.
______. *The Other Side of the Moon: A Biography of David Niven.* New York: Harper & Row, 1985.
Morris, Bob. "The Night; and They Call It an Oasis." *The New York Times.* March 20, 1994. Retrieved November 23, 2021, from http://www.nytimescom.
Munn, Michael. *Jimmy Stewart: The Truth Behind the Legend.* London: Robson, 2006.
Nelson, Miriam. *My Life Dancing with the Stars.* Albany, GA: BearManor Media, 2009.
Neuhaus, Mel. "Article: Right Cross." *Turner Classic Movies.* November 19, 2004. Retrieved June 11, 2021, from http://www.tcm.com.
______. "Article: 'Till the Clouds Roll By.'" *Turner Classic Movies.* April 24, 2008. Retrieved April 11, 2021, from http://www.tcm.com.
Nixon, Rob. "Article: The Reformer and the Redhead." *Turner Classic Movies.* May 20, 2003. Retrieved June 7, 2021, from http://www.tcm.com.
______. "Article: Remains to Be Seen." *Turner Classic Movies.* November 28, 2011. Retrieved July 3, 2021, from http://www.tcm.com.
______. "Article: You Can't Run Away from It." *Turner Classic Movies.* April 13, 2007. Retrieved September 2, 2021, from http://www.tcm.com.
O'Brien, Scott. *Ann Harding—Cinema's Gallant Lady.* Albany, GA: BearManor Media, 2010.
OConnor, John J. "The Academy Awards Ceremony." *The New York Times.* March 26, 1986. Retrieved November 1, 2021, from http://www.nytimes.com.
______. "Critic's Notebook: Revered or Reviled in the Name of Biography." *The New York Times.* March 20, 1997. Retrieved December 1, 2021, from http://www.nytimes.com.
______. "TV Weekend; All, Absolutely All, About Old M-G-M." *The New York Times.* March 20, 1992. Retrieved November 17, 2021, from http://www.nytimes.com.
______. "TV Weekend: Clifford Talks of Truman and Johnson." *The New York Times.* March 6, 1981. Retrieved October 16, 2021, from http://www.nytimes.com.
Parish, James Robert, and Bowers, Ronald L. *The MGM Stock Company: The Golden Era.* London: Allan, 1974.
Parish, James Robert, and Pitts, Michael R. *Hollywood Songsters: A Biographical Dictionary.* New York: Garland, 1991.

Passafiume, Andrea. "Article: Woman's World." *Turner Classic Movies.* December 14, 2015. Retrieved July 27, 2021, from http://www.tcm.com.

Pasternak, Joe. *Easy the Hard Way: The Autobiography of Joe Pasternak as Told to David Chandler.* New York: Putnam, 1956.

Peros, Mike. *José Ferrer: Success and Survival (Hollywood Legends).* Jackson: University Press of Mississippi, 2020.

Phillips, Brent. *Charles Walters: The Director Who Made Hollywood Dance.* Lexington: University Press of Kentucky, 2014.

Pickard, Roy. *James Stewart: A Life in Film.* New York: St. Martin's Press, 1993.

Porter, Darwin. *Humphrey Bogart: The Making of a Legend.* Blood Moon, 2010.

Pryor, Thomas M. "Arthur Kennedy Gets Movie Lead." *The New York Times.* September 12, 1951. Retrieved June 18, 2021, from http://www.nytimescom.

______. "At the Music Hall." *The New York Times.* May 13, 1949. Retrieved May 27, 2021, from http://www.nytimes.com.

______. "... June Allyson to Play Nun." *The New York Times.* October 18, 1956. Retrieved September 5, 2021, from http://www.nytimes.com.

______. "... Ladd, Allyson to Co-Star." *The New York Times.* May 14, 1954. Retrieved August 15, 2021, from http://www.nytimes.com.

______. "Metro's New Team Is Lamas-Allyson." *The New York Times.* May 18, 1953. Retrieved July 4, 2021, from http://wwwnytimes.com.

______. "'My Man Godfrey' Suspended Again." *The New York Times.* March 4, 1957. Retrieved September 6, 2021, from http://www.nytimes.com.

______. "New Role for June Allyson." *The New York Times.* November 9, 1951. Retrieved June 23, 2021, from http://www.nytimes.com.

______. "... Powell/Allyson Schedule." The New York Times. January 10, 1956. Retrieved September 10, 2021, from http://www.nytimes.com.

______. "U-I Finds Co-Star for June Allyson." *The New York Times.* September 26, 1956. Retrieved September 5, 2021, from http://www.nytimes.com.

______. "Universal Sues Actor It Ousted." *The New York Times.* February 21, 1957. Retrieved September 6, 2021, from http://www.nytimes.com.

Purdum, Todd. "At Home With: Esther Williams; Swimming Upstream." *The New York Times.* September 2, 1999. Retrieved December 7, 2021, from http://www.nytimes.com.

______. "James Stewart Seen as Rich in What Counts." *The New York Times.* July 8, 1997. Retrieved December 1, 2021, from http://www.nytimes.com.

Quin, Eleanor. "Article: High Barbaree." *Turner Classic Movies.* December 29, 2008. Retrieved April 16, 2021, from http://www.tcm.com.

Quirk, Lawrence J. *The Films of Lauren Bacall.* Secaucus, NJ: Citadel, 1986.

Rooney, Mickey. *Life Is Too Short.* New York: Villard, 1991.

Sagolla, Lisa Jo. *The Girl Who Fell Down: A Biography of Joan McCracken.* Boston: Northeastern University, 2003.

Sanders, Coyne Steven. *Rainbow's End: The Judy Garland Show.* New York: Morrow, 1990.

Schary, Dore. *Heyday: An Autobiography.* Boston: Little, Brown, 1979.

Schechter, Scott. *Judy Garland: The Day-By Day Chronicle of a Legend.* New York: Cooper Square, 2002.

Schumach, Murray. "Hollywood Stirred by Death of Dick Powell." *The New York Times.* January 3, 1963. Retrieved September 22, 2021, from http://www.nytimes.com.

Shapiro, Michael J. "Just One More Time." Saraband, 1974.

Sheppard, Dick. *Elizabeth: The Life and Career of Elizabeth Taylor.* Garden City, NY: Doubleday, 1974.

Shipman, David. *The Great Movie Stars 2: The International Years.* Boston: Little, Brown, 1995.

Simon, George T. *Glenn Miller and His Orchestra.* New York: Da Capo, 1980.

Smith, Starr. *Jimmy Stewart: Bomber Pilot.* St. Paul, MN: Zenish, 2005.

Spada, James. *Peter Lawford: The Man Who Kept the Secrets.* New York: Bantam, 1992.
Spoto, Donald. *Elizabeth Taylor.* London: Little, Brown, 1995.
Staggs, Sam. *All About 'All About Eve': The Complete Behind-the-Scenes Story of the Bitchiest Film Ever Made.* New York: St. Martin's, 2001.
Stahl, John M. *"Tomorrow Never Comes."* Universal/John M. Stahl Productions, 1939.
Steinberg, Jay. "Article: The Stratton Story." *Turner Classic Movies.* July 25, 2003. Retrieved May 27, 2021, from http://www.tcm.com.
Sterritt David. "'GI Jive': Tapping to the '40s." March 14, 1980. *The Christian Science Monitor.* Retrieved October 16, 2021, from http://www.csmonitor.com.
Strom, Robert. *Virginia O'Brien: MGM 's Deadpan Diva.* Albany, GA: BearManor Media, 2017.
Thames, Stephanie. "Article: The Bride Goes Wild." *Turner Classic Movies.* April 13, 2007. Retrieved April 26, 2021, from http://www.tcm.com.
______. "Article: Two Sisters from Boston." *Turner Classic Movies.* May 24, 2004. Retrieved April 7, 2021, from http://www.tcm.com.
Thomas, Barbara. "For June Allyson, A Lot Hangs on Depends." *The Washington Post.* January 1, 1988. Retrieved October 17, 2021, from http://www.washingtonpost.com.
Thomas, Bob. *Golden Boy: The Untold Story of William Holden.* New York, NY: Berkley, 1984.
______. *I Got Rhythm!: The Ethel Merman Story.* New York: Putnam, 1985.
Thomas, Tony. *The Busby Berkeley Book.* Greenwich, CT: New York Graphic Society, 1973.
______. *The Films of Gene Kelly, Song and Dance Man.* Secaucus, NJ: Citadel, 1974.
______. *A Wonderful Life: The Films and Career of James Stewart.* Secaucus, NJ: Citadel, 1988.
Thomas, Tony, and Solomon, Aubrey. *The Films of 20th Century Fox. a Pictorial History.* Secaucus, NJ: Citadel, 1979.
Thompson, Howard. "...June Allyson, Queen of the Box Office." *The New York Times.* February 10, 1952. Retrieved June 25, 2021, from http://www.nytimes.com.
______. "They Only Kill Their Masters.'" *The New York Times.* November 23, 1972. Retrieved October 2, 2021, from http://www.nytimes.com.
Thomson, David. *Humphrey Bogart (The Great Stars).* London: Penguin, 2009.
TMP. "A Fight Film from Metro Studios." *The New York Times.* December 16, 1950. Retrieved June 12, 2021, from http://www.nytimes.com.
______. "The Screen in Review: 'Her Highness and Bellboy.'" *The New York Times.* September 28, 1945. Retrieved March 31, 2021, from http://www.nytimes.com.
______. "The Screen: 'Thousands Cheer.' *The New York Times.* September 14, 1943. Retrieved March 15, 2021, from http://www.nytimes.com.
Tolchin, Michael. "Carter's Aides Push His Energy Program." *The New York Times.* May 20, 1977. Retrieved October 9, 2021, from http://www.nytimes.com.
Torme, Mel. *The Other Side of the Rainbow: With Judy Garland on the Dawn Patrol.* New York: Galahad, 1974.
Tranberg, Charles. *Not So Dumb: The Life and Career of Marie Wilson.* Albany, GA: BearManor Media, 2017.
T.S. "At the Capitol." *The New York Times.* December 3, 1943. Retrieved March 8, 2021, from http://www.nytimes.com.
Turner, Lana. *Lana: The Lady, the Legend, the Truth.* New York: Dutton, 1982.
Van Gelder, Lawrence. "FOOTLIGHTS." *The New York Times.* March 25, 1999. Retrieved December 7, 2021, from http://www.nytimes.com.
Vermilye, Jerry. *Barbara Stanwyck: Illustrated History of the Movies.* New York: Pyramid, 1975.
Wayne, Jane Ellen. *Lana: The Life and Loves of Lana Turner.* New York: St. Martin's, 1995.
Weiler, A.H. "Tamed 'Shrike'; Film Wife Less Deadly Than One in Play." *The New York Times.* July 8, 1955. Retrieved August 10, 2021, from http://www.nytimes.com.

Williams, Esther, with Diehl, Digby. *The Million Dollar Mermaid: A Fresh and Funny Expose of Hollywood's Golden Era.* San Diego: Harcourt, 2000.

Yudkoff, Alvin. *Gene Kelly: A Life of Dance and Dreams.* New York: Back Stage Books, 1999.

Zacharek, Stephanie. "Article: The Girl in White." *Turner Classic Movies.* March 8, 2014. Retrieved June 22, 2021, from http://www.tcm.com.

Index

Abbott, George 12, 15, 16, 17
The ABC Comedy Hour 154
ABC's Wide World of Entertainment 158
Airwolf 171
Albert, Eddie 153, 161
All About Eve 84–85
All Girl Revue 14
All Star Party for "Dutch" Reagan 171
All Star Tribute to Elizabeth Taylor 162
Alton, Robert 46, 58, 64
American Masters 180
America's All-Star Tribute to Elizabeth Taylor 172
The Annual Friars Club Tribute Presents a Salute to Gene Kelly 171
Arnaz, Desi 44, 89
The Arthur Murray Party 81
Ashrow, David 150, ***151***, 156–157, 159–161, 165–166, 174, 179, 181
Astaire, Fred 8, 26, 79
Astor, Mary 66, 68, 123

Bacall, Lauren 43, 48, 56, 95, 143
Ball, Lucille 25, 26, 28, 29, 30, 31, 35, 44, 89
Bankhead, Tallulah 126, 135
Battle Circus 85–86, 88
Benny, Jack 56, 119, 125, 141
Bergen, Candice 102, 104
Bergen, Edgar 56, 57, 76, 141, 142
Bergen, Frances 56, 57, 101, 102, 120, 141, 142
Berkeley, Busby 22, 74
Best Foot Forward (film) 2, 18, 21, 22, 24–**25**, 26, 175
Best Foot Forward (stage) 2, 17–***19***, 29, 62
Bing Crosby's White Christmas USO All Star Show 123, 125
Biography 3, 177, 179
Bixby, Bill 162, 165
Blackout 162
Blair, Betsy 15–16, 27, 34
Blondell, Joan 18, 29, 31, 35, 45, 50, 54, 117–118, 119, 138, 139, 141
Bogart, Humphrey 43, 48, 56, 85, 86, 88, 143
The Bride Goes Wild 60–61, 75
Brooks, Richard 85, 86
Burke's Law 148, 176
Burns, George 56, 69, 125, 141
Burns, Gracie 56, 69
Burt Reynolds Conversations With ... 172–173

Cagney, James 43, 102, 141
Chandler, Jeff 91, 94, 123
Charisse, Cyd 125, 175, 178
Colbert, Claudette 51, 53, 70, 114, 116, 173
Collins, Joan 116, 117, 118, 119, 179
Command Performance 36,
The Conqueror 96–97, 105, 110, 141
Crawford, Christina 55
Crawford, Joan 54–55, 69, 104, 167, 180
Crazy Like a Fox 171
Cronyn, Hugh 40, 61
Culp, Robert 128, 153
Curse of the Black Widow 161–162

Dahl, Arlene 60, 95
Dates and Nuts 9
The David Frost Show 153
Davis, Nancy 104
De pelicula 169
The Dean Martin Celebrity Roast: Jimmy Stewart 163
The Dean Martin Show 158
DeHaven, Gloria **25**, 26, 30, 31, 32, 33, 36, 37, 50, 68, 77, 143, 153, 160, 181
Depend 3, 166–167, 174, 175, 181
The Dick Cavett Show 167
The Dick Powell Show 137, 138, 143, 144
The Dick Powell Theatre see *The Dick Powell Show*
Did America Kill John Wayne? 166
Dime a Dance 9,
Donohue, Jack 22, 29, 42
Duke, Patty 161, 162
Durante, Jimmy 31, 33, 37, 40

The Ed Sullivan Show see *Talk of the Town*
The Edgar Bergen Show with Charlie McCarthy 76–77, 94

Eisenhower, Mamie 139, 140
Executive Suite 91–**92**, 93–94

Ferrer, Jose 96, 97, 98, 100,
The 15th Emmy Awards 144
The 58th Annual Academy Awards 171
The Film Society of Lincoln Centre Annual Gala Tribute to James Stewart 172
Fischer, O.W. 120, 121, 122
Forty Carats 2, 152–153
The 43rd Annual Golden Globe Awards 171
Freed, Arthur 18, 21, 46, 47, 50, 54, 60, 62, 74, 79

Gardner, Ava 77, 180
Garland, Judy 1–2, 12, 23–24, 30, 34, 46, 50, 54, 56, 58, 69, 74, 79, 80, 91, 105, 111, 113, 123, 136, 145, 146, 147, 152, 155, 173, 175, 177, 178, 180
Garner, James 154, ***155***
The Gay Divorcee 8, 79
General Motors 50th Anniversary Show 122
G.I. Jive 165
Giesler, Jerry 132, 134,
Girl Crazy 21–**22**, 23–24
The Girl in White 2, 3, 82–84, 91
A Girl, 3 Guys, and a Gun 179
The Glenn Miller Story 90–91, 94, 100, 163, 164, 169, 177, 178
Good News 3, 54, 58–***59***, 60, 146, 158, 173, 175, 178
Goodbye Ghost 150, 151, 154
Grable, Betty 74, 91
Grayson, Kathryn 26, 30, 40, 42, 175, 178

Hallmark Playhouse 74
Happy 100th Birthday, Hollywood 171–172
Happyland see *Dime a Dance*
Hart to Hart 168–169
Hayward, Susan 89, 94, 97
Hayworth, Rita 159, 160
Hepburn, Katharine 24, 66
Her Highness and the Bellboy 38–39, 46, 146
High Barbaree 53–54
Higher and Higher 13–14
Holbrook, Hal 154, ***155***
Holden, William **92**, 93, 94
The Hollywood Greats 164–165
Hollywood Without Make-Up 148
Hopper, Hedda 49, 55, 102, 142
House Calls 2, 165
Houseman, John 91, 94
Hughes, Howard 88, 105–106, 139
Hutton, Betty 2, 15, 22, 74, 145

In Performance at The White House 172
In the Good Old Summertime 2, 69
The Incredible Hulk 165
Inside the Dream Factory 176–177
Interlude 2, 119–120
I've Got a Secret 136

Jack Benny Christmas Special 119
Janus 149
The Joey Bishop Show 151
Johnson, Van 17, 21, 27, 31, 32, ***33***–34, 46, 53, 54, 60, 64, 81, ***83***, 86, 88, 105, 130, 153, 159, 161, 164, 165, 167, 169, ***170***, 173, 178, 180
Jones, Carolyn 145, 148, 155
The Judy Garland Show 145–147
The June Allyson Show 125, 126–131, 135–136
Jurgens, Curt 104

Kaye, Danny 9
Kelly, Gene 26, 27, 34, 61, 62, 171, 173, 176
Kelly, Grace 95, 112, 113, 116, 180
The Kid with the Broken Halo 168
The Knight Is Young 12–13
Koster, Henry 37, 38, 42, 74, 121, 122, 172

Ladd, Alan 3, 97, 106, 107, 108, 109, 110, 111, 112, 113, 120, 138–139, 148, 164
Ladd, Sue 107, 108, 109, 110, 111, 112
Lamarr, Hedy 38, 39
Lane, Rosemary 17, 18, 25
Lansbury, Angela 62, 86, 169, ***170***
Larry King Live 179–180
Lawford, Peter 34–35, 42, 43, 58, ***59***, 60, 65, 68, 154, 173, 177, 180
Lawrence, Steve 146, 147
Leigh, Janet 65, 68, 71, 162, 164, 173–174
Lemmon, Jack 114, ***115***, 116
Leonard, Robert Z. ***52***, 82
Le Roy, Hal 9 , 10, 12, 13
LeRoy, Mervyn 65, 66,
Letters from Three Lovers 158
Lifestyles of the Rich and Famous 169
Little Women 2, 65–***67***, 68–70, 74–75, 77, 78, 155, 162, 172, 173, 178, 180
The Love Boat 2, 164, 168, 169
Lux Radio Theater 50, 78, 82, 91, 94

Mail Call 36, 57
Mann, Anthony 90, 96
Maree, A. Morgan 46, 140, 142, 143
The Match Game 149
Maxwell, Glenn 3, 148, 149, 150–151, 153
Mayer, Louis B. 30, 31, 34, 35, 36, 43, 44, 45, 56, 62, 66, 73, 80, 82, 88, 122, 173, 175
The McConnell Story 97, 106–112
Meet the People 28–29, 31
Merman, Ethel 14, 15, 74
The Merv Griffin Show 153, 158

Index

MGM: When the Lion Roars 173
The Mike Douglas Show 149, 151
Miller, Ann 117, 172, 175, 178, 179
Miller, David 117, 118
Minnelli, Vincente 13, 46, 177
Misfits of Science 169, 171
Mitchell, Tommy 16, 20, 44, 45, 54
Mitchum, Robert 104, 114
Monroe, Marilyn 78, 130, 139, 180
Montalban, Ricardo 77, ***78***
The Movie Game 153
Murder, My Sweet 43, 100
Murder, She Wrote 169, ***170***
Murphy, George 56, 57, 73, 81, 104, 141
Music for Millions 37–38, 74, 169
My Daughter, Your Son 158–159, 165–166, 167
My Man Godfrey 2, 120–122

The Name of the Game 152
Night of 100 Stars 167
Niven, David 121, 122, 144
Nixon, Richard 139, 141, 159
No No Nanette 154, 155

Oberon, Merle 56, 105
O'Brien, Margaret 37, 38, 56, 65, 68, 153, 160, 162, 178, 181
Old Gold Comedy Theater 38
Olympic Fund Telethon 85
The Opposite Sex 2, 3, 116–119
Osborne, Robert 177, 178

Panama Hattie 2, 11, 14–15, 17, 145
Parkinson 166
Parsons, Louella 45, 49, 56, 80, 110, 112
Pasternak, Joe 26, 27, 31, 37, 38, 40, 84, 116, 153
The Perry Como Show 148
Person to Person 113
Personality 152
Pidgeon, Walter 51, 93, 141
Pixilated 8–9
Porter, Cole 11, 14, 36, 172
Powell, Dick 2, 3, 8, 18, 28, 29, 30, 31, 35, 36, 38, 43, 44, 45, 46, 47–50, 53, 54, 55, 56, 57, 69, 70, 71, 73, 74, ***75***, 76, 77, ***78***, 79, 80, 81, 82, 88, 91, 94, 96, 97, 100, 101, 102, ***103***, 104, 105, 106, 108, 109, 110, 111, 112, 113, 114, 116, 118, 119, 120, 122, 123, 125, 126, 127, 128, 131, 132, 133, 134–135, 137, 138, 139, 140, 141, 142, 143, 144, 145, 148, 150, 153, 157, 159, 163, 166, 173, 178, 180
Powell, Ellen 50, 70, 102, 110, 118, 140, 142
Powell, Jane 30, 79, 127, 172–173
Powell, Norman 50, 138, 142
Powell, Pammy 70, 77, 101, 102, ***103***, 112, 129, 137, 140, 141, 148, 155, 156, 160, 181
Powell, Ricky (aka Dick Powell, Jr.) 81, 101, 102, ***103***, 104, 112, 134, 137, 141, 143, 151, 152, 153, 156, 159, 160, 166, 181
Premier Krushchev in the USA 126
The Prisoner of Swing 10
Private Screenings 177–178
Pros and Cons 173

Reagan, Ronald 56, 69, 104, 141, 171, 172, 180
Reed, Donna 37, 71
The Reformer and the Redhead ***75***–76, 77, 78, 81, 82, 102
Remains to Be Seen 85, 86–***87***, 88, 91
Reynolds, Debbie 85, 174, 175–176, 179, 181
Richard Diamond Private Detective 80
Right Cross 77–***78***, 173
Rodgers, Richard 11, 13, 14, 15, 17, 28, 50
Rogers, Ginger 8, 38, 172–173
Rollin' in Rhythm 13
Ronald Reagan: The Hollywood Years, the Presidential Years 180
Rooney, Mickey 21, **22**, 23, 50, 54, 64
Royal Wedding 2, 78, 146, 177
Russell, Jane 91, 181

The Sailor Takes a Wife 39–40
Schary, Dore 74, 88
Schools, Victoria 17, 18
Screen Actor's Guild 75
Screen Director's Playhouse 74
Screen Guild Theater 77
The 2nd Annual American Cinema Awards 171
The Secret Heart 50–***52***, 53
See The Man Run 153
The 17th Golden Globe Awards 128
The 79th Annual Academy Awards 181
Sheilah Graham in Hollywood 113
Sheridan, Ann 117, 119
Shore, Dinah 56, 91
The Shrike 2, 96, 97–***99***, 100
Sidney, George 26, 46, 62
Simon & Simon 168
"Sing for Sweetie" 10
Sing Out the News 11–12, 16
The Sixth Sense 157–158
Spelling, Aaron 137, 144, 145, 148
Stanwyck, Barbara 93, 94, 141
A Star Is Born 91, 113, 177
Stewart, Gloria 73, 80, 163, 177
Stewart, James 16, 70, 71, ***72***, 73, 90, 91, 96, 125, 141, 163, 164, 167, 169, 172, 177, 180
A Stranger in My Arms 2, 123–***124***
Strategic Air Command 91, 95–96
The Stratton Story 70–***72***, 73, 78, 90, 163, 164, 167, 177
Sturges, John 77, 82, 84

Sullavan, Margaret 17, 149
Swing for Sale 8
Switch 161

Talk of the Town 88, 119, 153
Taurog, Norman 22, 61, 64
Taylor, Elizabeth 65, 66, 68, 75, 79, 162, 172
That's Entertainment! 158
That's Entertainment!: The Masters Behind the Musicals 60, 181
That's Entertainment! III 175, ***176***
These Old Broads 179
They Only Kill Their Masters 2, 154, ***155***
The 13th Annual Screen Actors Guild Awards 181
The 30th Academy Awards 122–123
The 30th Annual Golden Globe Awards 158
The 31st Annual Academy Awards 125
The 31st Annual Golden Globe Awards 158
This is Your Life 3, 153, 175
Thompson, Kay 29, 34, 47, 58
Thorpe, Richard 32, 38, 39
Thousands Cheer 26–27
The Three Musketeers 2, 61–62, ***63***
Three on a Date 162–163
Till the Clouds Roll By 46–***47***, 146, 173, 175
Tonight! 113
The Tonight Show Starring Johnny Carson 153
Too Young to Kiss 2, 74, 81, 82, ***83***, 85
Torme, Mel 146, 147
Turner, Lana 37, 56, 62, 76, 78, 163, 173, 180
The 20th Annual Golden Globe Awards 143
The 25th Academy Awards 88
The 27th Academy Awards 113
Two Girls and a Sailor 2, 3, 31, 31–32, ***33***, 35, 36, 38, 49, 117, 167, 173
Two Sisters from Boston 2, 40, 42

Ups and Downs 9, 10, 13

Vega$ 164
Very Warm for May 13
Vicki! 173–174

Walker, Nancy 17, ***25***, 30, 35
Walker, Robert 38, 39, 40, ***41***, 46
Walters, Charles 22, 24, 26, 29, 38, 58, 59, 60, 74, 79, 89, 181
Wayne, John 96, 97, 144, 145, 166
What's My Line? 106, 126, 129, 136, 137
Whorf, Richard 34, 39, 46
Wilfrid's Special Christmas 172
Williams, Esther 56, 69, 73, 116, 162, 172–173, 175, 177, 178
Wise, Robert 93, 94
Woman's World 94–95
The Women (1939) 116, 118
Words and Music 3, 62, 64, 158
Wyman, Jane 56, 69, 78, 104, 141

You Can't Run Away from It 2, 114–***115***, 116, 119
Young, Gig 62, 82

Zane Grey Theatre 130